Fremantle's Submarines

Fremantle's Submarines

How Allied Submariners and Western Australians
Helped to Win the War in the Pacific

MICHAEL STURMA

Naval Institute Press
Annapolis, Maryland

This book has been brought to publication with the generous assistance of Marguerite and Gerry Lenfest.

Naval Institute Press
291 Wood Road
Annapolis, MD 21402

© 2015 by Michael Sturma
All rights reserved. No part of this book may be reproduced or utilized in any form or by any means, electronic or mechanical, including photocopying and recording, or by any information storage and retrieval system, without permission in writing from the publisher.

Library of Congress Cataloging-in-Publication Data

Sturma, Michael, 1950-
  Fremantle's submarines : how Allied submariners and Western Australians helped win the war in the Pacific / Michael Sturma.
     pages cm
  Includes bibliographical references and index.
  ISBN 978-1-61251-860-2 (alk. paper)
 1. World War, 1939-1945—Naval operations—Submarine. 2. World War, 1939-1945—Australia—Fremantle (W.A.) 3. World War, 1939-1945—Campaigns—Pacific Ocean. 4. Fremantle (W.A.)—History, Military. I. Title. II. Title: How Allied submariners and Western Australians helped win the war in the Pacific.
 D780.S77 2015
 940.54'516—dc23

                                                            2015014404

 Print editions meet the requirements of ANSI/NISO z39.48-1992 (Permanence of Paper).
Printed in the United States of America.

23 22 21 20 19 18 17 16 15   9 8 7 6 5 4 3 2 1
First printing

Contents

List of Illustrations vii
Acknowledgments ix

Introduction 1
1. On the Edge 5
2. Like Heaven 16
3. Wilkes 20
4. Lockwood 27
5. Torpedoes and Tragedies 37
6. Christie 45
7. Traveling North 53
8. Sailors' Women 60
9. Hunter and Hunted 65
10. Trouble in Paradise 76
11. War of Attrition 83
12. Support and Supply 93
13. Cruel Months 97
14. The British Arrive 105
15. Adjustments and Special Missions 114
16. Battle of Leyte Gulf 120
17. Transitions 126
18. Tribulations 135
19. Cooperation at Sea 141
20. War's End 149
Epilogue 156

Notes 163
Bibliography 203
Index 227

Illustrations

Map
Pacific Theater   x

Photos
American submarines with the USS *Pelias*   9
John Wilkes   21
USS *Searaven*   23
Charles A. Lockwood Jr.   30
John Mosby   32
Ralph W. Christie   46
USS *Puffer*   71
Crewmen on the USS *Cabrilla*   72
Anthony Miers   74
USS *Harder*   85
Alistair Mars   111
James Fife Jr.   129
Survivors from the *Rakuyo Maru*   131
USS *Athedon*   139
USS *Cavalla*   142
USS *Cabrilla* ship's party   151
Ernest "Zeke" Zellmer and Babs Miller   157

Figure
Ships sunk by U.S. submarines based at Fremantle, 1942–45   123

Acknowledgments

> And so you people of the land 'ere you lay
> your heads to dream,
>
> Just pass a fleeting thought for the men
> who serve in a submarine.
>
> —A. B. Bristowe, "A Visit to a Submarine"

Over the years I have spared more than a fleeting thought for the men who served in submarines. In this endeavor I have accumulated a considerable debt, most of all to the submariners who have left oral histories and personal memoirs. I am also grateful for the assistance of numerous archivists and colleagues. Sally May, head of the Department of Maritime History, generously provided access to the recollections of Dutch, British, and American submariners held by the Western Australian Maritime Museum. Charles R. Hinman at the USS *Bowfin* Submarine Museum at Pearl Harbor has helped guide me through the museum's resources over several visits. I thank George Malcolmson for his help in locating relevant material at the Royal Submarine Museum in Gosport, England. Thanks to Caitlin MacNeil for her assistance at the Victorian Archives Centre (Melbourne). Bob Price assisted by going through a selection of "Boat Books" held at the Submarine Force Museum in Groton, Connecticut. Craig McDonald generously shared information about some World War II submarine veterans from USS *Puffer*. Ernest "Zeke" Zellmer not only recorded his detailed memories as a submariner but put me in touch with some of his former crewmates from USS *Cavalla*. Thanks to Peter Nunan for sharing ephemera from the papers of Les Cottman.

At Murdoch University, Dr. Ian Chambers has afforded valuable technical and editorial assistance. Pam Mathews and Yolie Masnada have assisted in the ordering of research materials. As in the past, my longtime friend Professor Mike Durey provided a valued sounding board. My wife, Ying, is a continuous source of support. To all of these people my heartfelt gratitude.

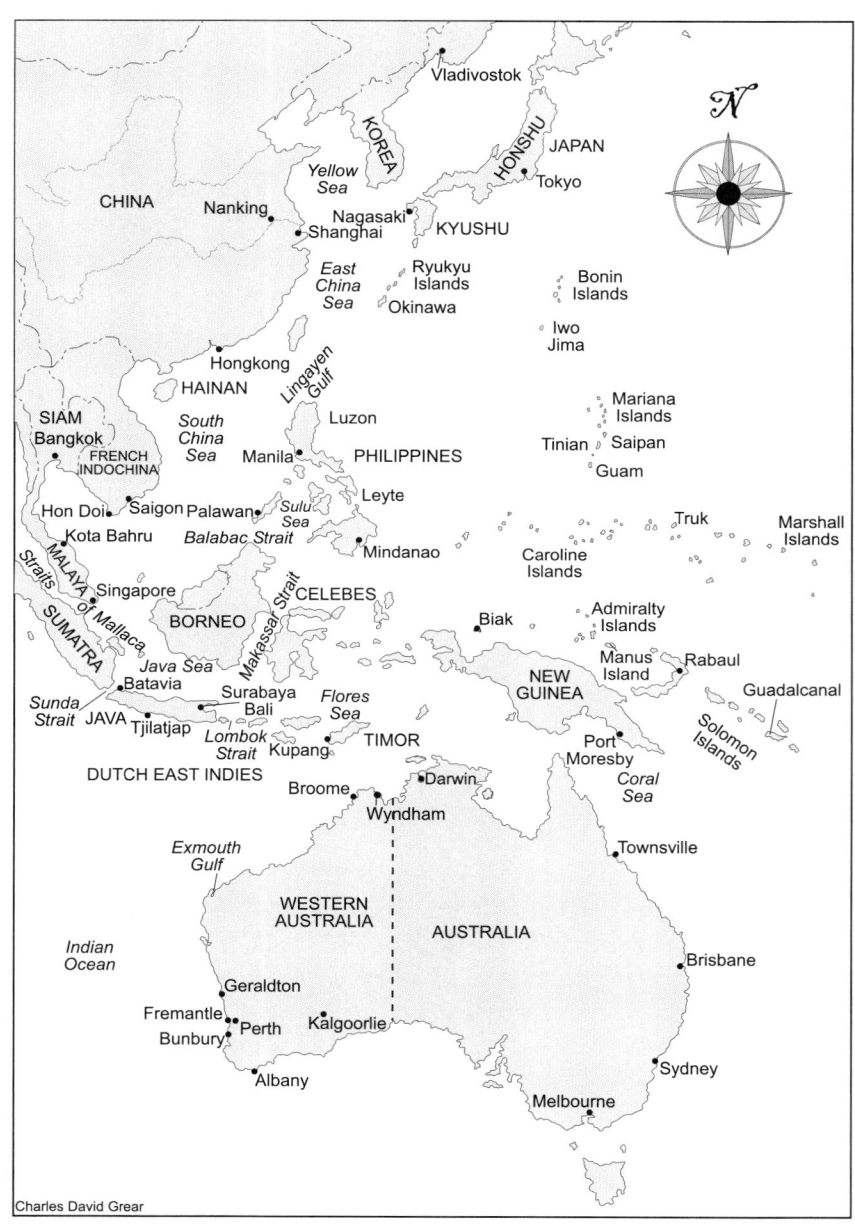

PACIFIC THEATER

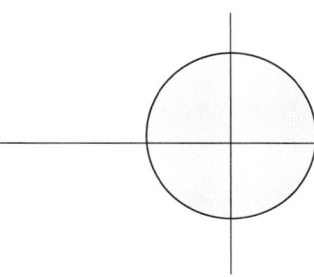

INTRODUCTION

The submarine base at Fremantle, Western Australia, evolved from unpromising circumstances. Faced with the onslaught of the Japanese in World War II, U.S. submariners retreated to Fremantle as a port of last resort. While the American submarine base at Pearl Harbor was largely undamaged by the Japanese attack on December 7, 1941, the base in the Philippines with the main contingent of U.S. submarines was devastated by an attack on December 10. A bomb sank USS *Sealion* as it underwent repairs at the Cavite Naval Yard, while the remaining twenty-eight American submarines stationed at Manila hurried out to sea in an attempt to both stem the Japanese invasion and avoid destruction.

With their base lost in the Philippines, the American submariners moved to the Netherlands East Indies, where for nearly two months Allied patrols were made from Surabaya and Tjilatjap on the island of Java. Soon, however, those bases too were overrun by the Japanese. Darwin, on the northern coast of Australia, was briefly considered as an alternative base, but, apart from the physical limitations of its harbor, any base there would be within striking distance of Japanese aircraft operating from recently captured islands to the north. From March 1942 on, Fremantle became America's main submarine base in the Southwest Pacific through default. The port had the advantages of a good harbor and of being outside the range of land-based Japanese aircraft, but it also had disadvantages; it was far away from the areas where submarines carried out their patrols, and it was difficult to reinforce should the enemy launch a naval assault.

Despite the port's shortcomings, Fremantle became the most significant Allied submarine base in the Pacific after Pearl Harbor. During the war 127 American submarines made 353 war patrols from Fremantle, roughly a quarter of all U.S. patrols in the Pacific. Early in the war a small number of Dutch submarines were sent to Western Australia, and a total of ten Dutch boats made patrols from Fremantle. From August 1944 Royal Navy submarines established a substantial presence there, and thirty-one made patrols from Fremantle. Taken together, Fremantle submarines made a total of 416 war patrols and took a huge toll on enemy shipping.[1]

In relating the story of Fremantle submarines during the Second World War, three major themes emerge: courage, cooperation, and community. Submariners certainly had no monopoly on courage during the war, but as naval historian Malcolm Murfett observes, "Even so, it is difficult not to see submariners as a special breed of seamen."[2] Shared danger and shared responsibility for the group's survival was a key factor that contributed to the special status of submariners. Comradeship and loyalty to the group helps explain the willingness of men to face the hazards of submarine patrols again and again. Some of the most spectacular submarine patrols of the war were made from Fremantle under the command of such legends as Reuben Whitaker, Walt Griffith, and Sam Dealey. Allied submariners took enormous risks not only sinking enemy ships but conducting covert operations and rescuing beleaguered comrades from behind enemy lines. Eight U.S. submarines (*Barbel*, *Bullhead*, *Flier*, *Grayling*, *Grenadier*, *Growler*, *Harder*, and *Robalo*) were lost on patrols from Fremantle, remaining on "eternal patrol," as the sailors phrased it. Another ten American submarines previously based at Fremantle (*Bonefish*, *Grampus*, *Grayback*, *Gudgeon*, *Pickerel*, *S-39*, *Seawolf*, *Sculpin*, *Swordfish*, and *Trout*) subsequently perished on patrols from other bases. The Dutch submarine *O-19* was also lost on patrol from Western Australia, and HMS *Porpoise*, which carried out missions from Fremantle and was lost with all hands on a patrol from Trincomalee, became the last British submarine of the war lost to enemy action.

The courage of submariners may appear self-evident, but the degree of cooperation between allies is not always so clear. In an early effort at combined operations, the British general Sir Archibald Wavell was appointed head of the American-British-Dutch-Australian (ABDA) command on January 15, 1942. The combined naval forces included a total of forty submarines: twenty-eight U.S., three British, and nine Dutch.[3] British submarine commander William King, however, believed that the grand name ABDA "amounted to damn-all" since in practice elements of the fleet mainly operated independently.[4] The first joint action by ABDA confirmed King's skepticism, when the Battle of the Java Sea, fought on February 27, 1942, resulted in the loss of the Dutch cruisers *De Ruyter* and *Java*. Without adequate air cover, common training, shared methods of fire control, or common codes or flag signals, the Allies were hopelessly disadvantaged. Given the Dutch-English language barrier, one captain of an American destroyer described the communications as "farcical."[5] The

Japanese Fifth Cruiser Squadron, on the other hand, had trained together for years.

The light cruiser HMAS *Perth* and heavy cruiser USS *Houston* survived the Battle of the Java Sea, but after encountering an enemy landing force in Sunda Strait a few days later, they again found themselves outnumbered and outgunned by the Japanese. At the Battle of Sunda Strait *Perth* was sunk shortly after midnight on March 1, 1942, a particularly bad omen for Western Australians not only because the ship was named after their capital city but because many on board had been purposely recruited from the state. Of the 681 men on *Perth*, only 218 would survive the war to return to Australia. USS *Houston* went down forty minutes later; less than a third of its crew survived. The British cruiser *Exeter* was also lost in the battle when an enemy shell exploded in its boiler room. The same day, March 1, the ABDA fleet was dissolved; the combined command established on January 15 had lasted a mere six weeks.[6]

Despite such spectacular early failures and disappointment with the ABDA command, the success of the Fremantle base depended largely on cooperation between allies at many levels. At the national level, collaboration between America and Australia was paramount. Dwight D. Eisenhower, at the time newly appointed to the War Plans Division of General George Marshall's staff, initially recommended the primacy of Australia as a base in the Pacific.[7] Once Gen. Douglas MacArthur was appointed supreme commander in the Southwest Pacific, he developed a strong personal and working relationship with Australia's prime minister, John Curtin. More locally, the Australians, with no submarines of their own, supported the base at Fremantle largely through the mobilization of workers and resources. Militarily, Australian commandos who traveled on U.S. submarines to be inserted behind enemy lines and later routinely accompanied war patrols epitomized the trust that developed between allies at an individual level. Australia's minister for external affairs, H. V. Evatt, concluded in 1945 that "seldom, if ever, has history evidenced a better example of military cooperation between a greater power and a lesser power."[8]

Cooperation at Fremantle also extended from early in the war to a small number of Dutch submarines that made patrols under American operational control. The degree of cross-national support became much more evident once British submarines began making patrols from Fremantle in August 1944. Despite a suspicion of Royal Navy participation in the Pacific by some senior U.S. naval staff, most notably Adm. Ernest King, it is clear that American and British submariners worked well together. Significantly, Anglo-American cooperation between submariners predated agreement by Prime Minister Winston Churchill and President Franklin Roosevelt at the Octagon summit in September 1944 over participation of the British Pacific Fleet in the war against Japan.[9] While not without friction, the Allies developed a reciprocity that far outstripped the Axis powers.

Still within the realm of cooperation, the most striking feature that emerges from the story of Fremantle submarines is the close bonds of community that developed between Western Australian civilians and Allied submariners. The submariners initially stationed in Western Australia had every reason to feel demoralized; continually on the retreat, they had achieved few successes against the enemy. Quickly, however, Fremantle gained an enviable reputation as a port of leave for submariners. The hospitality and sense of belonging offered to visiting submariners by Western Australians far exceeded anything in their previous experience. Among those submariners assigned to Fremantle during the Second World War, there was virtual unanimity that the port, along with the nearby city of Perth, was the best leave center in the Pacific. From the standpoint of morale, the submarine base at Fremantle was arguably the most successful military outpost of World War II.

CHAPTER 1

ON THE EDGE

Australia had already been officially at war for more than two years before the outbreak of the Pacific War. Traditionally Australia looked to Britain for leadership and protection, so when the mother country entered the Second World War in September 1939, Australia's prime minister, Robert Menzies, announced to the nation almost immediately that as "a result, Australia is also at war."[1] Four months later the first Australian troops, members of the Second Australian Imperial Forces, were dispatched to fight in the Middle East, and by 1941 three Australian divisions were fighting in the eastern Mediterranean theater. As one historian puts it, the first two years of the war afforded Australia "with a long warm-up session" for what followed.[2]

In November 1941 the war crept closer to Australia when the German raider *Kormoran* sunk the cruiser HMAS *Sydney* a little over a hundred miles off the Western Australian coast. Although not a single member of the crew of 645 on the *Sydney* survived, the attack on the U.S. Pacific Fleet at Pearl Harbor the following month came as a much greater shock. John Curtin had only taken office as Australia's prime minister on October 7, the same month that he turned fifty-one. Informed of the Japanese attack during the early hours of December 8, Curtin told Australians in a radio broadcast that evening, "This is our darkest hour." He also informed his audience that "our efforts in the past two years must be as nothing compared with the efforts we must now put forward."[3] Three days later, Curtin warned that "the enemy is seeking the earliest possible hour in which he can set foot on our soil."[4]

The quick succession of disasters that followed further eroded public confidence. The sinking of the British warships *Repulse* and *Prince of Wales* by aircraft off Malaya on December 10 sank the myth of Royal Navy supremacy in the Far East. Wake Island, Manila, Guam, Hong Kong, Thailand, North Borneo, Singapore, and the Netherlands East Indies all succumbed to the enemy offensive with a speed that surprised even the Japanese. Especially with the surrender on February 15, 1942, of Singapore, long considered the linchpin of regional security, the possibility of an invasion of Australia from the north seemed very real. With the fall of Singapore, 62,000 Allied soldiers, including 15,000 Australians, became prisoners of the Japanese. Only four days after the fall of Singapore, the Japanese launched a massive air attack on Darwin, Australia's northernmost city. In a memorable phrase, General Thomas Blamey characterized Australians as "a lot of gazelles in a dell on the edge of a jungle."[5] With a national population of only seven million and more than 12,000 miles of coastline to defend, Australians felt intensely vulnerable.

Isolated on the edge of the continent, with an even sparser population and longer coastline than the other states, Western Australia was especially vulnerable. Occupying 965,000 square miles, about one-third of Australia's total land mass, the state had a population of about half a million. It seemed the nightmare of an Asian invasion, long ingrained into the Australian psyche, might materialize. A meeting of Australia's defense chiefs on February 28 discussed the difficulties of reinforcing the west as well as Fremantle's potential as a Japanese fleet base, fears that were exacerbated when radio propagandist Tokyo Rose boasted that Perth would soon fall to the Japanese.[6] At Fremantle, considered by some an obvious target for a Japanese attack, residents held a public meeting as early as December 1941 calling on the government to draw up evacuation plans.[7] By March 1942 more than a hundred ships crowded with refugees from the Japanese onslaught in Southeast Asia arrived at Fremantle, sometimes forced to moor four abreast in the harbor.[8] The escapees from Java included seven Australian corvettes and four old U.S. destroyers that reached Fremantle on March 4.[9] Despite military censorship, the flow of people and shipping south afforded abundant evidence of the war's proximity.

Among the refugees arriving at Fremantle were British seamen who survived the sinking of their destroyer HMS *Electra* in the Battle of the Java Sea. They had spent hours in the water before a submarine suddenly approached on the night of February 28. Many expected to be machine-gunned by the Japanese, but the submarine proved to be American. Under the command of Henry Glass Munson, *S-38* took on board some forty-three men and then continued the search for survivors until eventually recovering another eleven sailors. Within the cramped confines of *S-38*, survivors recalled that the Americans "couldn't do enough for us," surrendering their bunks and providing clothing.[10]

On the morning of Tuesday, March 3, 1942, Japanese air raids brought the war directly to Western Australia. Flying from Penfoei airstrip at Kupang on the western end of Timor, Japanese Mitsubishi AGM2 "Zero" fighters raided the northern towns of Wyndham and Broome. The planes strafed the airfield and destroyed a fuel dump at Wyndham, while another group of planes staged a more spectacular raid on Broome some 435 miles southwest. The sleepy pearling port of Broome, more than 1,200 miles north of Perth, had assumed a new importance as a staging point for moving supplies north to Java and then as part of an escape route from the Dutch East Indies as people fled from the Japanese assault. A formation of nine Japanese Zero fighters wiped out all the aircraft based at Broome save one small floatplane that managed to escape south. Many of the planes were crammed with Dutch refugees. Seventy years later, Elly Koens, who was a ten-year-old at the time of the attack, recalled sitting on the wing of a burning plane before swimming for her life. She and her family had just flown from Java on a Dornier seaplane, one of fifteen flying boats that set down in Roebuck Bay to refuel earlier that morning. Another six aircraft were destroyed on the ground at the Broome airfield. Between seventy and eighty people were killed in the raid, some victims apparently taken by sharks as they swam for their lives from the burning aircraft in Roebuck Bay.[11] As recollected by Dorothy Hewett, a university student in Perth at the time, the attack on Broome had a profound effect. "Here we were, who had always been so safe and so isolated and suddenly we'd been bombed by the Japanese. Even if it was a long way up the coast, it was still the Western Australian coastline."[12]

Western Australians found themselves assaulted not only from the air but from the sea. On the same day as the air attacks on Wyndham and Broome, March 3, Japanese submarines made their presence known off Western Australia's coast. That morning the 8,667-ton Dutch freighter *Siantar* was torpedoed by *I-1* northwest of Shark Bay. Of *Siantar*'s crew of fifty-eight, twenty-one men were lost with the ship. The same day, *I-3* attacked the 8,988-ton steamship *Narbada* northwest of Fremantle en route to Colombo. Armed with a 4-inch gun, *Narbada* exchanged fire with *I-3* for nearly an hour before the submarine broke off its attack. That afternoon *I-3* made another attack, this time on the 8,720-ton armed New Zealand steamer *Tongariro* en route from Wellington to Fremantle. The same day, survivors from the ill-fated Dutch freighter *Parigi* were recovered. On the evening of March 1, at 8:03 local time, *I-2* had sunk the 1,172-ton *Parigi* west of Cervantes while the ship was en route from Tjilatjap to Bunbury, Western Australia. The survivors, in two lifeboats, were picked up by the southbound corvette HMAS *Yarra* two days later.[13]

Sensing the prospect of further Japanese attacks on Western Australia, regulations promulgated on March 11 ordered the removal of all road signs within twenty miles of the coast. By the end of the month, blackout conditions were implemented at Fremantle and the beachside suburb of Cottesloe. Some families living on the coast headed inland, or at least sent their children to what they believed to be safer areas. Gordon Baker, a teenager growing up in East Fremantle, was dispatched to live with cousins in the farming community of Wickepin and only returned to Fremantle the following year.[14] Maurie Jones, a Perth schoolboy in 1942, recalls his parents debating whether to send him to relatives in the country. In the end they decided that he should remain in Perth, reasoning that in the event of a Japanese invasion there might be more control over occupying troops in the city than "marauding bands" in the countryside.[15]

Although Perth was too far south to be reached by land-based Japanese planes, many anticipated attacks from aircraft carrier–based planes. Gordon Scott's family lived in Rose Street, South Fremantle, and like many other local residents built an air raid shelter in the backyard. They dug a trench about five feet deep, covered it with railroad ties and sand bags, and stocked it with a medicine chest and a stash of Mills & Wares biscuits.[16] The Western Australian director of civil defense, however, warned parents not to allow their children to dig trenches unsupervised; Perth's sandy soil was prone to caving in.[17] Even in the country there were preparations for air attacks, such as in the wheat belt town of Northam, where schoolchildren dug slit trenches and carried books showing the profiles of enemy planes so that they could be identified.[18]

Periodic air raid alerts sent residents of Perth and Fremantle scrambling for shelter. Phyllis May Atkinson, the first woman employed by Anchorage Butchers, recalled on one occasion hiding under a dining room table with her employer and his wife in their East Fremantle home, putting pieces of rubber in their mouths to guard against damage from the percussion of bombs.[19] Many businesses boarded up their shop fronts, while antiaircraft guns and searchlights were installed at the East Fremantle football oval. At the Westrail workshops in Midland, employees dug air-raid trenches around the premises, while many people began growing vegetables and keeping chickens in their backyards in anticipation of wartime austerity measures.[20]

Australia's prime minister, John Curtin, had a firsthand appreciation of the situation in Western Australia. He was the elected member of Parliament for Fremantle, and his family resided in the suburb of Cottesloe a short distance from the sea. With the British apparently unable to come

American submarines with the tender USS *Pelias* in Fremantle Harbour, Christmas Day, 1943   USS *Bowfin* Submarine Museum

to Australia's assistance, Curtin made his own views clear in a statement at the end of December 1941. In words later recognized as a historical watershed, Curtin told his countrymen, "Australia looks to America."[21]

It was against this backdrop of fear and anticipation that the first American submarines arrived at Fremantle. By March 10, 1942, ten U.S. submarines had reached the port, each carrying crews with their own stories of near disaster. Among the most demoralized was Tyrell Dwight Jacobs, commander of USS *Sargo*. Shortly after he arrived at Fremantle on March 5, 1942, Jacobs told a senior officer, "I've had it. I want to be relieved."[22] It had been barely a year since Jacobs assumed command of *Sargo*. Based at Manila when the Japanese bombed Pearl Harbor, Jacobs departed the following day for his first war patrol in the area off Cam Ranh Bay, a deep-water port on the coast of Indochina (today Vietnam) used by the Japanese fleet. The *Sargo* crew fired thirteen torpedoes at enemy ships, but all missed, and Jacobs had no explanation for this other than a belief that the torpedoes ran deeper than set or that the magnetic exploders were faulty. With a master's degree in ordnance engineering, Jacobs understood torpedoes well, and his suspicions that the weapons were faulty would eventually be confirmed. At the time, however, Jacobs received only criticism for his lack of success.[23]

With the destruction of the American submarine base in the Philippines on December 10, 1941, *Sargo* and its crew retreated to the Dutch naval base at Surabaya on the island of Java. Making its second war patrol from the Dutch East Indies, *Sargo* delivered a million rounds of .30-caliber ammunition to beleaguered Army troops on the Philippine island of Mindanao. During the patrol the *Sargo* crew picked up twenty-four members of the U.S. Army 14th Bombardment Squadron who had escaped from the island of Luzon. The extra men on board made the return voyage to Surabaya uncomfortable, especially after a refrigerating compressor broke down and temperatures in the submarine hovered at over 100 degrees Fahrenheit.[24]

An article published in the *Times* on February 27, 1942, boasted of American submarine successes in the vicinity of Java, claiming that the adjacent waters were "ideal for submarine warfare, and this is one of the most potent arguments in favour of holding Java as an allied base, whatever the cost may be."[25] The reality was quite different. Japanese air raids soon forced the abandonment of Surabaya, and *Sargo*'s next patrol included evacuating thirty-one Navy personnel to Australia. As *Sargo* approached Fremantle, cruising on the surface, lookouts spotted a plane about five miles away. Flying just under a heavy bank of cloud, the twin-engine aircraft appeared to be heading straight for them. Although supposedly in friendly skies, Jacobs ordered the submarine to dive. In heavy seas *Sargo* struggled to submerge, however, and while still partially surfaced a bomb rolled the submarine on its side and simultaneously lifted the stern out of the water. As *Sargo* reached a depth of fifty feet, a second bomb detonated with what Jacobs described as "terrific" force.[26] Many of the men on board reported seeing the submarine's steel hull bend in from the explosion. Concussion from the bomb damaged the conning tower hatch, burst light bulbs, broke depth gauges, and jammed the stern planes, plunging *Sargo* into a runaway dive toward the bottom of the sea. The crew managed to regain control of the dive, but an assessment of damage found the conning tower flooded, the periscopes wrecked, and three heads (toilets) destroyed.[27]

Such a beating from an enemy plane might have been palatable, but *Sargo* had been almost destroyed by an ally, a Royal Australian Air Force Lockheed Hudson. It was the first attack made on a submarine by the RAAF Western Area. Alerted to the likely presence of a Japanese submarine in the area by the destroyer USS *Whipple*, the Hudson's aircrew made a near-fatal assumption. No one had briefed them on U.S. submarines heading toward Fremantle.[28] Indeed, throughout the war Allied submarines remained vulnerable to "friendly fire." By the end of hostilities, British submariner Mervyn Wingfield had been attacked not only by Italian and Japanese aircraft but also by Norwegian, French, British, and American planes.[29] When the *Sargo* crew docked at Fremantle, the Australian aviators who bombed them were there to apologize, but Jacobs remained adamant that he wanted to be relieved. He told his division commander, Stuart "Sunshine" Murray, that he had lost all confidence in the torpedoes and that his nerves were shot.[30]

Another submariner to be relieved of command at Fremantle was USS *Searaven*'s skipper Theodore Charles "Ted" Aylward. *Searaven* had been undergoing an overhaul at the Cavite Navy Yard in the Philippines when Japanese bomb shrapnel punctured the submarine's superstructure and wrecked part of the deck. After making emergency repairs, the *Searaven* crew departed on December 13, 1941, only to be depth charged by destroyers at the entrance to Manila Bay. They were attacked again when patrolling off Cam Ranh Bay. While traveling south to Fremantle, they played cat and mouse with another submarine thought to be Japanese. Only after reaching port did the crew discover that the other submarine was USS *Swordfish*, which had been ordered to Fremantle while en route back to Surabaya. When USS *Searaven* limped into Fremantle, the crew's food supplies were nearly exhausted, and Aylward, suffering high blood pressure and other symptoms of stress, was replaced.[31]

John Wilkes, who commanded American submarines in the Philippines and then in Java, departed for Australia on USS *Spearfish* along with other senior officers and top-secret code equipment. *Spearfish* had already been depth charged off Celebes and then took another pounding as the Japanese invasion force approached Java. The submarine's skipper, Roland Fremont Pryce, sent a message that he was worn out and was relieved by Jack Dempsey. When *Spearfish* sailed for Fremantle, Pryce traveled as a passenger on his former command.[32] Getting *Spearfish* to Fremantle proved problematic. While the crew knew the latitude and longitude of Fremantle from a Dutch sailing table, they lacked detailed charts of the Western Australian coast and had to make do with an old map from a *National Geographic* magazine that one of the officers had acquired in Manila. When they were fifty or sixty miles out of Fremantle, they were met by a Royal Australian Navy destroyer that transferred some detailed charts on how to enter the harbor. At Fremantle they found the port crowded with ships; perhaps a hundred merchant vessels were tied up flying various national flags, along with destroyers and other warships that had survived the retreat from the Philippines. The most welcome sight was the submarine tender USS *Holland*. *Spearfish* pulled alongside the mother ship, and the crew boarded the tender to find out the latest news.[33]

Even in March 1942 the Americans were not the only submariners in Fremantle. At the time Germany invaded the Netherlands in May 1940, there were fifteen Dutch submarines in the Far East, including twelve K-class boats and three O-class boats. During the frantic period between the Japanese attack on the Philippines and the evacuation of Surabaya in early March, Dutch submarines based in the Netherlands East Indies in fact made a stronger showing than their U.S. counterparts. The Dutch managed to sink six enemy ships compared to three by U.S. submarines.[34] These early successes, however, were followed by a series of disasters in which one Dutch submarine was lost in a British minefield, one fell victim to a Japanese destroyer, one was sunk by a Japanese submarine, and another was scuttled after being badly damaged by a depth-charge attack. By the time the base at Surabaya was evacuated only seven Dutch submarines remained operational; four were sent to Ceylon and three to Fremantle.

Those that arrived in Australia (*K-VIII*, *K-IX*, and *K-XII*) were the oldest and needed repair the most. The K-class (*Kolonien* or colonial) submarines had been purpose-built for service in the Far East, equipped with air conditioning and gun armament and able to make lengthy voyages. By World War II, however, many of the Dutch K-class submarines, first based at Surabaya in 1924, were largely obsolete. It had been two years since any spare parts for submarines reached the Far East from the Netherlands, and any repair to the diesel engines required the arduous task of making parts locally. Of the three Dutch submarines that arrived at Fremantle, two never left Australian waters.[35]

K-VIII departed Surabaya on March 3, 1942, and reached Fremantle on the evening of March 17. With Surabaya burning, *K-VIII* had difficulty taking on sufficient fuel for the journey and ended up needing to be towed the final leg to Fremantle. Johannes Loep, who arrived in Fremantle with the submarine supply ship MV *Janssens*, was assigned to work in *K-VIII*'s engine room, but when the Americans inspected the submarine in May 1942 they declared it unfit for war patrols. Loep and five others were transferred to England to join another submarine.[36] With *K-VIII* decommissioned, it was pillaged for parts. The main battery and some electric motors were installed on the troubled *K-IX*, while the conning tower deck was used for the pilot boat *Lady Forrest*, today on exhibit in the Western Australia Maritime Museum. One of the submarine's propulsion electric motors ended up in a winch house used to service the submarine slipway later constructed at the west end of Fremantle Harbour, and the empty hull was towed to Jervois Bay south of Fremantle, where it lay abandoned for many years until determined to be a navigational hazard. The remains were finally blown up in 1957.[37]

Like *K-VIII*, the *K-IX* was originally built in 1922, but survived longer. After participating in antisubmarine training off Fremantle, the aging boat was sent to Sydney in May. With increasing Japanese submarine activity off Australia's coasts and without any submarines of its own, the Royal Australian Navy accepted *K-IX* as a training vessel to provide a target for Asdic (sonar) operators to practice on.[38] Only *K-XII*, originally commissioned in 1925, carried out operational missions from Fremantle during 1942. As Japanese forces closed on Surabaya, *K-XII* was the last vessel to leave the Dutch base on March 6. Its passengers included Rear Admiral Pieter Koenraad, the naval commander of Surabaya, along with his staff. The submarine originally headed for Ceylon, but after encountering two Japanese sub hunters and surviving a twelve-hour depth charging, *K-XII* diverted to Fremantle, arriving on the evening of March 20.[39] The *K-XII*'s crew had already distinguished itself by sinking a Japanese troopship and tanker off Kota Bharu, Malaya, in December 1941. On Christmas Day 1941 they recovered nine men from the crew of a shot-down British Catalina seaplane and delivered the men to Singapore two days later. After arriving at Fremantle the submarine was sent to Sydney for refit before returning to operate from Western Australia from September 1942 to May 1943.

The Dutch submariners had even more reason than the Americans to feel demoralized in the opening months of the Pacific War. While they had sunk more enemy ships, they had also lost far more men to enemy action and had to cope with the abysmal mechanical condition of their boats. Most of all they suffered the emotional strain of worrying about the fate of families and friends left in the Netherlands East Indies. Many of the men had no idea what happened to loved ones now under Japanese control.[40]

For the U.S. Navy, with recent memory of the Japanese attacks on Pearl Harbor, Manila, and Surabaya, the concentration of submarines at Fremantle created the specter of a similar disaster. It was decided to split the force, and on March 15 the submarine tender *Holland* and the

Catalina tender *Childs,* accompanied by the minesweepers *Lark* and *Whippoorwill* with the destroyer USS *Parrot,* escorted five submarines some 250 miles south to Albany. The *Holland* remained there for the next four months refitting submarines.[41] The *Lark* and the *Whippoorwill,* in addition to carrying out minesweeping and antisubmarine patrols, met incoming submarines at sea to escort them to base.

The quarantine station at Albany was used for housing some of the submarine force, while officers were put in the less-than-luxurious rooms of the Freemason Hotel. With a population of about four thousand, Albany mainly served the surrounding pastoral and agricultural districts. As with population centers farther north, the people of Albany prepared for the possibility of invasion, with barbed wire strung along Middleton Beach and machine-gun nests set up. Albany's inner harbor provided a good defensive position since it could be entered only through a narrow dredged channel. The submarine tender *Holland,* moored behind the dock in Princess Royal Harbour, was positioned so that its guns could sweep the entrance channel if necessary. On the other hand, the only land-based antiaircraft defenses were two outdated 6-inch guns.[42]

The potential threat to Albany was taken very seriously by Thomas Blamey, returning from the Middle East and shortly to be appointed the commander in chief of Australian military forces. When the *Queen Mary,* converted to a troopship, anchored at Fremantle on the afternoon of March 23, 1942, Blamey was among the passengers. More than thirty years earlier Blamey had worked as a schoolteacher at the Fremantle Boys' School, a school among those recently closed in the fear of an imminent attack. Although he spent only two days in Western Australia before flying east, Blamey was struck by the state's vulnerability. He believed the Japanese might seize Western Australia's potential wealth with a force no larger than the one used to capture Malaya, and he thought Albany in particular offered an attractive anchorage for the enemy.[43]

In reality, unknown at the time, the worst of the Japanese offensive on Western Australia was over. Although the Japanese bombed Broome three more times and eventually made a total of seventeen air raids on Western Australian territory, most proved to be "nuisance raids" or "diversionary tactics" rather than doing serious damage. The last Japanese submarine attack on shipping off the Western Australian coast came on August 4, 1942, when *I-32* shelled the 8,720-ton passenger ship *Katoomba* three hundred miles from Albany.[44] Based on the attacks of March 1942, however, most Western Australians assumed things would only get worse.

Periodic alarms about a possible Japanese attack continued to drive submarines south. When USS *Tambor* arrived at Fremantle on September 19, 1942, rumors of a Japanese assault resulted in the submarine spending the next eighteen days at Albany.[45] As late as March 18, 1943, John Curtin sent telegrams to Winston Churchill and Franklin Roosevelt singling out Fremantle as especially vulnerable to a Japanese naval bombardment or attack by carrier-based planes. It was not until July 1944 that Western Australia's premier, John Willcock, announced that "we feel we have now averted any threat of invasion."[46]

CHAPTER

LIKE HEAVEN

A shared vulnerability brought Western Australian civilians and Allied submariners together in a symbiotic relationship. For Western Australians, the presence of a major submarine base at Fremantle reassured them that they would not be simply abandoned to the invading Japanese. For Allied submariners, having faced death at sea and far from their homes, Western Australian civilians offered a semblance of normality. The anxieties of the local population quickly turned to gratitude, and they welcomed the visitors into their homes and hearts.

Corwin Mendenhall, an officer on USS *Sculpin*, reported after his first leave in Perth in March 1942 that "the Aussies had captured our affection. Their friendliness and hospitality were heart warming."[1] When *Sculpin* returned from patrol the following month, a loudspeaker announcement that the Rottnest Island navigational light was in sight brought a cheer through the entire boat. James Calvert, originally from Ohio and an officer on USS *Jack*, credited the light on Rottnest, located about eleven miles from Fremantle, with an almost mythical power. "It was safety; it was respite from the eternal vigilance for Japanese planes; it promised relaxation and letters from home; and it welcomed us to a place that would, we knew, be our home away from home."[2]

Subsequent visiting submariners were no less enthusiastic about Western Australia. With an extravagance typical of many other sailors, Hughston Lowder from USS *Batfish* pronounced "if ever there was a heaven on earth for submariners, it was Perth."[3] Tom Parks from USS *Sailfish* similarly declared that "coming to Fremantle and Perth was like entering Heaven."[4] News that a patrol was going to end at Fremantle inevitably created a wave of expectant excitement on board submarines. Wes Headington, on USS *Thresher* in 1942, recorded in his diary, "This is the one we've all been talking about because our destination is Perth, Australia."[5]

Pearl Harbor remained America's main submarine base in the Pacific, but despite the mystique of Hawaii as a romantic paradise, many sailors found their stopovers on Oahu disappointing. Submariners returning from patrol were put up at the lavish Royal Hawaiian Hotel on the beach at Waikiki, so there were few complaints about the accommodations. The hotel grounds, though, were circled by barbed wire, and strict curfews were enforced. Submariners who stayed at the Royal Hawaiian Hotel were only allowed to entertain women on the ground floor between the hours of 5:00 and 7:00 p.m., while the islands remained under martial law until October 1944.[6] Overcrowded with military personnel, it was said that if you saw a line in Honolulu it was either in front of a liquor store, movie theater, or brothel. James B. O'Meara, an electrician's mate on USS *Seahorse*, summed up his experience at Honolulu's Hotel Street as "an hour or two drinking the terrible stuff they called whiskey, getting your uniform all messed up, avoiding the shore patrol, and getting in line to get laid."[7]

There were few women to socialize with; most European females were evacuated after the attack on Pearl Harbor, and most of those remaining were in steady relationships. The journalist Robert Trumbull claimed of submariners in Hawaii that "they have practically no opportunity to meet the type of girl that the average young man from the States would care to entertain among his friends in his own home town."[8] When submariner Tim McCoy attended a dance at the Navy Recreation Center in Waikiki, he found it crowded with more than a thousand men and only thirty women.[9] Gordy Cox complained in a letter to his mother that "the only hula dancers over here are in photo shops where you pay 50 cents to get your picture taken with them, and half of the time they're not real Hawaiians."[10] In the absence of other female companionship, the brothels of Hotel Street in Honolulu were said to service 30,000 customers a day.

Much of the appeal of Western Australia for submariners was the large number of English-speaking, ethnically similar women who appeared as interested in the Americans as they were in them. In contrast to Hawaii, Robert Trumbull found the situation quite different in Australia, noting that "the Australian girls find the 'Yanks' attractive, and vice versa."[11] Numerous commentators have noted the heightened sex drive that seems to exist in times of war. The attraction appeared to be accentuated for young women brought up with Hollywood movies that gave the Americans a halo of glamor, while modest differences in language and customs appeared to enhance the thrill of discovery on both sides.[12] Betty Bloom, at the time a sixteen-year-old living in the Perth suburb of Shenton Park, recalls that she and her friends liked to look at the Americans and listen to them talk. "I started dating them, going out with different ones with my girlfriends to dances. I had a good time."[13] At least in the early stages of the American visitation, dating a sailor appeared almost a patriotic imperative.

As described by submariner Hughston Lowder, with pretty girls in abundance there was romance everywhere in Perth, and "some of us fell in love."[14] After their first leave at Perth in March 1942, several crewmen from USS *Sculpin* had already expressed their intent to marry Australian women on their return to port. By the middle of 1942 a number of *Sculpin* men had indeed married and three or four more had declared their intent to do so.[15] The Dutch submariners also quickly developed relationships with the local women. Only a few days after arriving in Fremantle, Jan van Hattam was invited to a wedding reception at the Orient Hotel in Fremantle. Six months later another officer he knew decided to marry. Although there was supposed to be a two-month waiting period, this seems to have often been circumvented. Van Hattam himself married an Australian woman a short time later.[16] At least for some couples, marriage seemed to offer a semblance of stability and emotional comfort in the midst of uncertainty.

Submariners had a reputation for keeping their own company; a journalist for *Life* magazine described those in Honolulu as generally "aloof" and "furtive."[17] As described by Paul Snyder, who served with *Guardfish* and *Seahorse*, crews on leave mainly socialized "within their own pod."[18] In Australia, however, the possibilities for social interaction expanded. In Western Australia submariners found not only an abundance of eligible women but a civilian population eager to extend hospitality. Not surprisingly, it was often young women who bridged the gaps and formed relationships between visiting submariners and local families. Albert Rupp, who served on relief crews at Albany and Fremantle before joining the crew of USS *Grenadier*, noted, "I found the young ladies to be very good company and was asked to their homes to meet their families, cementing the bond between us, as they were so much like cherished loved ones at home."[19]

Friendships seemed to form quickly and easily between submariners and civilians. Chris Kreiss from USS *Batfish* remarked, "I think it was actually the best port because the folks there treated submariners royally."[20] John McCain, later a U.S. senator and presidential candidate, recalled that his father, a World War II submarine commander, spoke about Perth all of his life because "people were so wonderful to the Americans."[21] An officer from USS *Gunnel* professed that at Fremantle "I feel that I was treated there like a native son, and for that I will be eternally grateful."[22] Albert Rupp claimed, "Truly, Perth was a very unique place with a very special people who opened up their hearts and homes to all the 'yanks' who passed through, maybe not knowing they would always have a part of the hearts of those who served there."[23]

Unlike Hawaii, one of Perth's drawing cards was a relative absence of other military personnel. While large numbers of Australian men were in the military overseas, the visitors helped to fill a vacuum. One American submariner, Cecil S. King, later enthused with typical hyperbole that "all the Australian men had gone overseas. There were a hundred beautiful Australian girls to each American sailor."[24] Although Perth hosted a Catalina air base, the city was largely viewed as the preserve of submariners. While clearly affected by the war, Perth also retained a semblance of normality that appealed to men on leave. According to journalist John Field, one of the pleasures of returning from a submarine war patrol was simply to "walk around to look at the streets, the stores and the green trees."[25]

To some submariners, Western Australia seemed to offer a simplicity nostalgic of America's recent past. Zeke Zellmer from USS *Cavalla* was struck by the butcher shops with sawdust floors that had long been supplanted by grocery chains in the United States. His crewmate Don Haseley thought many of the buildings in Fremantle and Perth had a look of the "wild west" about them.[26] At times, this association with an earlier era vexed men. Gordy Cox, attached to the submarine tender *Holland*, complained in a letter home in May 1942 that "there sure isn't much to do over here," adding, "all of the music over here was out before I left home."[27] Especially on public holidays, Perth could pose a challenge for those seeking a good time. Victor Radwick arrived back from patrol looking forward to a big leave to discover that on Sundays everything was closed including the movies. Radwick and two crewmates got together some snacks and alcohol, then roamed the nearly deserted streets looking for female company. Eventually they came across three women from the Australian army who agreed to celebrate the New Year with them at a nearby park.[28] Over time the amenities for servicemen improved, and as Fremantle's reputation spread among submariners, it became an ever more popular port of leave.

CHAPTER 3

WILKES

Capt. John Wilkes, after supervising the retreat from the Philippines, became the first commander of submarines based at Fremantle. A graduate of the Naval Academy in 1916, he attended the Submarine School at New London in 1922 and received his first submarine command two years later. He had served at the Mare Island Naval Yard before assignment to the Asiatic Fleet. With white hair and what some described as movie-star looks, Wilkes affected a forceful yet aloof management style.[1] While commanding submarines of the Asiatic Fleet at Manila, Wilkes had been scheduled to be detached in the first week of December 1941 and rotated back to the United States, but the Japanese attacks on Pearl Harbor and the Philippines changed this plan, and he would not be replaced until mid-May 1942.

Wilkes set up his Fremantle office at 7 High Street and also established a headquarters in Perth occupying a couple of floors in the Colonial Mutual Life Insurance (CML) building. The premises were protected by a home guard of Western Australian men in their late forties or fifties, described as mainly farmers. By the end of March, twenty-two submarines had reached Fremantle, but with the submarines' spare parts and torpedoes largely abandoned in the Philippines, Wilkes commanded a severely undersupplied force.[2] The Australian military provided protection for the port, with the Royal Australian Navy responsible for harbor defenses including operation of an antisubmarine net system. The defensive boom across the harbor entrance was first constructed in December 1940 and kept closed from sunset until sunrise. Coastal gun batteries and searchlights covered Gage Roads and the entry channels to Fremantle, while gun positions on North and South Mole protected the harbor entrance. Australian aircraft flew missions from Pearce air base to patrol the seaward approaches to Fremantle until May 1945.[3]

At Fremantle Harbour, the U.S. Navy gained the use of two wheat-loading sheds for repair and machine shops. Civilian contractors were also used to construct new buildings and renovate existing ones at North Wharf. For the time being, though, Fremantle lacked the facilities to carry out major overhauls on submarines, so an arrangement was struck with Pearl Harbor to exchange submarines a couple at a time. Fremantle submarines requiring overhauls were sent on patrols that ended at Pearl Harbor, while newly refitted submarines at the American harbor would make patrols to Australia. During April seven submarines made patrols from Fremantle, including two that returned to Pearl Harbor for overhaul. The total ships claimed sunk by Fremantle submarines from March through April 1942 was nine, later whittled down by postwar assessments to seven ships totaling 25,387 tons.[4] The relatively low tonnage claimed during these first months in Fremantle was in part because U.S. submarines largely carried out "special missions" supplying and evacuating troops stranded in the Philippines. Of sixteen patrols from Fremantle during March and April, five were special missions to the small island of Corregidor in Manila Bay.[5]

John Wilkes, commander of U.S. submarines at Fremantle from March to May 1942
U.S. Naval Institute Photo Archive

Among these missions, USS *Permit* was sent to Corregidor to evacuate Gen. Douglas MacArthur. A week after the fall of Singapore, President Roosevelt ordered MacArthur to leave the Philippines for Australia, and although MacArthur opted to leave Corregidor by PT boat instead of by submarine, *Permit* still evacuated thirty-six code-breaking specialists. Once transported to the island of Mindanao, MacArthur along with his wife and son next flew to Darwin in a B-17 bomber. From there it was a short flight to Alice Springs and then a train to Adelaide before traveling on to the state of Victoria. MacArthur's arrival in Melbourne on March 21, 1942, did much for Australians' morale, especially in the eastern states. When MacArthur arrived at Spencer Street station, five thousand Melbournians turned out to greet him, and later the crowd at his hotel had to be cleared by mounted police.[6] One Melbourne newspaper proclaimed him "the greatest tonic we have had in this war."[7] As supreme commander of all Allied forces in the Southwest Pacific area, he would exercise enormous powers.

American and Filipino forces on the Bataan Peninsula in the Philippines, suffering from slow starvation and rampant disease, surrendered on April 9. More than 70,000 men became prisoners of the Japanese, although a few thousand managed to escape to the island of Corregidor. USS *Spearfish* became the last submarine to visit Corregidor before the island fortress fell to the enemy on May 6, 1942. On May 3, *Spearfish* picked up eleven Army nurses, one Navy nurse, six Army colonels, six Navy officers, and one Navy wife, along with naval financial records. The evacuees were amazed to find a single-layer chocolate cake waiting for them in the crew's mess when they boarded the submarine; conditions, however, quickly deteriorated. The passengers and crew spent the next twenty-two hours submerged and would not see daylight again for seventeen days, during which time everyone on board experienced seasickness. Even so, one of the nurses, Lucy I. Wilson, concluded that submariners "are the world's best to me!"[8]

Arguably the most dramatic evacuation during this period, and one that helped solidify the bonds between Americans and Australians, took place in April 1942. USS *Searaven* departed Fremantle on Thursday, April 2, under the command of Hiram Cassidy, a native of Brookhaven, Mississippi. The submarine was to deliver a consignment of 3-inch antiaircraft ammunition to the Philippines, but this mission was aborted following the fall of Bataan on April 9, when it was believed the surrender of Corregidor would soon follow. *Searaven* was redirected to a patrol area, and on April 11 the crew received a message ordering them to evacuate a group of thirty-one Australians stranded south of Cape Kurus on the 290-mile-long island of Timor.

Under a long-standing agreement with the Netherlands East Indies, Australia was committed to reinforcing Dutch forces on Timor in the event of war in the Pacific. Australian troops, code-named Sparrow Force, arrived at Timor on December 12, 1941. For the Japanese the island was a staging point toward Java, and they invaded both Dutch West Timor and Portuguese East Timor on February 20, 1942. In the Portuguese sector Australia's 2/2nd Independent Company, a special-forces-style unit of more than three hundred men mainly recruited in Western Australia, retreated into the interior and continued to conduct a guerrilla campaign against the Japanese for the next twelve months. These men would later be evacuated in stages, with the last group picked up by the submarine USS *Gudgeon* on February 10, 1943. Those fighting in the Dutch sector, on the other hand, surrendered several days after the invasion began,

USS *Searaven* and its crew rescued thirty-one Australians from Timor in April 1942. U.S. Naval Institute Photo Archive

with more than a thousand Australians, mainly men of the 2/40th Battalion, becoming prisoners of the Japanese.[9]

Among those to evade capture was a contingent of the Royal Australian Air Force under Meteorological Officer Bryan Rofe, which retreated into the jungle. The group of stranded Australians was later joined by Flight Lieutenant Harold Oliver Cook and Pilot Officer Vivian Charles Leithhead, a native of Perth. Their Hudson aircraft had been shot down by Zeros during an air raid on Kupang the same day that *Searaven* reached the waters off Timor. Helped by local villagers, the airmen managed to travel forty miles to meet up with the other RAAF men, but Cook, suffering from infected shrapnel wounds, needed urgent medical attention.

The *Searaven*'s crew was not the first to attempt to rescue the Australians. The original plan had been to evacuate them by flying boat, and an aircraft was specifically scheduled for this task. Unfortunately, the flying boat was among those destroyed when Japanese Zeros laid siege to Broome on March 3. With the situation deteriorating throughout the Netherlands East Indies, any further rescue attempts appeared unlikely. But then the stranded Australians received a cryptic radio message via

Darwin: "Do you have a way of shining a light out to sea?"[10] Extracting these men by submarine was highly dangerous, and the crew of *Searaven* received warning that they might be entering a trap since the Australians used a dubious code in their radio messages. The proposed rendezvous spot was only twenty miles north of the Japanese base at Kupang. On April 13, as *Searaven* made its way down the west coast of the island, signals were detected from the beach. When the submarine surfaced at 7:00 p.m. the following evening there was a fire burning near the proposed rendezvous site.

Searaven carried a sixteen-foot wherry, but when it was hoisted over the side it was discovered that the boat's diesel engine no longer worked. The crew quickly fashioned a pair of makeshift oars out of two-by-fours and ammunition crates. Ens. George Carlton Cook of the U.S. Naval Reserve volunteered to lead the boat party, and also volunteering was Joseph McGrievy, along with a friend, Swede Markeson, quartermaster first class. Paddling to the beach proved unnerving, not only because of the prospect of ambush by the Japanese but because of the huge sharks that knifed through the water next to their boat. When they were near shore at about 9:00 p.m., Ensign Cook swam in to reconnoiter the beach. As he approached the fire, men scattered into the darkness of the jungle, and, unsure if they were Australians or enemy soldiers, Cook hustled back to the boat.

Searaven received instruction by radio to try again, and on Friday night, April 17, the boat party again paddled to shore. Some five hundred yards from the beach, they swam in trailing long lines to the wherry. This time they returned to *Searaven* with sixteen Australians, reaching the submarine just before dawn. Below decks the Australians were given bowls of hot tomato soup and sandwiches to warm them up. All were weak and emaciated, but another seventeen men in even worse shape had been left on shore.

After an anxious day with rumors of an imminent Japanese attack, the boat party returned to the beach, this time receiving a cheer of thanks from the Australians remaining ashore. The weakest Australians had their wrists tied together, which were then looped over the neck of a submariner for the swim to the wherry. This time the boat party included an extra sailor for the rescue operation, Machinist's Mate Johnny Lintz. Known for his strength, Lintz was to pull the weakened Australians into the wherry. When the Australians reached *Searaven*, four of the men were barely capable of moving and all but two had to be carried below by the submarine's crew. One Australian, a barely conscious P. J. "Phil" Kean, narrowly avoided being left on the afterdeck when *Searaven* submerged.

Fortunately, Kean spoke up as preparations were made to dive, reportedly saying in an Australian accent to a sailor "Hey, mite, wotabutemei?"[11]

The additional men on board taxed the submarine's oxygen supply; the patrol report recorded that "the air throughout the whole ship was most odorous due to the malaria sweat of so many sick men."[12] The strain of caring for so many ill became even more complicated when, four days after departing Timor, a serious fire broke out in the main electrical cubicle. After a three-hour battle to contain the fire, the crippled *Searaven* was only able to make about two knots on its way back to Australia. Luck seemed to smile on *Searaven*'s crew again, however, because another American submarine was able to come to their aid.

USS *Snapper*, under the command of Hamilton L. Stone, had recently completed its own special mission, delivering a cargo of food to the rescue ship *Pigeon* and taking on twenty-seven military evacuees from Corregidor. After receiving *Searaven*'s distress call, *Snapper* sighted the submarine the following morning and took it in tow. With rough seas, one of *Searaven*'s crew described the experience of being towed as "like a carp on the end of a fishing pole."[13] By late afternoon the Australian corvette HMAS *Maryborough* and the destroyers USS *Paul Jones* and USS *Parrott* were on the scene. *Maryborough*, with 1,750-horsepower engines capable of making fifteen knots, took over the job of towing *Searaven* to Fremantle. Before entering the harbor, the Australian evacuees were taken off *Searaven* for the hospital and the submarine was towed to the dock the following day. Both *Searaven* and *Snapper* arrived at Fremantle on April 25; appropriately for the rescued men it was Anzac Day, which commemorates the Australians' first military action during the First World War. While on leave in Perth, the *Searaven* men received a jubilant reception, including a party thrown for Cassidy and his crew by an Australian servicemen's organization. For *Searaven* crewman Joseph McGrievy, the rescue of the Australians proved the highlight of his thirty-year Navy career. He was awarded a Silver Star for his role in the operation, and he made some lasting friends. After the war he returned to Australia to attend a reunion of the men he helped evacuate from Timor.[14]

During Wilkes' tenure at Fremantle, both the likelihood and fear of a Japanese invasion declined. America initially proposed leaving Australia's west coast as a British responsibility, but following Australian protests Western Australia was incorporated as part of the Southwest Pacific Area. This was just as well, since the British Eastern Fleet under the command of Admiral Sir James Somerville was on the retreat in the Far East. In early April the Japanese bombed British bases on Ceylon. On April 5 more than 120 aircraft attacked Colombo and on the same day sank the cruisers HMS *Dorsetshire* and HMS *Cornwall*. Four days later a massive air raid damaged the British naval base at Trincomalee, while the aircraft carrier HMS *Hermes* and the Australian destroyer HMAS *Vampire* were sunk at sea. The Royal Navy's Eastern Fleet retired first to Bombay, India, and then to Kilindini, East Africa.[15]

British submarines had all but abandoned the Far East at this stage of the war. In March 1942 there were only two British submarines, HMS *Trusty* and HMS *Truant*, based at Ceylon, as well as four Dutch submarines under British operational control. The British submarines were soon recalled to England for refit, leaving only the Dutch boats for patrols. The situation remained much the same until mid-1943, when British operations in the Mediterranean became less critical and boats were transferred to the Indian Ocean.[16]

In April Western Australia's defenses were reinforced by the transfer of six thousand troops from Victoria. The same month, on April 17, Prime Minister Curtin placed all Australian forces in the Southwest Pacific area under General MacArthur's command.[17] By this time the number of Allied troops in Australia included 40,000 Americans, 100,000 men of the Australian Imperial Force (AIF), and 265,000 militia. Another 100,000 men, many veterans of the First World War, made up the Volunteer Defence Corps. These forces, though, could not be moved rapidly due to the deficiencies of Australia's road and rail infrastructure, especially in the west.[18] More decisive in alleviating Australians' fear of invasion was the Battle of the Coral Sea (May 5–8). On May 4 a Japanese invasion force sailed from Rabaul for the Allied naval base at Port Moresby on Papua New Guinea. Port Moresby was the largest port on New Guinea's southwest coast, and its capture would disrupt the flow of supplies linking Australia and the United States. Thanks to signals intelligence, the Americans anticipated this move, and following a series of naval actions between aircraft carriers, the Japanese force turned back. The Japanese lost ninety-two planes in the engagement, and the deaths of many experienced pilots would have a detrimental effect on their future operations.[19] The *West Australian* newspaper joyfully, albeit inaccurately, proclaimed "Japanese Fleet Destroyed" and that no U.S. ships were lost.[20] Despite such distortions, the battle did represent a significant turning point in naval warfare in that it was fought entirely by carrier planes and for the time being ensured Australia's safety. Nationwide there was a collective sigh of relief.

CHAPTER

LOCKWOOD

Wilkes' replacement at Fremantle was Capt. Charles Andrews Lockwood Jr., who at the time of the Japanese attack on Pearl Harbor had been in London as America's naval attaché. On hearing news of the attack an incensed Lockwood confided to his diary, "They [the Japanese] had best enjoy their sneaking victory for, by God, they'll pay for it. Now my job is to get away from here."[1] He immediately began writing to his Navy contacts in an attempt to escape from what he called the "paper-pushing brigade" to a posting in the Pacific.[2]

Born in Virginia on May 6, 1890, Lockwood grew up on a farm in southwest Missouri. He graduated from the Naval Academy with the class of 1912 and broke the academy record for the mile run the same year. Lockwood had served in the submarine service since 1914, and he enjoyed an iconic status among his peers that earned him the nickname "Uncle Charlie." Relatively short in stature at five-feet-eight-inches tall and with an affable disposition, Lockwood gained a reputation for his energetic approach and for cutting through red tape.[3] For the time being, he directed these talents toward getting transferred to a war zone.

At last, on March 12, 1942, Lockwood received orders detaching him from duty in London and instructing him to proceed to Washington, D.C., where he and his wife spent a hectic but pleasant month before flying to their home in Coronado, California. For Charles it was a brief stopover; he confided to his friends in London that he would soon be traveling "much farther West."[4] While in Washington, the chief of naval operations, Adm. Ernest King, personally ordered him to assume responsibility as commander of Submarines Southwest Pacific based in Perth. Lockwood flew first to Brisbane on April 28 before making his way to Perth at the beginning of May. Arriving at Fremantle on a rainy afternoon, he compared the streets to a "Kansas boom town."[5] With time, however, he considered the Perth landscape comparable to California and reported that he "felt very much at home."[6] On May 22 he formally relieved John Wilkes as commander and set about trying to relieve the palpable "atmosphere of depression" that he sensed.[7] The submariners' morale was low; Lockwood noted in his diary that "all this retreating has taken something out of them."[8] He fretted over the worn and emaciated appearance of men coming in from war patrols, predicting that some were destined for breakdowns unless properly rested.

Barely a week after Lockwood assumed command at Fremantle, events on the other side of the continent reminded Australians of the close proximity of the Japanese. On the night of May 31 three Japanese midget submarines slipped into Sydney Harbour to make an attack. The potential targets in port included the cruiser USS *Chicago*, which had recently taken part in the Battle of the Coral Sea. One of the submarines got caught up in the harbor's defensive antisubmarine net, while another was sunk by patrol boats. The third managed to fire its torpedoes, missing the *Chicago* but hitting HMAS *Kuttabul* at Garden Island. A former Sydney ferry being used as a depot ship, *Kuttabul* went down with nineteen men. As it happened, the Dutch submarine *K-IX* previously sent from Fremantle to Sydney for antisubmarine training was moored alongside *Kuttabul*, and as the ship sank it struck the submarine, damaging its battery and forward superstructure.[9]

Even before the Japanese midget submarine attack, *K-IX* was in pitiable condition. Lieutenant F. M. Piggott, who was assigned supervision of *K-IX*, professed, "When I first saw my new Command I nearly had a fit."[10] The submarine's last major refit had been four years earlier. At this stage bureaucratic problems added to *K-IX*'s physical limitations. After the damaged battery was removed and sold for scrap, Australian customs attempted to levy an import duty on the battery. An incensed Rear Admiral F. W. Coster, in charge of Dutch naval forces, withdrew his offer of the submarine to the Royal Australian Navy for training, and it took almost another year before the matter was resolved.

At the end of May there was at least some reason for personal celebration: Lockwood learned he had been promoted to rear admiral. Characteristically addressing his wife via his diary, Lockwood wrote, "I just can't tell you how I felt! Amazed—unbelieving—delighted all of those impressions flashed thru my mind—and on top of them all a very deep sorrow that you should not be here to hear the news with me."[11] Lockwood's wife, Phyllis, was the daughter of Rear Adm. Bull Irwin, who once commanded USS *Oklahoma*, so Lockwood may have felt special pride in the eyes of a woman eleven years his junior.

The following month there was more reason for celebration. America's success in the Battle of Midway proved more decisive than the Battle of the Coral Sea and further bolstered Allied spirits. Admiral Isoruku

Yamamoto looked to an attack on Midway as a way of cutting the lines of communication between the United States and Australia, as well as drawing U.S. aircraft carriers into a decisive battle.[12] In large part because the Americans had cracked the Japanese codes, the plan backfired horribly. Although the Americans lost the carrier USS *Yorktown*, the Japanese lost four carriers. Following this victory, Prime Minister Curtin informed his Advisory War Cabinet on June 16 that "I do not think the enemy can now invade this country."[13] The same month it was determined to establish airfields at Milne Bay on the eastern tip of Papua New Guinea. The subsequent attempt by the Japanese to take the airfields resulted in the first victory by Allied land forces in the Pacific War.[14]

At Fremantle, Lockwood immediately began campaigning for reinforcements to carry out overhauls on submarines so returning crews could have the luxury of a couple of weeks respite between patrols. With the submarine tenders overcrowded, some of the men were forced to sleep on their submarines even while round-the-clock repair work was taking place. Lockwood wanted something similar to the system in Hawaii, where submariners returning from patrol were immediately whisked off for two weeks of R & R. Following the precedent established at Pearl Harbor, he believed it important for both submariners' morale and "physical reconditioning" that they be well treated on shore.[15] Lt. Cdr. Tyrell Jacobs, following his relief as skipper of *Sargo*, was moved to the administrative staff, and by mid-June Lockwood put him in charge of looking after the welfare and morale of submariners on leave between patrols. In the city of Perth and the oceanside suburb of Cottesloe, two hotels were taken over for the exclusive use of submarine crews where enlisted men might spend their recreation leave at no cost.[16] A couple of buses were also rented to provide the men with transportation.

In the meantime, recreational activities for servicemen improved as dance halls and night clubs, virtually nonexistent before the war, proliferated. The Lido on the waterfront at Cottesloe was one of the first night spots to open. Two Perth sisters, Molly and Pat Wagner, set up a night club in the Karrakatta Club on St. George's Terrace, which they called the Cabarita. The United Service Club later opened on the east side of Barrack Street, where the hostess, Gwen, became known for her diaphanous gowns and Carmen Miranda–style turbans.[17] The Coconut Grove in Hay Street was a favorite of Dutch sailors, and on occasion a band from the ship *Tromp* played with the house band. Dutch submariners also frequented the Havana, Silver Dollar, and the National Hotel in Hay Street. There were also canteens that hosted dances at the Government

Charles A. Lockwood Jr., commander of the Fremantle submarine base from May to December 1942   U.S. Naval Institute Photo Archive

House ballroom and Perth Town Hall, while the YMCA Services Social Centre in Murray Street promised dances Tuesday, Wednesday, Friday, and Saturday nights with "Partners and Supper provided."[18]

Also attractive to men on leave were the many places to eat at for reasonable prices such as the Florentino Café, the Green Gate, Bernie's, and the Silver Buffet. Bernie's was known for its hamburgers and thick steaks cooked over charcoal in forty-four-gallon drums. Chinese restaurants attracted patrons to Perth's James Street and in High Street, Fremantle, while Molinari's near Karrinyup was known for its Italian food.[19] The United Nations Café in Barrack Street, Perth, offered a wide variety of fish, poultry, and beef dishes for a little over two shillings. The Pig'n Whistle Café at 4 Market Street, Fremantle, stayed open until 1:30 a.m. serving steaks and omelettes for similar prices, while hot toasted sandwiches and hamburgers could be had for about a shilling.[20]

Submariners on leave widely embraced outdoor activities like horseback riding and picnics at Mundaring Weir. At the time, horseback riding was permitted in King's Park, and many sailors went for picnics in the hills.[21] Going to the beach was also a popular pastime, although potentially hazardous to men who had just spent sixty days cooped up in a submarine. Charley Odom ended up with blisters all over his body from sun bathing, which the locals treated with lanolin, and Edward "Fitz" Fitzpatrick later missed USS *Blenny*'s patrol from Fremantle after falling asleep in the sun and getting severely sunburned.[22]

Many sailors were determined to get outside the main population centers and visited sheep stations or went kangaroo hunting in the bush, while others stayed on farms in the southwest. Sunshine Murray recalled that "the boys got a big kick out of farming, because a lot of them came from farms."[23] Farmers also appreciated having them around, especially in fruit-picking season. Looking for places where they were unlikely to run into others from the military, George Seiler and Irwin "Moose" Hornkohl from USS *Gudgeon* ended up at Mt. Barker. Seiler took a train to Kalgoorlie as well, later reflecting on the large number of hotel pubs located there. On yet another trip he visited Sawyer's Valley and professed, "I loved to go to these places that are way off the beaten track."[24] Bob Hunt and some of his crewmates took the train to the small community of Katanning, some 170 miles east of Perth. To Hunt, the place reminded him of the small town where he grew up. Local farmers extended dinner invitations, and he was quickly accepted into the family of one of the local young women. At one point Hunt unadvisedly tried to live up to the locals' image of him as a cowboy by riding an unbroken horse, and he ended up crashing into a house.[25]

The love affair between submariners and the local women continued unabated. Lockwood observed that "the girls of Western Australia were exceptionally fine looking, usually of the athletic type, so it was not surprising that our lads were attracted to them."[26] Some American sailors became engaged within days of meeting women. American submariner Andy Anderson met his future wife three days after arriving in Western Australia; he was quickly "adopted" by his girlfriend's family and

American submariner John Mosby, golf clubs in hand, visits a friend's farm at Meckering, Western Australia. Note the blackout shrouds on the car headlights in background. Bruce Teede

stayed with them on all of his subsequent leaves. Soon after the submarine tender *Holland* arrived at Albany, Homer White visited the Allied Service Club, where he first met Ethel Hassell, whose parents owned a nearby farm. By July 1942 the couple were engaged, and they were married the following month.[27] Adm. Herbert F. Leary had established a six-month "cooling off" period for those intending matrimony in Australia. Lockwood believed the waiting period should be reduced to three months, and he was prepared to make the time even shorter if a pregnancy was involved. Nevertheless, enlisted men still had to wait six months after filing marriage applications, and their prospective brides required character references, letters from parents, and doctor's certificates. The legality of these regulations, though, was questionable, and it is apparent that some sailors married without waiting for official approval.[28]

To some sailors it appeared that distance meant they had license to temporarily forgo commitments to girlfriends and wives at home. Although already married, Alastair Mars recalls being advised by a senior officer to "grab yourself a blonde" while on leave in Perth.[29] Despite also being already married, James Calvert, an officer on USS *Jack,* fell head over heels for a young Fremantle woman named Kathie Aberdeen, a university student and Navy driver.[30] William Ruhe, executive officer of USS *Crevalle*, was alarmed to discover just how many of his crew wanted to be transferred to shore duty in Perth. They were, in Ruhe's term, mainly "Perth happy" fellows infatuated with the local women. Fearing that their performance on patrol might be affected, he threatened to have any men who didn't do their jobs properly assigned to the stark Aleutian Islands.[31]

Those men who had shore assignments gained an obvious advantage in forming relationships with local women. In 1942 Gordy Cox accompanied the tender USS *Holland* to Albany, where the men received a liberty every fourth day. He soon wrote home that he had found a girlfriend, an attractive blonde named Linley Austin, Lin for short. About every liberty Cox would join Lin and her parents for dinner before going to a movie or dance. Cox turned nineteen while in Albany, while Lin was apparently still a student; they attended a high school ball. Cox observed, "I can't dance very good, but nobody knows the difference." Such quickly formed relationships, however, could end just as suddenly. Once Gordy Cox was transferred to the tender *Pelias* and sent back to Fremantle, the romance faded. Cox reported to his family that he had heard from Lin only once in the two months since he had left Albany, "so I have practically forgotten her."[32] Charlie Rush was another sailor whose love life benefited from shore duty. Taken off USS *Thresher* after suffering dental problems, he was put in charge of assigning men to relief crews and outgoing patrols. He acquired a girlfriend in Fremantle whom he was able to see almost every night. As Rush remembers it, life was good, but all too soon he was sent back to submarines for a war patrol.[33]

Similarly, Chuck Vervalin was able to spend two happy months in Western Australia after being transferred from USS *Gudgeon* to a relief crew on the tender *Pelias*. Working on overhauling diesel engines by day, he pursued other interests at night, which included relationships with a number of Australian women before encountering the girl of his dreams while strolling through a shopping arcade. This was nineteen-year-old Gwen Haughey, a private in the Royal Australian Women's Army, who lived with her family in Victoria Park. Chuck was not even put off when her mother accompanied them on their first date, a screening of the movie *Penny Serenade* starring Cary Grant. As Gwen later remembered it, Chuck "looked like Gary Cooper, and was very gentlemanly . . . and looked great in his uniform."[34] Like Charlie Rush, though, all too soon Vervalin returned to submarine duty, in his case with tragic results.

In August 1942 social relations between Americans and Australians at Albany underwent a brief crisis following the alleged rape of a local woman by an African American serviceman. Charles Lockwood described the case as "very nasty," and at least for a time black personnel at Albany were prohibited from going ashore after dark for fear that locals might try to retaliate against them.[35] As a result of this case, Lockwood advocated replacing African American stewards on submarines with Filipinos and Chamorros (indigenes of the Mariana Islands). Less seriously perhaps, Lockwood urged skippers making patrols out of Fremantle to bring back Filipino survivors who might serve as mess attendants. Lockwood reported that the first batch of such "recruits" returned to port with USS *Tautog*, four young Filipino survivors picked up after the submarine sank a Japanese fishing sampan in the Sulu Sea.[36]

Like most American institutions at the time, the U.S. Navy segregated African Americans and limited their opportunities for advancement. The U.S. secretary of war, Henry Stimson, unashamedly defended such policies, claiming that blacks were "less capable of handling modern weapons."[37] On U.S. submarines African Americans were limited to the positions of stewards and mess attendants, and at sea their duties included serving the officers' meals and cleaning their quarters. On most submarines, though, stewards and mess attendants assumed responsibilities far beyond this. They might be assigned lookout duties or serve on gun crews for example. Like everyone else on board, stewards went through the process of qualifying as submariners and were accorded the privilege of wearing the dolphins on their uniforms. Like the rest of the crew, they also shared the very real risks of a submarine patrol. During the course of the war ninety-seven men from the steward's branch, including seventy-four African Americans, were lost on submarine patrols.[38]

Despite Lockwood's reservations, African Americans continued serving in Western Australia, sometimes spending lengthy periods on shore duty. As with other submariners, stewards were rotated to serve on relief crews and assigned to tenders. Donald Fenner, originally from Smithfield, Virginia, was assigned to the submarine tender *Otus* after making two patrols with USS *Snapper*. He worked on a relief crew from April to July 1942 before joining the crew of the ill-fated USS *Grampus*. Robert Coley from Alabama made one patrol with USS *Bugara* before getting off at Fremantle, where he worked with a relief crew and remained for three years on shore duty.[39]

While it appears that African Americans were generally well integrated into submarine crews at sea, the dynamic could quickly change on shore. According to Richard Lucas, a steward's mate on USS *Raton*, "When ashore, we went our way, they [white shipmates] went theirs."[40] Similarly, Hosey Mays, who served as steward on USS *Crevalle*, recalls that "when we went over the gangway on liberty, we went our separate ways because of the times and segregation. . . . We didn't associate generally with the crew or with the white elements on the beach."[41] Instead Mays spent his leave with the other African American steward from *Crevalle*, Timothy Pennyman. Whether through choice or exclusion, small groups of stewards sometimes found their own housing rather than staying at hotels leased by the Navy.

That stewards were sometimes excluded from ship's parties signified their liminal status. Robert Goens from USS *Icefish* attended his submarine's party in Perth, but to do so he had to ask his crewmates to treat him as a "dark-skinned Caucasian" for the evening.[42] On the other hand, crew loyalty at times transcended racial differences on shore. Steward's Mate Elvin Mayo recalled an incident in Perth when men from another submarine started abusing him with racial taunts. One of his crewmates defended him, telling the men "Mayo is part of my crew."[43] There were also friendships between black and white crewmates that carried over to shore leaves; from USS *Pampanito*, Charles A. "Red" McGuire hung out with John Lewis Johnson, steward's mate first class and one of two African Americans on the *Pampanito*.[44]

Some of the places frequented by African American submariners in Perth included the Westralia Café, the China Café, the All-Night Restaurant, and the bar of the Newcastle Hotel.[45] Local authorities appeared particularly concerned about the interaction of black servicemen with the Aboriginal population that congregated in East Perth, and African Americans were forbidden from associating with Aboriginal women. There was increased surveillance in the area by police, the Native Affairs Department, and American shore patrols. Nevertheless, there were so-called safe houses where the Americans hung out with black Australians.[46]

Given the "White Australia" policy of the day, which restricted immigration, one might imagine African Americans received a frosty reception in Western Australia. When the Australian colonies federated in 1901 to become a nation, much of the impetus for union came from xenophobia and the desire to ensure that Australia remained predominantly of British stock. One of the first acts passed by the new Federal Parliament was an Immigration Act that effectively excluded nonwhites. Australia's Advisory War Council objected to black troops, and the first group of African Americans to arrive at Melbourne were prevented from landing by customs officials. The United States overrode these objections, however, and by the end of 1942 there were about eight thousand African Americans stationed in Australia.[47] Most of the evidence suggests that they were generally accepted by the community. At least some African American submariners later recalled Australia as a "paradise" where the people were friendly and unprejudiced. Hosey Mays, originally from Denver, Colorado, made war patrols on USS *Crevalle* and USS *Bowfin*, then spent the remainder of the war as a relief crewman on the tender *Howard W. Gilmore*, based at Fremantle. According to Mays, "Australia was a good place. We were called 'Black Yanks' and the kids wanted to feel our hair and skin. We were taken into people's homes—there was no prejudice."[48]

CHAPTER

TORPEDOES AND TRAGEDIES

Apart from improving the morale and fitness of his men, Lockwood's most immediate concerns were with the number and material condition of the submarines in his charge and the performance of their torpedoes. One of his major preoccupations was replacing the aging S-boats with more modern fleet submarines. The twenty-six U.S. Navy S-boats in operation at the beginning of the Pacific War had been built between 1918 and 1924. The five S-boats initially based at Fremantle were transferred to Brisbane on the other side of the continent after a base began operations there in April. Even so, Lockwood continued to fret over their capacity to make war patrols. Without air conditioning and with a relatively slow surface speed of fourteen knots, their operations in the South Pacific were severely handicapped.[1] There was a saying among those who served on S-boats that their luck seldom turned except for the worse.[2] Lockwood informed Vice Adm. Herbert Leary that the S-boats were "entirely unsuitable for the job they are now performing."[3] In a similar vein Lockwood later complained to his friend Capt. C. W. "Gyn" Styer that "the crying need at the moment is for more boats in the most productive areas and for Fleet replacements of the 'S' class."[4] The latter were falling apart, and although they had begun to install air conditioning in them locally, they were plagued by decrepit machinery. Because Australia was at the end of the Pacific pipeline, spare parts were in short supply, a problem aggravated by the country's national transport system, in which each state had a different railway gauge.[5]

The shortage of torpedoes was particularly acute. The primary American weapon was the Mark-14 steam torpedo, armed with 660 pounds of Torpex (an explosive 50 percent more powerful than TNT) and capable of running 4,500 yards at high speed (i.e., 1,500 yards per minute or forty-six knots). At this stage of the war, such complex weapons were being manufactured in only small numbers. In the rush to evacuate the Philippines, 230 of the precious torpedoes had been abandoned in storage.[6] Just as critical, there were increasing reports of the torpedoes malfunctioning. The poor performance of the torpedoes offered a possible explanation for the lackluster performance of American submarines in the opening stages of the war. Of eight submarines that departed Fremantle for patrols in April 1942, James Wiggins "Red" Coe's *Skipjack* was the only one to sink any enemy ships.[7] Although Fremantle submarines claimed six ships the following month, complaints about the torpedoes continued. On Lockwood's watch, however, submariners in Western Australia made a major contribution toward unraveling the defects of the torpedoes.

After returning to Fremantle from a patrol off Indochina, skipper "Red" Coe added his own complaint to a growing fund of stories about torpedo problems. A big man with pale skin, thinning red hair, and bulging eyes, Coe's earlier success at sinking ships gave him a credibility some other skippers lacked. Coe included a detailed summary of torpedo problems in his patrol report.[8] Prompted partly by Coe's critique and pushed by his chief of staff, Capt. Jimmy Fife, Lockwood ordered a test of the torpedoes. On June 20, 1942, USS *Skipjack* fired its last three torpedoes at five hundred feet of fishnet stretched across Frenchman's Bay some six thousand yards offshore near the mouth of King George Sound, Albany. The fishnet had been purchased from a local fisherman to calibrate the depth at which the torpedoes hit their target. Fired from a range of one thousand yards, the torpedoes hit the net before heading into the shallows where they could be recovered.[9]

If not exactly shots heard round the world, they certainly resounded through the U.S. submarine service. All three torpedoes ran deeper than the depth at which they were set. The first two torpedoes fired were supposed to run at a depth of ten feet, but they actually hit the fishnet at eighteen and twenty-five feet. The third torpedo, set to run on the surface, ricocheted off the bottom of the harbor before it hit the fishing net at a depth of eleven feet. The tests confirmed what many submarine skippers had been claiming for months: the torpedoes ran deeper than set and often undershot their intended target.

James Fife, with a representative of the Bureau of Ordnance present, supervised the test from the tender USS *Fulton*. Still, the Bureau of Ordnance insisted that the experiment was not sufficiently scientific to draw a definite conclusion. Lockwood scheduled a second series of tests conducted on July 18 that confirmed the original findings. In the meantime, he wrote to Rear Adm. W. H. P. "Spike" Blandy at the bureau urging him to conduct his own tests.[10] In his same letter to Blandy, Lockwood lamented the continuing shortage of torpedoes. The loss of torpedoes stored at the Cavite Navy Yard in the Philippines continued for more than a year to create a shortfall in the weapons available to submarines in Australia. At the time the U.S. Navy was producing only sixty torpedoes a month, and even after the production was stepped up, transport problems slowed delivery to the Southwest Pacific.[11] Many submarines set out on patrol with less than a full complement of twenty-four torpedoes, frequently making up the shortfall with a load of mines to be laid.[12]

On August 1, 1942, the Bureau of Ordnance at Newport revealed that new tests by its engineers confirmed that the Mark-14 torpedoes ran ten feet deeper than set, finally vindicating the claims made by Lockwood and numerous skippers.[13] Time would prove that the American torpedoes not only ran deep but were riddled with additional faults that only became apparent after the correction of other mechanical defects. No other issue created so much anger among submariners as the defects of their torpedoes.

Despite torpedo problems, U.S. submarines continued to sink ships, although in fewer numbers than many skippers imagined. USS *Sturgeon*'s skipper, William "Bull" Wright, had earned his nickname for his gift as a storyteller rather than for his disposition or physique. By the time he reached Fremantle, Wright had two war patrols under his belt and had already entered submarine lore when, after claiming two hits on an unidentified ship during the second patrol, he radioed the message "Sturgeon no longer virgin."[14] The claimed hits were never confirmed, but Wright's quip became famous.

After a period recuperating in Western Australia, USS *Sturgeon*'s crew departed Fremantle on the evening of June 5, 1942, for their fourth patrol still under the command of Bull Wright. Among the officers on board *Sturgeon* was Lt. Chester W. Nimitz Jr., son of the American Pacific Fleet's commander in chief. On June 30 at about 10 p.m., under a nearly full moon, the submarine crew spotted an unlit Japanese ship making a zigzag course north of Luzon in the Philippines. *Sturgeon*'s crew believed it to be a troop ship, and initially the submarine was unable to keep pace. "This fellow was really going," Wright recorded in his patrol report.[15] He decided to persist, and about midnight his quarry inexplicably slowed down. The ship was in fact waiting to rendezvous with two destroyer escorts, but this proved a fatal error. At 2:25 in the morning of July 1, *Sturgeon* launched four torpedoes from four thousand yards, two of which connected with the target. In a matter of minutes the ship began going down by the stern, and through the periscope Bull Wright let his crew have a look at the dying ship as men jumped from its decks.

On July 22 the men of the *Sturgeon* were again back in Fremantle for a period of leave after a successful patrol. What was not known at the time, and would only be discovered after the war, was that *Sturgeon*'s attack on July 1 had caused the greatest loss of life in Australia's maritime history. Contrary to the *Sturgeon* crew's belief that they had sunk a ship transporting Japanese soldiers, those on board were mainly Australian prisoners of war. Had this fact been known at the time, it would most likely have seriously strained relations between U.S. submariners and Australians. The ship, later identified as the 7,267-ton *Montevideo Maru*, had sailed from Rabaul on the boomerang-shaped island of New Britain, which had been mandated to Australia from Germany following the First World War. Amid growing tensions in the Pacific, small garrisons of Australian troops were established on various northern islands to form a forward observation line. Like the Australian force on Timor, the one on New Britain was given a bird code name, Lark Force. The Second Australian Imperial Force 22nd Battalion arrived at Rabaul in April 1941, but again, as in the case of the Australians on Timor, the force was grossly inadequate. Following massive raids by carrier planes, a Japanese force of five thousand troops invaded the island on January 21, 1942, and easily swept aside the underequipped, vastly outnumbered, and inexperienced Australian soldiers defending it.[16]

Faced with food shortages at Rabaul, the Japanese decided to send their Australian prisoners to the island of Hainan, and on June 22 about 845 enlisted prisoners were marched from their camps to the docks of Rabaul's harbor. Those boarding *Montevideo Maru* included not only captured soldiers but approximately two hundred civilian internees, among them planters, company managers, government officials, public servants, and missionaries. In addition to prisoners, the ship carried eighty-eight crewmembers and sixty-four naval guards. After the ship sank, many of the crew and guards managed to make it to land on Luzon, but most were killed by Filipino guerrilla fighters on the island. All the Australians perished; those who made it off the ship were kept from the lifeboats by the Japanese marines. As later recalled by one of the Japanese survivors, Yoshiaki Yamaji, to his amazement some of the Australians clinging to wreckage began singing "Auld Lang Syne."[17]

Although word of the sinking reached Rabaul little over a month later, the Japanese Navy Department did not report the loss to the Prisoner of War Information Bureau until January 1943, and it was only in late 1945 that Major Harold S. Williams from the Australian Army Directorate of POWs discovered the relevant files. According to the Japanese records there were 1,053 prisoners and internees on board; the Australian federal government only officially announced the deaths on October 5, 1945.[18]

Among those lost was Charles Ross Field, the director of public works at Rabaul. Aged forty-seven, he had survived the fighting at Gallipoli and the Somme during World War I. By the time the Japanese invaded Rabaul, his wife Nellie had been evacuated to Western Australia, where she set up a household in Mount Lawley with her teenage daughter and five-year-old son. At one stage they received a letter written by Charles while in captivity. In March 1942 the Japanese had permitted prisoners to write letters home, which were later dropped from the air over Port Moresby. Remarkably, hundreds of the letters eventually found their way to the addressees. Nellie died three months after they received the letter from Charles, leaving her young son Tony to be cared for by an aunt. He would not learn of his father's fate until he was a teenager.[19] Another of those lost with *Montevideo Maru* was twenty-four-year-old Fred Mansley, who had initially escaped into the jungle when the Japanese invaded, but surrendered after injuring his leg. Without clear information, his family held out hope for years that he was hiding somewhere in the islands, possibly suffering from amnesia.[20]

Such personal tragedies would be multiplied many times. *Montevideo Maru* was the first Japanese prison ship to be sunk by an American submarine, but it proved far from the last. By the end of the war more than ten thousand Allied POWs were lost as a result of U.S. and British submarine attacks. On July 1, 2009, a plaque was unveiled at Subic Bay in the Philippines commemorating the loss of those on the *Montevideo Maru* sixty-seven years earlier. A memorial at the Bita Paka War Cemetery on Rabaul also lists the victims of the disaster. Despite being confined to a wheelchair, Fred Mansley's sister, Doreen, attended an Anzac Day ceremony there in 2012.[21] To commemorate the seventieth anniversary of the ship's loss, a memorial statue was unveiled in Canberra at the Australian War Memorial on June 30, 2012, during a ceremony attended by more than a thousand people.

During his months at Fremantle, Lockwood kept up a rigorous routine, often rising at dawn and working well into the night. His quarters in a suburban home on Jutland Parade offered a reasonable commute to both his offices in Perth and the submarines docked at Fremantle, although he found the frequent loss of hot water while showering disconcerting. He also worried about putting on too much weight, complaining to his wife that lack of exercise and too much good food was taking its toll on his "girlish figure."[22]

By August 1942 Lockwood had surrounded himself with what he described as a "swell staff."[23] Stuart S. "Sunshine" Murray initially worked as operations officer and then served as Lockwood's chief of staff from August on. Born in Texas on March 22, 1898, Murray graduated from the Naval Academy in 1919. When the Japanese attacked Pearl Harbor, Murray had only recently arrived in Manila to command a submarine division of the Asiatic Fleet. As Murray later recalled, on December 7, 1941, he played a round of golf and paid his initiation fee to the Army-Navy Club in Manila. The $100 fee proved a poor investment; at 2:00 a.m. the following morning he was awakened to the news that America was at war and told to get his submarines on patrol.[24]

Once Murray became Lockwood's chief of staff, Heber Hampton "Tex" McLean headed operations. McLean had arrived on the tender *Pelias* from San Francisco in July 1942 to assume command of Submarine Division 21 and serve as assistant operations officer.[25] John Mylin "Dutch" Will also arrived with the tender *Pelias*. Described as a "tough and exacting" repair specialist, he ran the overhaul and relief crews, while Joe Connolly looked after materiel concerns.[26] Apart from Lockwood's genuine concern for his men, his personality made him popular with his staff as well. He was, according to one senior officer, "a perfect gentleman—smart, meticulous."[27] Lockwood respected the judgment of his subordinates, and while he was not above correcting his officers, he did it without rancor.

Many of his senior staff pestered Lockwood to go out on war patrols, and he was inclined to oblige them. Part of his reasoning was that most submarines were making disappointing patrols, and a senior observer might help sort out what was going wrong.[28] Tex McLean, described by one contemporary as having icy eyes and at times a mean disposition, talked Lockwood into letting him make a patrol with USS *Sargo*. The fifty-day patrol, though, proved disappointing. McLean characterized the skipper, Richard Victor Gregory, as someone better suited to making repairs than combat. *Sargo* sank only one ship on the patrol, first hitting it with a torpedo and then finishing it off with the deck gun. On his return to Fremantle in late October 1942, McLean became commander of Submarine Division 61 and assumed the role of operations officer.[29]

Lockwood's relationship with the Australian civilian workforce was more strained than with his staff in the submarine service. According to an American commentator writing in early 1942, Australia's productive potential was constrained not only by a small population and a shortage of skilled workers but by a "socialistic outlook."[30] Lockwood complained in November that "Aussie work is awfully slow" and prone to "go on strike with or without visible reason."[31] Like many servicemen, Lockwood tended to regard wartime strikes as a form of treason. Anticipating the possibility of labor disputes, he groused, "Perhaps we can make them believe that the Japs would give them even more unfavorable labor conditions."[32]

In reality, Lockwood encountered little industrial trouble. Most strike action took place in the coal mines and factories of New South Wales, and the Americans also tended to overlook the extent of industrial disputes on their own home front. While U.S. business and labor had called a temporary truce in the aftermath of Pearl Harbor, large-scale industrial conflict was soon back on the agenda.[33] Although the Americans sometimes took a jaded view of Australian production and labor practices, they nevertheless depended heavily on Australian workers and infrastructure.

Under the exigencies of war, the Australian government was able to implement the type of controls only dreamed of in peacetime. From January 1942 a Directorate of Manpower controlled the country's labor resources, able to order men and women into any civil or military occupation. Many skilled Australian workers had been prohibited from enlisting in the armed services and "manpowered" into supporting essential services and industries. Numerous men employed by the State Engineering Works, the Western Australian Government Railways Midland Workshops, and the East Perth Power Station were put to work repairing and maintaining Allied submarines. Despite the blackout restrictions on lighting that included fitting hoods over car headlamps, the flashes of welders continued to illuminate the night sky.[34]

In September 1942 a marine slipway, under construction since 1940, was completed. Located at the west end of Victoria Quay, the slipway was used for servicing and painting submarines and other naval vessels and merchant ships. It remained in operation until 1998 and is used today to display the *Oberon*-class submarine HMAS *Ovens* at the Western Australian Maritime Museum.[35] In the end, as described by American submariner Lloyd R. "Joe" Vasey, Fremantle was "an ideal base, well away from the air threat; had all the logistics, facilities, excellent railhead, skilled work force, a slipway, wonderful repair facilities."[36]

The main issue the Fremantle base faced during the second half of 1942 was the declining number of submarines available for patrol. Beginning in August with USS *Sculpin*, many fleet boats were transferred to Brisbane, mainly because of the American offensive in the Solomon Islands, which began that month. On August 7 the first U.S. Marines landed on the island of Guadalcanal as well as Tulagi, twenty-five miles to the east. The occupation of the islands began a long battle of attrition in the Solomon Islands that would not end until February 1943. As the Americans stepped up operations in the Solomon Islands, eleven more submarines were transferred from Fremantle to Brisbane over the next three months, so that patrols emanating from Western Australia dropped to only about four a month.[37]

The only patrol made by a Dutch submarine during this period was that of *K-XII*. Returning to Western Australia after refit in Sydney, *K-XII* was mainly used for "special missions" landing and picking up reconnaissance patrols behind enemy lines. The *K-XII* crew made its first mission in September 1942, when, during Operation Mackerel, the submarine landed three Dutch men of the Netherlands East Indies Forces Intelligence Service (NEFIS) on the south coast of Java.[38]

During 1942, twenty-six U.S. submarines made a total of sixty-one patrols from Fremantle, with activity peaking in July, when ten submarines departed for patrol. The most patrols were made by *Seadragon*, *Searaven*, and *Swordfish*, each making four runs from Fremantle. In total, according to official postwar assessment, Fremantle submarines were responsible for sinking forty enemy ships with a combined tonnage of 158,849.[39] This was achieved despite a shortage of torpedoes and defective torpedoes. Still more dramatic was the turnaround in the morale of the submarine force based at Fremantle. Once a depot for the demoralized men who had retreated from the Philippines and Netherlands East Indies, Fremantle now provided the best rest and recreation facilities in the Pacific.

CHAPTER

CHRISTIE

The beginning of 1943 saw a major shake-up in the U.S. submarine service. On January 19 the commander of Submarines Pacific, Adm. Bob English, and many of his senior staff were killed in a plane crash near San Francisco. Charles Lockwood was anointed the new head of submarines in the Pacific. Lockwood was keen to take up his new post at Pearl Harbor, but leaving Perth was not without a sense of loss. In light of the hospitality he had received, Lockwood described his departure as "like parting from life-long friends."¹ During the period of more than a month between Lockwood's departure and the arrival of his successor, Capt. Allan R. McCann acted as commander of submarines in the Southwest Pacific. McCann had originally arrived in Fremantle as squadron commander of the tender *Pelias* and twelve submarines, but for this brief period was the senior naval officer in Western Australia.²

The officer named as Lockwood's successor at Fremantle and commander of Submarines Southwest Pacific was Ralph Waldo Christie, recently promoted to rear admiral. At the time of the Japanese attack on Pearl Harbor, Christie was based at Newfoundland, commanding a division of submarines used for antisubmarine training. When the first American submarines began arriving at Fremantle, Christie had been en route to Brisbane with a division of S-boats from the Panama Canal. Departing Balboa in early March, the submarines traveled 12,000 miles to arrive at Brisbane on April 15, 1942. Remarkably, the six antiquated S-boats survived the forty-two-day journey without a major breakdown. At Brisbane the submarines were joined by five more S-boats formerly part of the Asiatic Fleet to make up Task Force 42 under Christie's command.

Christie's first impressions of Australia were less than favorable. Although he found the weather "delightful," he described Brisbane as "a nine o'clock town, dreary and drab." He was especially annoyed at the reluctance of Australian quarantine officials to let him land his pet dog, Pepper, commenting to a friend, "They have, however, no objections to us saving them from the Japs."³ While Christie headed submarine operations from Brisbane, his relations with Lockwood at Fremantle

Ralph W. Christie, commander of the Fremantle submarine base from 1943 to 1944   U.S. Naval Institute Photo Archive

were sometimes strained. They competed for the limited number of new fleet boats and trained men available to the Navy in 1942. More explosive, however, was the issue of torpedoes. Christie, who held a master's degree in mechanical engineering from MIT, had been involved in the development of the Mark-VI exploder at Newport, Rhode Island, at one stage becoming head of the torpedo section.

While in Australia, Christie continued to defend the American torpedoes even as evidence of their faults accumulated. He believed poor maintenance was responsible for many of the problems, and he deeply resented Lockwood's tarring the torpedoes' reputation in his patrol report endorsements.[4] Nevertheless, although their respective staffs were well aware of the tensions between the two men, for the most part Lockwood and Christie kept a lid on their differences. Lockwood wrote to Christie in November 1942, "We are all in this business together so let's keep all our fighting for the Japs and not indulge in unproductive bickering among ourselves."[5] The same month the torpedo issue had reached a critical stage, and the Bureau of Personnel informed Christie he was being transferred to the Torpedo Station at Newport in the role of inspector of ordnance in charge.[6] In no hurry to relinquish his Brisbane command, Christie stalled his departure until the end of December, when he was replaced by Lockwood's former chief of staff, James Fife. No sooner had Christie reached Newport, however, than events conspired to bring him back to Australia.

Given the comparable roles played by Christie and Lockwood at Fremantle, comparisons between the personalities of the two men seemed inevitable. Four years older than Christie, Lockwood came across as the more stolid, dedicated, and hard-working. Some described him as a "gentleman" with an easygoing disposition and good sense of humor. Submarine skipper Reuben Whitaker felt Lockwood's only fault was a tendency to be overly loyal and to keep some ineffective officers on his staff.[7] Christie, handsome and looking much younger than his age, impressed people with his vigor. Proud of his athleticism, Christie boasted to Adm. Richard S. Edwards that he was "fit as a fiddle and can still trim anyone in the squadron in either golf or tennis."[8] His energy also extended to the opposite sex; some admired him as a reputed ladies' man while others questioned his morals.

Christie's initial impressions of Perth were more generous than those of his first arrival in Brisbane, describing the city as "quiet, pleasant and beautiful."[9] He took up residence at 4 Crawley Avenue in the expansive premises known as "Bend of the Road." John Wilkes and Charles Lockwood had occupied a nice two-story home on Jutland Parade after the owners, anticipating a Japanese attack, had "taken to the hills."[10] Bend of the Road had become available under similar circumstances. The home was owned by one of Western Australia's most intriguing women, Miss Alice Cummins, who was not only one of Australia's few female barristers at the time but most likely the nation's only female brewmaster. Convinced that Perth would be bombed by the Japanese, she loaned her home to the U.S. Navy and moved inland to Kalgoorlie.[11]

Christie resided at Bend of the Road with a half dozen of his senior staff. After Sunshine Murray transferred to Pearl Harbor to resume his role as Lockwood's chief of staff from March 1943 on, Christie's new chief of staff was another Texan, Heber "Tex" McLean. McLean, who had formerly been working as the operations officer in Fremantle, characterized his shared accommodation at Bend of the Road as comfortably furnished, but more functional than lavish.[12] The home offered an excellent view of Crawley Bay and easy access to leafy King's Park. They were served by mess cooks who had survived the sinking of USS *Houston*, and Christie had a Packard car for the ten-minute drive to his offices in Perth. The car was driven by an attractive and vivacious Dutch refugee from Java, Mary Hartman, who made a strong impression on the submariners who met her. Alvin Jacobson, a young officer on USS *Flier*, believed her family had fled from Jakarta when the Japanese invaded, and he wrote to his family that her grandfather had been one of the owners of the Dutch electrical giant, Phillips. While on leave, Jacobson contrived to spend as much time as he could with her.[13] Tex McLean was similarly enchanted by Hartman and recalled her as a "wonderful" person whom they treated as a daughter.[14]

While working long hours, Christie also gave free rein to his competitive instincts and self-professed love of gambling. The routine at Bend of the Road included playing darts for money each evening before dinner. Christie also played three or four rounds of golf each week, inevitably wagering on the outcome. Among naval men Christie was hardly alone in these pursuits; Britain's submarine admiral Max Horton played a round of golf virtually every day, and the Japanese admiral Isoroku Yamamoto had a passion for off-duty gambling.[15] In Christie's case, though, there were some who thought he took advantage of his rank. Skippers returning from patrol were invited to Bend of the Road for games of darts and poker, sometimes losing significant sums of money. From Christie's point of view, such informal recreation helped loosen up the men into giving him a truer picture of what was happening at sea, but some critics accused him of getting the officers drunk and then fleecing them of their pay.

One of the skippers less than impressed with Christie was Lawson Peterson Ramage, who was quoted after the war as saying he "was for the birds" and "I never could stand him."[16] Originally from Massachusetts, Ramage graduated from the Naval Academy in 1931 and was nicknamed "Red" for his shock of wavy auburn hair. He departed Fremantle on December 29, 1942, for his third patrol as the *Trout*'s skipper. On the morning of February 14, 1943, in what proved to be the last attack of the patrol, Ramage sighted a ship he described as a 7,700-ton tanker emerging from a rain squall off Balikpapan, Borneo. He had considerably overestimated the size of his target; the ship was later identified as the 1,911-ton *Hirotama Maru*. The *Trout* crew fired two torpedoes at the ship from only seven hundred yards. One of the torpedoes struck the ship's bow, but the other failed to explode. It was the third dud torpedo of the patrol, and a frustrated Ramage ordered a battle surface on the craft, sending the crew to the deck guns and opening fire.

The crew of *Hirotama Maru*, determined to go down fighting, sprayed *Trout* with machine-gun fire from the bridge and stern. As the gun battle continued Ramage decided "it was going to take another torpedo to complete this job."[17] He turned *Trout*'s stern to *Hirotama Maru* and fired. This time the torpedo exploded and sank the ship within five minutes. Ramage, though, had crewmembers in need of medical attention. Seven of his men were hit, mainly in the legs, by enemy bullets or flying metal, and another three crewmen suffered ruptured eardrums from firing *Trout*'s deck guns.

Trout headed for Fremantle, but when it arrived on the evening of February 24 the harbor's submarine nets had been closed. Despite his protests, Ramage and his crew were forced to spend the night anchored outside the harbor until the nets opened the following morning. At near midnight, medical officers boarded *Trout* to tend the wounded, but to Ramage it was a ludicrous situation. Incensed that there were also five large troopships anchored outside the harbor awaiting entry, Ramage felt these potentially fat targets could be easy pickings for any enemy submarines in the vicinity. As Ramage put it later, "here were the five greatest targets in the world sitting right there at anchor and they wouldn't open the gate to let us in."[18]

A meeting with Christie once *Trout* docked did little to placate him. Ramage claimed that of fourteen torpedoes fired on the patrol, one had exploded prematurely and five were duds. Christie, however, argued that Ramage's lack of success was due mainly to human error. The official endorsements of the patrol also criticized the failure to use more torpedoes in attacks on two tankers that were left damaged instead of sunk.[19] A tense standoff over the torpedoes was only ended when Christie's operations officer, Capt. "Tex" McLean, insisted it was time for Ramage to leave Christie's office.[20]

Despite his dislike of Ralph Christie, Red Ramage still declared that "Fremantle is the best port for R & R in the Pacific."[21] Even more than the enlisted men, submarine officers were catered to during their periods of leave in Western Australia. Many officers visiting Perth stayed at a residence known as the Lucknow, at 2 Queenslea Drive in the suburb of Claremont. A former rest home overlooking the Swan River, the house afforded a spacious community room and adjacent dining room where the men shared family-style meals. With each officer contributing £14, they were kept in food, liquor, and beer for two weeks. Activities were supervised by a type of house mother, whom one submariner described as resembling an aging version of the actress Joan Bennett with a penchant for revealing clothing. Staying at Lucknow allowed officers to meet officers from other submarines and swap stories about recent war patrols.[22]

As befitting their rank and responsibilities, submarine commanders resided in even greater luxury while on leave. On Oahu, skippers lived in a suite at the Royal Hawaiian Hotel, while enlisted men stayed four to a room. In Perth, skippers stayed at two private bungalows leased in the lush residential area of Dalkeith on Birdwood Parade. At times executive officers might also be put up at the captains' rest home, known as Birdwood. The hostess and manager was Gwen Plaiston, who assisted in organizing recreational activities. According to Corwin Mendenhall, the days were mainly filled with tennis, swimming, the beach, picnics, and horseback riding.[23] George Grider, skipper of USS *Flasher*, recalled his time there as idyllic. He woke each morning to be served orange juice by a house boy, and there were quart bottles of Australian beer available with all the meals.[24]

One of the perks skippers enjoyed was access to automobiles, often with a uniformed female driver. Shirley B. Pearce, twenty-two years old, was one of the local women who acted as a driver, as well as working a switchboard at the U.S. Navy establishment at Fremantle's North Wharf. The women wore uniforms similar to the American officers, except with a skirt hemmed just below the knee and no necktie. Christie had some 150 young women in his employ, who in addition to a uniform received £5 a week. Christie believed the women were more excited by the uniform than by the money.[25]

Like enlisted men, some officers sought experiences away from the city. John R. Bertrand, the ensign and commissary officer on USS *Bowfin*, headed for Tinglewood, some three hundred miles away from Perth, during his leave. With a Texas farming background, Bertrand equated normality with fishing and milking cows. Bertrand had studied toward a PhD at the University of Missouri Agricultural Experiment Station before joining the submarine service, and he also made contact with the University of Western Australia to learn about local agriculture. The

UWA academic Dr. Hartley Teakle not only escorted Bertrand around the state's vineyards but frequently hosted him at his home during the three periods of leave Bertrand spent in Perth.[26]

For skippers wishing to escape the city, there were retreats where they could stay in relative luxury as well as isolation. After a brief splash on the town, Tommy Dykers took a seaplane to the south coast and could take any officers who wanted to accompany him.[27] Following one patrol of USS *Flasher*, several of the officers were flown in Admiral Christie's seaplane to a camp some 240 miles south near Albany. There the men amused themselves hunting, fishing, and playing cards.[28]

Some officers found their way to country areas through family connections. George Ridgway, in his early teens during the war, recalls leading a kangaroo hunting party of Americans at the family property at Moora. His aunt lived in Albany, where she served on a welcoming committee for the crew of USS *Pelias*. One of the *Pelias* officers, J. E. Madden, was keen to shoot a kangaroo, so George's aunt arranged for him to visit Moora, about 110 miles north of Perth. Madden arrived at the Ridgway homestead with a gunner's mate, Joe Wokter, and a photographer named Llewellyn Perkins. George was given the task of leading the men through the bush to find a kangaroo. This proved difficult, especially since the Americans were wearing white uniforms, and at the end of the day they returned empty-handed. George's father took the men out that night, however, and they managed to shoot a kangaroo spotted in the car's headlights. According to George, the Americans took the kangaroo with them, and Madden later propped the animal in a truck's passenger seat and drove up and down Fremantle's North Wharf while honking the horn.

George and his father were later invited to visit *Pelias*, by this time based in Fremantle, where they were treated to lunch and dinner and given a guided tour through one of the U.S. submarines. There was also a postscript. During the kangaroo hunt the photographer, Perkins, had lost his watch. It had great sentimental value because it had been given to him by his wife before he departed San Francisco, but despite a lot of backtracking they were unable to find it. Perkins promised George that if he could find the watch and return it by post he would send him a tennis racket. Eventually George found the watch and sent it to Fremantle, and true to his word, Perkins sent him a tennis racket.[29]

No less than the enlisted men, submarine officers were impressed by the hospitality of Western Australians. Albert Strow, a lieutenant on USS *Gudgeon* originally from western Kentucky, believed the Australians were the friendliest people he had ever known. Recently married and homesick, leave in Perth offered some solace after dangerous periods on patrol. When one family invited him to dinner, he discovered that they had named their cat Douglas MacArthur.[30] At least some local residents also perceived a qualitative difference between the behavior of officers and rank-and-file submariners. Mrs. Marjorie Ward, the proprietor of the Derward Hotel in Murray Street, Perth, described the officers she met as "very nice," but she believed some of the enlisted men "went a bit crazy."[31]

Apart from organized ship's parties, enlisted men were unlikely to encounter their officers while on leave, unless by accident. Chuck Vervalin, while walking with his girlfriend in downtown Perth, recalled running into his skipper, James Fitzgerald, from USS *Grenadier*. Fitzgerald struck Vervalin as very amiable and polite.[32] Overfamiliarity, though, was discouraged. Even more than other officers, submarine skippers were segregated from their crews. Relative isolation was seen not just as a privilege of rank but in some ways a psychological necessity. According to one skipper, "As the captain of a crew whose lives depended on my instant decisions and with whom I lived in very close quarters, I could not now relax with any of them."[33] Given the immense responsibility they endured on patrol, submarine commanders were arguably most in need of a period for recovery.

CHAPTER 7

TRAVELING NORTH

The Guadalcanal campaign in the Solomon Islands wound down at the beginning of 1943, with the Japanese abandoning the fighting there in February. As a result, fewer submarines were based at Brisbane, but these boats were shifted to Pearl Harbor rather than to Fremantle. The number of patrols from Fremantle remained modest, with only six submarines departing the port during January and February 1943 to conduct patrols in the Java Sea, Flores Sea, and South China Sea. Postwar assessments indicate that these patrols claimed six ships for a total of 18,790 tons of Japanese shipping.[1]

The following month four submarines departed Fremantle for war patrols. These included USS *Trout* commanded by Red Ramage, which laid twenty-three mines in Api Passage off Borneo and then searched Japanese shipping lanes to Singapore. As on Ramage's previous patrol, there were more torpedo misses and duds, until the crew vented its frustration on April 23 with gun attacks on two trawlers estimated to be two hundred tons each. Traveling south after passing through Sibutu Passage, *Trout*'s crew surfaced about noon and opened up on the small craft with their 3-inch and 20-mm guns. Although the trawlers responded with machine guns, in less than an hour both were left burning wrecks with only a few survivors spotted in the water amid the burning oil.[2]

Trout arrived back at Fremantle in the early hours of May 3, escorted into the port by HMAS *Dubbo*. Christie relieved Ramage of *Trout*'s command soon after his return. While Christie described the patrol as "aggressive" in his endorsement, he attributed the poor results to a combination of factors including "control errors."[3] In his diary, Christie noted that "Red had a miss last patrol—many chances and many failures."[4] Ramage was sent back to the States for new construction, putting USS *Parche* into commission.

USS *Grenadier* also departed on patrol in March, but with far more dire consequences. Ramage and the *Grenadier*'s commander, John A. "Jack" Fitzgerald, were old friends. Fitzgerald had been on the boxing team at the Naval Academy and was described by one contemporary as

"185 lbs. of pure determination."⁵ On a previous patrol *Grenadier* had already made a major, although at the time underappreciated, contribution to the Allied war effort. On May 8, 1942, the submarine sank the 14,457-ton *Taiyo Maru* making its way to the Dutch East Indies to service recently captured oil fields. Nearly eight hundred oil experts and technicians, mainly from the Mitsubishi Company, were lost with the ship. The lure of unlimited petroleum largely spurred Japan into the war, but the destruction of the *Taiyo Maru* dealt a major blow to the Japanese timetable for developing oil supplies. *Grenadier* had also distinguished itself as the first submarine to plant mines in Japanese shipping lanes, placing its deadly cargo in the Gulf of Tonkin off the Indochina harbor of Haiphong in October 1942.⁶

Grenadier began its sixth and what proved to be its last patrol when it slipped out of Fremantle on March 20, 1943. Fitzgerald and his crew headed for the Straits of Malacca, the first U.S. submarine to patrol what was normally the preserve of the British. Because of the area's shallow and confined waters, operations officer Tex McLean had voiced his reservations about the patrol. On the other hand, the British had specifically requested that the Americans investigate enemy shipping in the area between Singapore and Rangoon. *Grenadier* was to photograph island harbors and determine the sea routes being used by the enemy.⁷

On the morning of April 21, as *Grenadier* stalked a two-ship convoy in the Straits of Malacca, the lookouts spotted an incoming Japanese torpedo plane and ordered an emergency dive. As the submarine reached a depth of 120 feet it heeled over from a huge explosion, which Fitzgerald described as like "two express trains collid[ing]."⁸ The aircraft had dropped an aerial torpedo armed with five hundred pounds of TNT, driving the submarine to the bottom of the sea. *Grenadier* immediately lost power, and a fire broke out in the maneuvering room; water also sprayed in from at least three major leaks. A bucket brigade frantically tried to keep the rising water away from the main propulsion motors. After fifteen hours submerged, *Grenadier* finally surfaced in darkness without locomotion or a functioning radio. So desperate was the situation that the crewmen even rigged an improvised sail from sewn-together mattress covers in an attempt to move closer to islands seen in the distance, but to no avail. Damage from the attack also left the submarine virtually defenseless, unable to fire the torpedoes or use its 3-inch deck gun. The only functioning weapons remaining, stored below deck during the bomb attack, were a 20-mm gun on the afterdeck of the conning tower and two .30-caliber machine guns mounted port and starboard.⁹

Although the crew was initially able to drive off an attacking plane, as enemy ships approached from north and south it became clear they would have to abandon ship. *Grenadier*'s men destroyed all classified documents on board as well as any Australian money before scuttling the submarine. Skipper Jack Fitzgerald instructed his men, "We can't let the Japs know where our home port is."[10] He told them, if interrogated, to say they came from San Francisco rather than Fremantle. When it came time to abandon *Grenadier*, Fitzgerald instructed the men: "On my command, all hands will go over the side. Swim as rapidly as possible away from the boat, and God bless you all."[11] When scuttled, the submarine slid slowly underwater stern first. Watching *Grenadier* sink, crewman Albert Rupp felt as though he had lost not only his home, a "little piece of America, in this alien place," but also "a very close friend."[12]

After the seventy-six men of *Grenadier*'s crew were picked up by a Japanese merchant ship, the prisoners were taken to Penang, where they endured 103 days of torture and confinement in a former convent. Later they were driven away in two trucks and put on board a small freighter, *Hir Maru*. They landed in Singapore, stayed for a short time, and then boarded *Asama Maru* on September 24, 1943. After some days at sea, around midnight, the *Grenadier* men heard the unmistakable sound of torpedoes detonating. They assumed that U.S. submarines sank at least one of the ships in their convoy since the guards subsequently vented their anger by beating each prisoner.[13] On October 9 they arrived at the port of Shimonoseki on the island of Honshu. From there the *Grenadier* men were taken to Fukuoka Camp Number 3 to join some twelve hundred other Allied prisoners of war and were put to work at a steel mill. Half of the *Grenadier* crew, including all of the officers, were transported to the Japanese navy camp at Ofuna in the hills about fifteen miles southwest of Yokohama, where they were subjected to more brutal cross-examination. An Australian pilot named Geoffrey Lempiere helped some of the Americans settle in at Ofuna. During interrogations, when he translated questions from the Japanese, he managed to slip in additional information for the prisoners.[14]

Until the sinking of *Grenadier*, Fremantle submarines had survived for more than twelve months without a loss. Unfortunately, the next loss of a Fremantle submarine would come in less than six months, and unlike with *Grenadier*, there would be no survivors. USS *Grayling* first arrived at Fremantle in December 1942 and on April 25, 1943, only days after the loss of *Grenadier*, returned to port after a successful patrol. Later in the year, under the command of Robert M. Brinker, *Grayling* delivered supplies to guerrilla fighters on the Philippine island of Panay and attacked a number of cargo ships, but then disappeared with all crew in early September after apparently being rammed in shallow water by a Japanese ship. More sad news came the following month when it was reported that James "Red" Coe, who had made his reputation at Fremantle in command of *Skipjack*, was lost with all hands in the new boat USS *Cisco*.[15] Although American submarines were becoming more effective in sinking Japanese shipping, the Japanese had also become more effective in antisubmarine warfare.

In April 1943 Admiral Christie visited Exmouth Gulf, some seven hundred miles north of Fremantle, to consider the practicality of establishing a submarine base there. The idea for a base originated with Charles Lockwood, who hoped to cut down on the transit time to and from patrol areas. If submarines could be refitted at Exmouth Gulf, it would save the extra two days each way that it took traveling to and from Fremantle. Historian Clay Blair suggests that Lockwood's enthusiasm for a base at Exmouth stemmed partly from his acrimonious relationship with Vice Adm. Arthur "Chips" Carpender, who assumed overall command of U.S. naval forces in Western Australia from July 1942 on. Exmouth, code-named "Potshot," would provide Lockwood a place to escape from Carpender's immediate supervision. On the other hand, even after Carpender departed the west coast for a posting in Brisbane, Lockwood continued his interest in the Exmouth plan. The same day Carpender shifted his command, September 11, 1942, Lockwood made a reconnaissance visit to Exmouth Gulf.[16]

Following his inspection in April, Christie concluded that the base could not be made satisfactory "without expenditure of time, manpower, and money all out of proportion to the purposes intended."[17] When Corwin Mendenhall had visited the Gulf in February 1942, he described it as "one of the most unsettled, wildest parts of the continent."[18] For much of the year Exmouth Gulf was exposed to strong winds and occasional cyclones, and there were reports of enemy coast watchers in the area.[19] Given that there was virtually nothing in terms of infrastructure at Exmouth, the project would require sinking a well for fresh water, installing a land wire for telegraphic communications, setting up Quonset huts for personnel, as well as constructing antiaircraft defenses and landing fields. Oil tanks would also be built on the west bank of the bay.[20] The key to the plan, though, was the availability of a submarine tender that could be permanently stationed there.

Despite Christie's reservations, in early May he sent the 14,200-ton submarine tender *Pelias* to Exmouth Gulf. As many had predicted, however, the experiment proved short-lived. Even before the cyclone season, strong winds buffeted submarines in the gulf, frequently making it impossible to moor alongside *Pelias*. The idea of ferrying returning submarine crews to Fremantle for leave while their submarine underwent refit at Exmouth was quickly abandoned. In the end, the only submarine actually to undergo refit at Exmouth was USS *Trout*, then under the command of Ramage's replacement, Albert H. Clark, which moored alongside *Pelias* on May 7.[21]

The final demise of plans for a major forward base at Exmouth Gulf came the same month, after Japanese bombers mounted an attack on the nights of May 20–21. On Thursday night, May 20, a single bomb was dropped, apparently directed at *Pelias*. The following night three bombers dropped a total of nine stick bombs in the area, although none close enough to threaten the tender. Yet another aircraft was detected in the early hours of May 22, but this time no bombs were dropped.[22] USS *Trout*, still undergoing refit at the time, was forced to clear *Pelias* and remain submerged during the air raids. When USS *Thresher* arrived at Exmouth a couple of days later from patrol, there were not only stories of the bombings but reports of Japanese submarines lurking in the area.[23] The following month Christie informed Charles Lockwood that Potshot was "definitely of no value as a submarine advance base."[24] Ironically, the same conclusion had been reached fifteen months earlier when Exmouth Gulf was initially surveyed by the U.S. Navy.

Submarines did continue refueling operations at Exmouth until virtually the end of the war. For a time the Dutch tanker *Ondina* was stationed there, later replaced by a fuel barge. By topping off their fuel tanks both going and coming back from patrol, submarines effectively added four days to their cruising radius.[25] Weather, however, continued to be a hazard, and the Dutch submarine *K-XIV* was damaged there during a cyclone.[26]

After topping off fuel tanks at Exmouth Gulf, the first place submariners anticipated trouble was Lombok Strait, the usual route taken through the string of islands referred to as the Malay Barrier. The chain of islands extending through the Dutch East Indies and Timor had once been conceived as a line of defense, but they were now in the hands of the Japanese. Lombok Strait formed a twenty-seven-mile-long sluice gate from the Indian Ocean to the Java Sea and offered a forbidding aspect. Although the southern entrance to the strait was about ten miles wide, the towering mountains looming on either side made it appear much narrower. To the west the volcanic Mount Agung on Bali reached 10,000 feet, while on the Lombok Island side to the east the mountain Rinjani rose to 12,000 feet.[27] As described by one submarine lookout, the volcanic mountains "were so close it looked like you could reach out and touch them."[28]

Strong currents and unpredictable tidal streams added concealed dangers to Lombok Strait's menacing entrance. The current running from north to south could reach nine knots, making it impossible for a submarine to negotiate the strait while submerged.[29] Charley Odom recalled that when USS *Billfish* tried to make the passage submerged, the bow of the submarine broached and the Japanese fired on them.[30] Red Ramage encountered similar rough going when he tried to take USS *Trout* through on its eighth war patrol, comparing the experience to being "inside a washing machine."[31] Most submarine commanders elected to make the passage at night on the surface at high speed.

The Japanese augmented Lombok Strait's natural hazards with gun batteries, minefields, and patrol craft that narrowed the navigable passage still further. There were Japanese artillery emplacements on either side of the southern entrance to the strait, and on Lombok Island at Cape Pandanan the Japanese established large guns on 1,500-foot-high cliffs. The shadows cast by the mountainous slopes of Bali and Lombok also helped disguise the presence of lurking Japanese patrol boats. Perhaps a bit too cavalierly, a sailor from USS *Rock* claimed the patrol boats "were good enough to make one stay alert for them, but not good enough to worry about."[32] With their faster surface speeds and effective radar, American submarines could usually outrun the patrol craft, but the Dutch and the British submarines that later operated from Fremantle had much greater difficulty.

The first six months of 1943 had brought more disappointments than successes. Fremantle had suffered its first submarine loss with USS *Grenadier*, and the attempt to establish a base closer to the enemy at Exmouth Gulf had been thwarted. The number of patrols made from Fremantle remained relatively low, averaging about four a month, and because of this the number of enemy ships sunk remained modest. At the time it was claimed that thirty-five Japanese ships were sunk during this period, but postwar assessment cut this figure to nineteen. Similarly, the claimed total tonnage sunk, 190,500, was reduced to 87,350 tons by later analysis. The latter figures have been hotly debated, but throughout the war and regardless of the area, it seems submariners claimed roughly twice the number of ships and tonnage that could be verified by extant records.[33]

Still, there had been some standout performances. USS *Gudgeon*, in two patrols under William S. Post Jr., sank four confirmed ships totalling 38,000 tons. USS *Tautog*, under the command of William R. "Barney" Sieglaff, had also done good work, sinking four confirmed ships for 12,300 tons. Between them, the two submarines accounted for more than half of the tonnage sunk by Fremantle submarines in the first half of 1943.[34] Soon there would be more submarines based at Fremantle, and more submarine aces under Christie's command.

CHAPTER

SAILORS' WOMEN

A month after the short-lived experiment of basing a submarine tender at Exmouth Gulf, the Americans began using Midway Island as a rest center for submariners between patrols. Using the same logic as he had with Western Australia, Charles Lockwood pressed Admiral Nimitz to establish a forward submarine base at Midway on the basis that it was eleven hundred miles closer to the enemy than was Pearl Harbor and would save crews time in getting to their patrol areas. The tiny atoll was of immense strategic importance, but, as Norvell Ward observed, "it was not a good spot for rest and recreation."[1] Midway offered little other than swimming, softball, and beer for recuperating submariners. Eugene Fluckey, skipper of USS *Barb*, wrote to his family from Midway describing it as "a strange place. . . . Not a female in sight. White coral sand every place."[2] Kenneth Ruiz from USS *Pollack* summed up Midway in similar terms: "There were no girls, no hard liquor, no night life, and no entertainment. There was little to do but drink beer and watch the gooney birds [Leysan albatross] mate."[3] Ned Beach, who knew Midway well, claimed that most men "heartily disliked" the place.[4]

The prospect of having to spend two weeks' leave on Midway made Fremantle an even more desirable location in the world of submariners. In many ways, Fremantle appeared the polar opposite of Midway, particularly in terms of the availability of female company. To George Grider, skipper of USS *Flasher*, it seemed that "the girls were everywhere . . . at the clubs, in the stores, on the streets."[5] From a command point of view, however, women could complicate military life. While in charge of submarines in Brisbane, Ralph Christie fretted about the incidence of venereal disease among sailors. Writing to Charles Lockwood in July 1942, he complained that despite establishing extra prophylactic stations and docking the pay of men who became infected, "the damn fools won't take the prophylaxis."[6] In a more strident letter to Adm. R. S. Edwards the following month, Christie described the rate of venereal disease as "terrific" and claimed little could be done "unless we cut off their cojones."[7]

Cases of venereal disease among American troops in Australia apparently spiked in May 1942 with a rate of 45.8 cases per thousand troops, before falling off to more modest levels.[8] Christie had less to say on the topic in Fremantle, although it is likely venereal disease remained a concern. Fremantle's brothels, concentrated in Bannister Street, were within easy walking distance of the docks. Of these, The Palms, under the supervision of Ms. Jessie Jones, became the best known. Some enterprising boys made pocket money by selling newspapers to the men who lined up outside.[9] In the city of Perth nine brothels were concentrated in Roe Street. One submariner recalls that on his first trip to Perth, as the train moved slowly by Roe Street, prostitutes lined a fence "showing quite an amount of bare flesh."[10] On one occasion near the end of the war, six crewmen from USS *Puffer* hired a bawdy house in Roe Street for a week, where they played host to their friends until their antics were discovered by the police and the *Sunday Mirror*. Eventually, Christie's successor, James Fife, placed the Roe Street brothels off limits to American submariners and deployed patrols to enforce the ban.[11]

Concern about the spread of venereal disease, along with the putative moral danger to young women consorting with servicemen, prompted the appointment of four plain-clothes police officers in Fremantle specifically to deal with vice. The vice squad patrolled not only parks but the back seats of cinemas. Female police officers also patrolled hotels and dance halls in search of underage girls, while women designated as prostitutes could be compelled to undergo medical examinations.[12] Terrifying lectures on the consequences of venereal disease served to deter some young women from sexual activity. Nancy Graham, who grew up in a small country town before moving to Fremantle and joining the army, professed that she "had never seen anything so absolutely frightening. I never ever kissed a boy for two year after that."[13]

The Navy also relied mainly on "educational" talks, along with prophylaxis stations and the indignity of so-called short-arm inspections to curtail the spread of disease, but some sailors went to sea infected. Charles Taylor contracted gonorrhea while on leave in Fremantle before departing for patrol on USS *Grenadier*. After the capture of *Grenadier*'s crew by the Japanese, he suffered even more horribly than most of his crewmates as a result of the disease.[14]

How many submarine sailors frequented brothels remains unknown, but most men on leave were looking for "romance" if not just sex. As Robyn Arrowsmith points out, "The wartime perception of the powerful military males as hero and saviour, and the passive young female waiting to be wooed created an atmosphere of heightened romance, rather than simply one of physical pleasure."[15] The strong attraction between American submariners and Western Australian women has already been noted, although by mid-1943 these relationships had lost some of their gloss for a portion of women and the public. While some women may have been swept off their feet by the aura of glamour associated with the Americans, others adopted a cynical approach. Dorothy Hewett recalls that although she once dated an American submariner, "I didn't find him very interesting."[16] She found Australian men better company and felt embarrassed by the American habit of showering girls with gifts. Wes Headington from USS *Thresher* recorded in his diary a song sung by an Australian girl at a party, describing it as intended "to get the Yanks' goat."[17]

> *Oh, the Yankees sure think they are wonderful guys,*
> *They're all full of self-conceit,*
> *They think Aussie gals are as dumb as their wives,*
> *And the line they hand out is quite neat.*
>
> *They imitate Gable, James Cagney, and Bing,*
> *And even old Al Capone,*
> *They try to impress us, instead they depress us,*
> *And make us all wish they were home.*

Some parents forbade their daughters to go out with the Americans. Doreen White and her sister, who lived in the Perth suburb of Subiaco, were warned by their father that "if he caught us out with a Yank he would break our legs from beneath us."[18] But then her father introduced her to submariner John Battle, bringing him home to dinner after meeting him at a pub. John and Doreen ended up married. Despite parental disapproval, the expansion of war work meant that many Australian women were experiencing a new degree of independence. By mid-1943 more than 190,000 women were in direct war work, and the total number of women in employment (including the armed services) peaked at 849,000 in September 1943.[19]

For many contemporaries, the platitude that the Yanks were "overpaid, oversexed and over here" seemed accurate enough. One downside of blossoming relationships between the Americans and local girls was that some, especially Australian troops, resented them. George Grider blamed local newspapers for creating much of the animosity.[20] The tabloid *Mirror* doubled its Perth circulation during the war, largely on the strength of its titillating reports on the liaisons of U.S. Navy personnel and the resulting local divorce cases. Perhaps the most fabulous story, which combined upper-class decadence with American crudity, purportedly took place at a Perth socialite party. As the story goes, the party featured a champagne fountain; young women dipped their exposed breasts into the champagne, which was then sucked off by eager Americans. One woman had to be hospitalized after an overenthusiastic sailor bit her nipple off.[21]

Even the Americans conceded that much of their attraction for women was their free-spending attitudes. Don Haseley from USS *Cavalla* was nineteen when he visited Western Australia and maintains that most of the men coming in from war patrols felt like they had a good deal of money after receiving two months' pay. This, combined with an uncertain future, meant that many submariners were keen to spend before leaving on their next patrol. As Haseley put it, many girls were happy to be along for the ride.[22]

Despite cynics on both sides, the reality was that romances between the Americans and Western Australian women continued to flourish. Submariners making their first visit to Perth frequently relied on more experienced shipmates for introductions. Ernest "Zeke" Zellmer from USS *Cavalla* was taken under the wing of a fellow officer who had befriended a local family during a previous stay. The family had a son serving in India and two charming daughters in their twenties. Zeke had several dates with one of the daughters for dinners and movies, but the relationship stopped short of anything serious.

When *Cavalla*'s next patrol ended in Fremantle, one of Zeke's friends from the U.S. Naval Academy came on board to greet him. Lt. (jg) Albert "Hap" Trottier was about to head off on patrol, but before he left he told Zeke about a young woman he thought he would like. Her name was Laurel Brenda "Babs" Miller, and she worked for the U.S. Navy service force as a "yeomanette." Hap gave Zeke her phone number. "What a friend!" Zeke thought, and he called Babs the same night arranging to go out for dinner and a movie. The first date, on a Monday evening, went well—so well that they went out every night for the remainder of Zeke's leave.[23]

George McPherson, who arrived at Fremantle on USS *Puffer*, also had a date arranged by one of his shipmates who had visited Western Australia before. The shipmate had a girlfriend who lived at Mount Hawthorn with her parents, and he fixed George up with her sister. A shy nineteen-year-old, he recalls being pleased to meet "a very nice young lady, which made my time in Perth very pleasant." Their outings included a picnic lunch at Mundaring Weir and a crew party on Rottnest Island. According to George, "The young Australian ladies had very few young Australian men available, so it really benefited everyone."[24] Beryl Lynch, at the time a sixteen-year-old working in a Subiaco chemist shop, met her future husband, torpedoman Chuck Colvin, when he presented a note of introduction from another American she had dated. In fact, she had dated so many Americans that her mother finally forbade her to go out with any more. As Lynch later recalled it, however, she told her mother that "I couldn't help it, he followed me home."[25]

Submariners sometimes inherited the girlfriends of crewmates who had been transferred from Western Australia. Lloyd Schuermann, a motor machinist on USS *Tambor*, dated a woman in Perth before being redeployed back to the United States. His former crewmate, Bob Hunt, then began dating the same woman. The sweater she had been knitting for Lloyd was to become Bob's, but he too was transferred. When Lloyd and Bob later ran into each other at Midway, they pondered which sailor had ended up with the sweater.[26]

CHAPTER 9

HUNTER AND HUNTED

The Dutch submarine *K-IX*, transferred from Fremantle and damaged in the midget submarine attack on Sydney Harbour in May 1942, was finally commissioned into the Royal Australian Navy on June 22, 1943. *K-IX* was staffed by some experienced British submariners with the balance of the crew made up of Australian volunteers. Unfortunately, *K-IX*'s mechanical problems continued unabated until finally, on the morning of January 22, 1944, its battery exploded in Sydney Harbour after the ship spent a total of only thirty-one days at sea. Decommissioned on March 31, 1944, the RAN decided to cut its losses and converted *K-IX* into a lighter. It was not until 1967 that another submarine was commissioned into the Royal Australian Navy.[1]

The lack of an antisubmarine training vessel may help to explain the relatively disappointing performance of the RAN against Japanese submarines. The RAN was handicapped not only by relatively little live training but also by delays in receiving the technical innovations that made the British and American units more effective. The Australians were not entirely without successes; the destroyer HMAS *Arunta* managed to destroy the Japanese submarine *RO-33* off Port Moresby on August 29, 1942, and in the Indian Ocean the Australian corvettes *Ipswich* and *Launceston*, assisted by the Indian sloop *Junna*, destroyed *RO-110* in the Bay of Bengal while escorting a convoy from Colombo to Calcutta.[2] These were slim pickings, however, compared to the success of the Americans.

June 1943 saw not only the commissioning of *K-IX* into the Royal Australian Navy but, more significant for U.S. submarines, a change in torpedo policy. With the blessing of Adm. Chester Nimitz, commander in chief of the Pacific Fleet, Charles Lockwood ordered submarines under his command to deactivate their Mark-VI exploders on June 24. Ralph Christie, however, under the authority of the Seventh Fleet's Adm. Arthur S. "Chips" Carpender rather than Nimitz, insisted that submarines in the Southwest Pacific continue using the magnetic exploder. He believed that reports of the exploders' defects were exaggerated and that they continued to be useful against escorts, warships, and tankers. Only after Adm. Thomas Cassin Kinkaid replaced Carpender as the senior naval officer for the Southwest Pacific in November 1943 did the policy change. Kinkaid directed deactivation of the magnetic exploders on all torpedoes, and Christie passed the order to submarine commanders on January 20, 1944.[3]

Despite the continued limitations of the American torpedoes, by mid-1943 two wartime innovations helped locate enemy craft and gave the U.S. Navy an enormous edge. The advent of SJ surface radar significantly improved the chances of submarines locating enemy targets, especially in poor visibility or at night. The first SJ radar set was trialed on USS *Haddock* in August 1942, and although not without teething problems, thanks to radar the night surface approach increasingly became the preferred mode of attack for U.S. submarines.[4]

Still more important to locating the enemy was the intelligence provided by radio intercepts and crypto-analysis about the movements of Japanese shipping, commonly referred to as "Ultra." Through Ultra, submarines were often provided with precise projections of the route and speed of Japanese convoys and warships. In early 1943 the so-called maru code was broken, allowing code breakers to anticipate the movements of merchant shipping and convoys with startling accuracy. Since Japanese merchant skippers methodically reported their positions twice a day, this often provided Allied intelligence with a bonanza of information.

Adm. Ralph Christie claimed that the code breakers sometimes knew more about submarine patrols than the skippers who conducted them, especially in assessing the damage done by attacks. At his Perth office in the Colonial Mutual Life Insurance building, Christie had some thirty to forty ensigns working on codes and communications around the clock.[5] From 1943 on naval cryptographers were able to send intelligence directly to submarine commanders via a special code. So secret was the Ultra information that only the commanders of submarines were privy to it, and they were officially bound never to disclose its existence. Between January and October 1943, more than eight hundred Ultra messages were transmitted to submarines on patrol.[6]

During the second half of 1943 (July through December), operations by Fremantle submarines accelerated as a total of thirty-two war patrols were made, with most concentrated in the South China Sea. Postwar investigations by the Joint Army-Navy Assessment Committee (JANAC) confirmed that the patrols resulted in the sinking of forty-seven Japanese ships, totalling 208,640 tons.[7] This was well over twice the tonnage claimed in the first half of the year.

During this period, one of the most successful submarines of the Pacific War—USS *Bowfin*—operated from Fremantle. Launched on December 7, 1942, exactly one year after the Japanese attack, *Bowfin* was nicknamed the "Pearl Harbor Avenger." After departing on patrol from Brisbane, *Bowfin* arrived at Fremantle on October 10, 1943, to be greeted by a Navy band along with a crowd of people who offered fresh fruit and milk. During the patrol *Bowfin*, under the command of Joseph Harris Willingham, claimed the destruction of three freighters in a convoy. In his endorsement of the patrol, Adm. Chips Carpender characterized the engagement as "a brilliant action in which three enemy ships totalling 23,753 tons were dispatched in 18 minutes."[8] Postwar investigations, however, confirmed only the loss of the 8,120-ton ship *Kirishima Maru*.

In addition to the attack on a Japanese convoy, *Bowfin* had carried out a special mission that would have far-reaching implications. On Thursday, September 30, *Bowfin* picked up nine men at a cove west of Binuni Point off the northern coast of Mindanao in the Philippine Islands. Once they boarded the submarine, the evacuees were taken below to meet Commander Willingham and then given new clothes. The passengers included Luis P. Morgan, a former captain of the Philippine constabulary and self-styled colonel in the resistance. Described as being of "questionable character," he had created dissension between various guerrilla factions on Mindanao and was sent to Australia to get him out of the way.[9] At the Fremantle docks he was met by military police and led off in handcuffs. The other evacuees were of unquestioned valor, and some openly wept with joy on arrival at Fremantle. Three of the men (Francis J. Napolillo, Elwood H. Offret, and Paul A. Owens) had served on the PT boat that had whisked Gen. Douglas MacArthur from Corregidor to Mindanao for his flight to Australia in March 1942. After MacArthur's departure from the Philippines they refused to surrender to the Japanese, preferring to join the Filipino resistance. Also brought to Australia on USS *Bowfin* were Dewitt L. Glover of the U.S. Navy, Tracy Tucker and Leonard Minter (both sergeants in the Army), Lt. Samuel C. Grashio, and Edward M. Kuder.[10]

Kuder, a forty-eight-year-old originally from Virginia who had served as a long-time school superintendent on Mindanao, helped organize resistance and acted as the director of civil affairs on the island once the war began. He spent nine months living with the local Moro people in Mindanao's mountain forests and only agreed to be evacuated after contracting a life-threatening disease. When *Bowfin* arrived off Mindanao he was carried to the beach on a horse, and then ferried by launch to the submarine. On *Bowfin*, Kuder stayed in the after-torpedo room, too ill to leave his bunk even for meals. On arrival at Fremantle his body was so swollen and racked with pain that he had to be taken off *Bowfin* on a stretcher. Diagnosed as having an abscessed liver, Kuder underwent an operation and recovered sufficiently in early 1945 to publish a series of five articles in the American magazine *Saturday Evening Post* titled "The Philippines Never Surrendered."[11]

Another *Bowfin* passenger, Sam Grashio, was also destined to have his exploits published. When *Bowfin* surfaced off Liaugan Bay, Mindanao, and hoisted the American flag, Grashio recalled trembling with excitement. He had been a fighter pilot on Bataan before becoming a Japanese captive, and after managing to escape the Japanese, he joined the guerrilla fighters on Mindanao. Once he boarded *Bowfin*, Grashio professed that he felt truly safe for the first time since the Japanese attacked the Philippines on December 8, 1941. He later concluded that "overall, I have never seen a more outstanding group of servicemen than the crew of the Bowfin."[12] Although Grashio had escaped Japanese captivity five months earlier, he remained emaciated and continued to suffer the effects of malaria and dysentery. After his arrival at Fremantle he spent the next three days in the hospital, where he was doted on by volunteers who supplied him with food and candy. Many of the crew from *Bowfin* also visited him, smuggling in a sack full of beer on one occasion.[13]

In Australia Grashio experienced the frustration of having to remain quiet about the conditions in Japanese prison camps. As he saw it, the bureaucrats were "far too concerned about the reactions of the Japanese and too little about the fate of Americans abroad and the anxieties of their loved ones at home."[14] So secret were the submarine evacuations that for a time he was even denied permission to contact his wife and parents. Once back in the United States, Grashio suffered alternately from insomnia and nightmares about his captivity. It wasn't until January 28, 1944, that the stories of Japanese mistreatment of prisoners began to be published in the media.[15] Some commentators claimed their revelations were as shocking as the attack on Pearl Harbor. Sam Grashio toured the country promoting war bonds, and at one munitions factory he personally signed a 400-pound bomb with a message for General Tojo: "In appreciation of your hospitality."[16]

A month after Commander Willingham arrived at Fremantle, Christie incorporated him into his senior staff and put him in charge of a submarine division. In Willingham's stead Christie selected Walter Thomas

Griffith to take command of *Bowfin*. At thirty-three years of age and a graduate of the Naval Academy class of 1934, Griffith was considerably younger than Willingham; originally from Mansfield, Louisiana, he had enlisted in the Navy on his seventeenth birthday.[17] As recalled by one of his crewmen, Griffith was a "gung ho" type, and his executive officer, Bill Thompson, described Griffith as a "fearless fighter" but also as someone with a "poetic" side to his character.[18]

Assuming command only six days before departing on patrol, Griffith's aggression quickly earned Christie's admiration. When the *Bowfin* returned from its first patrol out of Fremantle on December 9, 1943, the submarine claimed the sinking of fourteen vessels totalling 70,948 tons. This proved not only the best patrol out of Fremantle in 1943 but, at the time, a U.S. record. Some of the vessels sunk were small craft destroyed in gun actions, but the toll also included two large tankers and a host of freighters.[19] Postwar investigations later confirmed the sinking of five of the larger ships. Christie described *Bowfin*'s run as "the classic of all submarine patrols" and awarded Griffith a Navy Cross.[20] When Christie's cocker spaniel Pepper had puppies, he even named one of them Bowfin.

At least in part, Christie's jubilation over *Bowfin*'s success was related to the performance of its torpedoes. Griffith had kept the Mark-VI magnetic exploders on the torpedoes activated, apparently with devastating effect on enemy shipping. Christie also determined to make at least a partial war patrol in order to witness *Bowfin* in action firsthand. On January 25, 1944, he flew to Darwin, regularly used since 1943 by Fremantle submarines for refueling and minor repairs.[21] When *Bowfin* arrived to take on more torpedoes and fuel, Christie joined the crew and was able to observe at close quarters Griffith's bold night surface tactics. On the bridge when *Bowfin* fired torpedoes at a Japanese seaplane tender from only one thousand yards, Christie later recounted, "I was slammed against the bridge railing by the force of the explosion and broke my binocular strap and lost my cap."[22]

On the way back to Fremantle, Christie disembarked at Exmouth Gulf and flew back to his headquarters after a nine-day absence. He had become the first submarine force commander and admiral to make a war patrol. The patrol had been made, though, without the permission of Thomas Kinkaid, and this likely contributed to a growing rift between the two men. Christie had also potentially put one of the greatest secrets of the war at risk; if he had fallen into Japanese hands, they might have extracted from him that the Americans were breaking their codes.

While *Bowfin* proved itself a successful hunter, two other Fremantle submarines nearly became victims of Japanese depth-charge attacks.

During the First World War depth charges had remained relatively unreliable and in short supply, with most submarine sinkings occurring on the surface. By the Second World War, however, depth charges had become a much more formidable antisubmarine weapon. A Japanese depth charge exploding within fifty or sixty feet of a submarine would cause damage, while an explosion within twenty feet was likely to be lethal.[23] Of the fifty-two American submarines lost during World War II, at least twenty were victims of depth-charge attacks.[24]

USS *Puffer* survived possibly the most prolonged depth-charge attack of the Pacific War in October 1943. In the 450-mile-long passage between Borneo and Celebes known as Makassar Strait, the submarine remained submerged for thirty-seven hours. With all machinery including air conditioning turned off during "silent running," temperatures in the boat shot up to barely endurable levels. With the buildup of carbon dioxide in the atmosphere, each exhaled breath contributed to the crew's slow poisoning. As carbon dioxide accumulated in their bloodstreams, they experienced dizziness, headaches, palpitations, spasms, and loss of mental function.[25] Many men suffered from severe dehydration and sank into a stupor. As the lack of oxygen took its toll on the crew, discipline began to disintegrate. At one stage the skipper proposed surfacing and fighting their tormentors with the deck guns; his officers pressured him to put the matter to a vote, and the men elected to remain below the surface.

Puffer arrived back at Fremantle on October 24. Skipper Marvin John Jensen was relieved of command to become assistant operations officer, remaining in that post until November 1944.[26] According to one of his contemporaries, Jensen talked incessantly about the episode, and it seems likely at least some of the crew were similarly scarred.[27] Robert "Dusty" Dornin, executive officer of USS *Gudgeon* and later skipper of USS *Trigger*, postulated that the older the submariner, the longer he remained jumpy after experiencing a depth-charge attack. In fact, some submariners continued to exhibit the effects long after the war.[28]

The new commander of *Puffer* became Frank Selby, formerly the executive officer on USS *Billfish*. As it happened, Selby's former crewmates experienced an ordeal not unlike that of *Puffer* the following month. *Billfish* had first arrived in Fremantle about the same time as its sister ship *Bowfin*, and after departing Fremantle on November 4, 1943, for its second war patrol, *Billfish* again ran into trouble in Makassar Strait. Although the depth-charge attack was not as prolonged as the one experienced by *Puffer*, the atmosphere on the submarine was poisoned by a leaking refrigeration line and chlorine gas as seawater contaminated the batteries. At one point *Billfish*'s third officer began screaming "We're all

USS *Puffer* and its crew survived one of the most prolonged depth-charge attacks of the war in October 1943.   U.S. Naval Institute photo archive

going to die! . . . The next one is going to kill us!" before being sedated.[29] In the meantime, both the skipper and executive officer appeared too stunned to act. While there was no crew vote about whether to surface or not, even more dramatically, the engineering officer, Charles W. Rush Jr., relieved the skipper of command. Rush, originally from Greensboro, Alabama, had served on USS *Thresher* and managed relief crews at Fremantle before joining the *Billfish*.

The story of these dramatic events only became public much later. At the time, *Billfish*'s patrol report falsified the chaos on board during the depth-charge attack and Rush promised to keep the details secret on condition that the skipper, Frederic Colby Lucas Jr., resign. Back at Fremantle, Ralph Christie recorded in his diary: "I am obliged to detach Lucas from command of Billfish at his own request. He is convinced that he is temperamentally unsuited to submarine command."[30]

The year ended with a harbinger of the British submarine presence at Fremantle in the form of Commander Anthony Miers. In September 1943 Charles Lockwood wrote Ralph Christie to let him know that Miers, the British submarine liaison officer, was on his way from Pearl Harbor to Australia. Describing Miers as a "stout fellow," Lockwood took a dig at Christie, adding, "Incidentally, he plays a much better game of tennis than you do."[31] Within the British submarine service Miers had developed a reputation for both his personality and his submarine exploits. He was renowned for his short temper; not only did he dish out vicious tongue-lashings to his subordinates in a stentorian voice, but he occasionally physically assaulted them.[32] Despite his temper, there were those who swore undying loyalty to Miers. Fellow submariner Edward Young typically remarked on his "pugnacious audacity" while describing him as "generous-hearted."[33] Miers had put his aggressive instincts to good use in the Mediterranean as commander of the submarine *Torbay*, and following a daring raid on shipping inside the anchorage at Corfu, Crete, he was awarded Britain's highest combat award, the Victoria Cross, by King George VI on July 28, 1942.

By the time he completed his eleventh patrol in *Torbay*, Miers, at the age of thirty-six, was virtually geriatric by submarine-service standards. Even more than the Americans, the British saw submarines as the purview of the young and reckless. Considered over the hill for war patrols, Miers became the Royal Navy's submarine liaison officer with the Americans. At Pearl Harbor, Charles Lockwood welcomed Miers into the fold for almost eight months. As naval attaché in England, Lockwood had advocated maintaining close relations with the British submarine service, arguing that this would "produce dividends in the line of obtaining from them all the latest gadgets and wrinkles in the business of killing Huns, Italians and Japanese."[34] At Pearl, the burly Miers gained a reputation for challenging the American officers to wrestling matches and usually winning.[35]

Crewmen on USS *Cabrilla* relax during a war patrol.
USS *Bowfin* Submarine Museum

For the trip to Australia, Miers joined the crew of USS *Cabrilla* for a war patrol from Pearl Harbor and arrived at Fremantle in November. No sooner had Miers arrived than Christie hustled him off for a tennis match. Boasting of his stamina, Miers wrote to Admiral Claude Barry that the Americans were "amazed that the day after return from patrol I went to a tennis party with the Admiral and played 4 sets of tennis, all sets going '5 all.' "[36] Christie, on the other hand, gave a less flattering appraisal of the match, prompting Lockwood to comment in his next letter that "I was surprised to hear that his [Miers'] tennis game has deteriorated so badly."[37] Apart from tennis-court diplomacy, Miers challenged the Americans in other ways, again confiding to Admiral Barry that on USS *Cabrilla* he "was easily the most aggressive officer on board (although the oldest)." While he found the *Cabrilla*'s commander, Douglas T. Hammond, always polite, he described him as "too self-centred to be interested in my comfort and too self-satisfied to pay any attention to advice or suggestions."[38] Miers was particularly galled by Hammond's refusal to mount a gun action against a schooner and two unarmed trawlers observed while at San Bernardino Strait in the Philippines. Hammond thought such small vessels weren't worth exposing his position, whereas Miers argued that they might be supplying the enemy and could be attacked with relatively little risk.[39] Hammond's caution may have been partly motivated by *Cabrilla*'s special mission in the Philippines; on October 20 they picked up Maj. Jesus Villamor and four other intelligence operatives off the west coast of Negros. In the first submarine mission to the Philippines supporting the guerrilla movement, USS *Gudgeon* had landed Villamor and five other Filipinos at a deserted beach on Negros the night of January 14, 1943. Already a national hero, Villamor operated behind enemy lines until retrieved by *Cabrilla* ten months later.[40]

Miers was warmly received by both the submarine fraternity and the locals in Western Australia. He predicted to Admiral Barry that if British submariners were stationed there, "they will be really well looked after and won't want to go home!" At the same time, there was a note of cynicism about their alliance with the United States: "I do feel while this glorious liaison lasts, we must get all we can out of it and it is on the material side that we have most to learn from the Americans."[41] Over the next few months, Miers kept up a hectic schedule traveling not only around Australia but to Ceylon, New Guinea, and Guadalcanal. He concluded that he had "done more than a little to cement good relations between the two submarine services and also between our people and those of Western Australia."[42] After meetings in February 1944 with Gen. Douglas MacArthur and Thomas Kinkaid, commander of the U.S. Seventh

Anthony Miers, Royal Navy submarine liaison officer Royal Navy Submarine Museum, Gosport

Fleet, Miers reported both men were "very favourable to the projected reinforcements of British submarines."[43]

After eighteen months as the British submarine liaison officer, Miers was replaced in May 1944 by Lieutenant Commander Richard "Barclay" Larkin. Miers in the meantime went to command British submarines of the Eighth Submarine Flotilla at Trincomalee, Ceylon, where his hospitality for returning submarine crews became legendary. One former submariner boasted that "there will be many who will remember all their days the parties and the merriment that Commander Miers caused to be made when they had secured alongside."[44] It would not be long, though, before Miers was back in Fremantle.

CHAPTER 10

TROUBLE IN PARADISE

In early 1944 Western Australians experienced a spasm of panic reminiscent of the scares two years earlier. Although the possibility of a Japanese invasion was remote, fears of a naval attack remained, and with elements of the Japanese fleet on the move in March 1944, it appeared the assault on Fremantle might materialize. The Japanese first moved a number of warships, including seven battleships and two carriers, from their naval base at Truk in the Caroline Islands to Singapore. When it was learned that the armada sailed from Singapore on March 4, many believed that Fremantle was the intended objective.

In response to an anticipated Japanese strike, some submarine crews were recalled from leave to vacate Fremantle Harbour in the event of an attack. Five submarines departed on reconnaissance patrols, while the tenders *Pelias* and *Orion* were sent south to Albany for protection. Merchant ships at Fremantle were also dispersed, and more than a thousand members of the Volunteer Defence Corps were activated to defend the port. The Australian chiefs of staff reported on March 8 that reinforcements had been sent to the west coast and that submarines were forming a picket line seaward. From Darwin two fighter squadrons were shifted to Perth, and another three squadrons sent to Exmouth Gulf.[1]

The presumed seriousness of the threat is further suggested by the precautions taken at the Hollywood Military Hospital in Perth. Put on full alert, the staff wore steel helmets and carried gas masks, while patients were put on mattresses under their beds. In the meantime, ambulances evacuated as many patients as possible to the wheat-belt town of Northam sixty miles away.[2] Fortunately, the anticipated Japanese attack proved to be a false alarm; the Japanese ships did not turn south, and on March 20 the air squadrons sent to Western Australia returned to their original stations. At least some considered Western Australia's defenses to be inadequate, and the emergency underlined Fremantle's continuing isolation. A British naval intelligence officer in Perth at the time of the crisis believed the state remained "pretty wide open" to attack, noting that of the eighty-six aircraft directed to Western Australia, only about a quarter arrived within two days.[3]

The following month there was trouble of another kind, as Western Australia experienced its most notorious episode of collective violence of the war. On a Tuesday afternoon, April 11, 1944, a brawl erupted outside the National Hotel in Fremantle. At its height, an estimated five hundred people were involved, including New Zealanders, Americans, Australian soldiers, English sailors, and merchant seamen, all apparently egged on by a large crowd of civilians. Two soldiers, New Zealanders, died of stab wounds, and many others were hospitalized. A nursing aid at the Hollywood hospital recalled the aftermath as one of the most "heartbreaking" of her career. Many of the combatants were injured by broken bottles and glasses: "We had patients with heads laid open, eyes gouged out, horrible jagged stomach and abdomen wounds."[4] Significantly, though, the melee mainly involved transient troops, and the police placed most of the blame on visiting New Zealanders. Also considered at fault was the shortage of military police in Fremantle, the lack of hotel supervision, and the high alcohol content of Australian beer.[5]

The strong Australian beer is one of the leitmotifs of submariners' experience in Western Australia. According to the war journalist John Field, what submariners on leave looked forward to most, after female companionship, was a drink.[6] Submariners who visited Western Australia almost universally remembered the beer, and one of the reasons it made such an impression was the higher alcohol content compared to its American equivalent. Zeke Zellmer from USS *Cavalla* vividly recalled his first arrival at Fremantle and going for a drink with some other off-duty officers even though it was still morning. After one mug of Swan Lager it seemed to Zellmer that his head had detached and begun floating around the room.[7]

Admittedly, Zellmer was not a big drinker and had imbibed on an empty stomach, but many other submariners attributed almost mythical powers to the local brew. Elton Brubaker, assigned to the submarine tender *Orion*, wrote to his family that the crew drank only beer and claimed it was so strong it initially hurt his kidneys.[8] Many submariners remember the local beer as one of the highlights of their Australian stays; as one submariner put it, "The beer was the best."[9] For men returning from war patrols, drinking could help block out recent dangers and celebrate what one submariner called "the blessedness of being alive."[10] On first returning to port, submariners often had a beer party and were frequently given a chit that could be exchanged for a case of beer.[11] Many men got seriously drunk at the beginning of their leave, but then took a more moderate approach for the remainder of their time ashore. Jack Glotzbach, who served as a radio operator on USS *Gar*, divided his peers into two categories: those interested in the local sights and history, and those whose leave revolved around local pubs.[12]

Once submariners were assigned to a hotel for their leave, they were pretty much left to their own devices. George "Tag" McPherson from USS *Puffer* recalls being instructed to obey the law and stay out of trouble, but otherwise he and his crewmates could do what they liked. With most of the men between eighteen and twenty-two years old, and after two months cooped up in a submarine, McPherson concedes they tended to be "excessively exuberant" and indulge in some "wild conduct."[13] Even so, McPherson believed most were reasonably well-behaved. On the other hand, the effects of drink, along with a mindset that they might not return from their next patrol, could lead to problems. As Don Haseley from USS *Cavalla* explained, "It was the thought of the next patrol could be our last and you wanted to do everything you could think of. [That] coupled with drinking was a bad combination."[14] Many believed that the more war patrols they made, the slimmer their chances of survival. Bill Grady from USS *Pampanito* became convinced he would not return from his next patrol and lived accordingly. He borrowed all the money he could during his leave, but, according to Grady, "We made it back to port and I had to pay back everything that I had earned for two months."[15]

Bob Hunt from USS *Tambor* sensed that the longer the men were away from the United States, the wilder their leaves became. Before departing for patrol in July 1943, Hunt got into a fight with another sailor outside the Ocean Beach Hotel at Cottesloe and gave the man a concussion.[16] Fighting was one of the main side effects of excessive drinking, accentuated by the macho posturing of military life. According to Jim Cashero, a torpedoman from USS *Seawolf*, fights sometimes erupted between submariners and sailors from surface ships. "Some of the guys on the regular ships didn't like submarine men and they used to beat the hell out of us."[17] Relations between U.S. sailors and the Dutch took a turn for the worse on December 20, 1943, after a brawl over a taxi in which a steward from HMNS *Van Galen*, Pieter van den Bos, was killed by a group of Americans.[18]

Although most fighting was nonlethal, occasionally submariners became involved in homicide cases. William Penzenik, a motor machinist's mate from USS *Puffer* transferred to tender duty, was convicted of killing a member of the Royal Australian Navy. On June 8, 1944, Penzenik took leave in Fremantle with a friend, and while drunk they got into a fight with two RAN sailors. One of the men, Arthur Reginald Flores, fell and hit his head on the pavement during the fight and died five days later. Penzenik was convicted of voluntary manslaughter, dishonorably discharged from the Navy, and sentenced to three years at the Portsmouth Naval Prison in New Hampshire.[19] The following year the mother of his victim wrote to the U.S. consul in Perth, stating, "I feel as though I should forgive this boy for what he did as I know he wasn't in his right mind when it happened."[20] She expressed her hope that Penzenik might be released, or that she could at least write to him, a sentiment that may explain why Penzenik's sentence was later reviewed by the judge advocate general and reduced to one year's confinement.

Another *Puffer* crewman, African American Steward's Mate John Alden Pruitt, was also charged with a serious offense while on leave. Pruitt had served with *Puffer* since its commissioning, and during the submarine's infamous depth charging in Makassar Strait he distinguished himself by passing out salt pills and reassuring crewmen that they would survive. On April 19, 1944, Pruitt was reassigned to the tender *Orion*, and a few weeks later, on the afternoon of May 9, he took a taxi to Roe Street in Perth with some fellow sailors. Pruitt spent some hours drinking in downtown Perth before allegedly assaulting Robert Wells, a Navy boatswain's mate, and his girlfriend Lavinia Mestichelli on their way to the movies. A short time later he was accused of stabbing the girl's father, Angelo Mestichelli. Pruitt was discharged from the Navy for bad conduct and sentenced to five years, prison for the offense.[21]

Apart from cases of violence, alcohol also figured in other deaths. After a night out drinking, Chief Machinist's Mate Lloyd Sandridge from USS *Seawolf* died after he stepped out into the road in front of an oncoming taxi. In addition to alcohol, the blackout conditions enforced at the time probably contributed to the accident.[22] Another submariner killed in a traffic accident was Peter Jongerling, a machinist on the Dutch submarine *K-XII*, although it is unclear whether alcohol was a factor.[23] Many other submariners suffered non-life-threatening injuries as a result of overindulging in alcohol. Ona D. Hawkins from USS *Pampanito*, for example, fell down a stairwell at the Ocean Beach Hotel while inebriated and spent New Year's Day in the hospital.[24]

Loss of inhibitions associated with drinking also contributed at least indirectly to a range of offenses. Following a ship's party, one crewman from USS *Puffer*, Leonard "Chickie-Bub" Evans, reputedly drove off in the first car he could find with a key in it. As it turned out, the car belonged to the chief of police.[25] The local police tended to see sailors as a problem for shore patrols. In Fremantle, while there were only two police constables on duty at a time, Navy military police wearing armbands and carrying batons were in conspicuous numbers. Many of the submariners who came to the attention of the police were let off lightly, most likely because at least some of the local police understood the hardships submariners experienced at sea and tended to make allowances for their behavior while on leave. Most offenders were disciplined by their officers, typically punished at captain's mast in which the skipper meted out a punishment he deemed fit.[26]

Along with drinking, gambling was another popular pastime among submariners on leave. Some of those who still had money at the end of their leave were happy enough to risk it in a card game or shooting craps. Frank Golay, an officer with USS *Puffer*, described losing money in a dice game as a "pre-sailing ritual."[27] His thinking was that it was better to leave someone with a fat bankroll rather than carrying money out to sea. Eric McNabb, a young Australian serving with the RAAF at Exmouth Gulf, was astounded by the amount of money that changed hands in a craps game. When he asked one of the submariners about this, the man replied, "What the hell, we are off on operations and I may not return to use the money, so why worry about it."[28]

Despite the incidence of drunkenness and other misbehavior by submariners on leave, Western Australians appeared relatively tolerant. Don Haseley from USS *Cavalla* recalled staying at the King Edward Hotel in downtown Perth when the Salvation Army band began playing outside the hotel one Saturday morning. "Here all of us U.S. sailors about half drunk from the nite [sic] before were hanging out the windows and acting crazy. The local citizens had every right to yell at us but they did not. I think they knew we were going on dangerous missions and left us alone."[29]

In Eastern Australia, a portion of the civilian population developed a fear and resentment of American troops that was mainly absent in Western Australia. As early as May 1942, Australian-American relations in Melbourne were tainted after a U.S. private, Edward Leonski, murdered three local women. In October 1942 the American military attaché in Melbourne alluded to "a distinct trend" away from the previously friendly relations.[30] After General MacArthur moved his headquarters to Brisbane, Queensland, in July 1942, the city also experienced a wave of anti-Americanism. The most famous clash became known as the Battle of Brisbane, when on the night of November 26, 1942, a riot erupted outside the downtown American PX (post exchange). During the melee one Australian soldier was killed and eight others were wounded by gunfire.

Two reasons may be suggested for the relative lack of friction between submariners and civilians in Western Australia. The most obvious is that the Americans were in smaller numbers. The state of Queensland saw the heaviest concentration; of about 100,000 American military personnel in Australia by August 1942, three-quarters were in Brisbane and north Queensland towns such as Rockhampton and Townsville.[31] In these towns inundated with U.S. forces, tensions rose as locals blamed the Americans for shortages in housing, food, and other commodities.[32]

Another significant factor was the perception of submariners as a special branch of the military, both by themselves and the broader public. Through their recruitment, selection, and training, submariners viewed themselves as part of an elite force. The men attracted to submarine duty were portrayed as eager to face the enemy and not afraid to put themselves in harm's way. Submarine recruiting posters promised the opportunity to "See Action Now" and "Hit 'Em Where It Hurts."[33] The rigorous selection process further defined submariners as superior to most enlistees. An article published in *Life* magazine insisted that those in the submarine service represented the Navy's "toughest, smartest men."[34] The physical requirements included 20/20 vision in each eye, acute hearing, an ability to withstand twenty-three minutes in a pressure chamber, and the ability to hold in one's breath for at least a minute. The men also had to take a battery of psychological tests. Those who failed to meet the submarine service's criteria were, in the telling vernacular of submariners, "surfaced" and reassigned to other parts of the Navy.[35]

Submarine training further narrowed the field of qualified men, with prospective submariners spending six weeks to three months at the submarine school based in New London, Connecticut. Located on the Thames River, the school dated from 1915 and included instruction on torpedoes, batteries, and engines as well as training on older-class boats. The men also took oral and written exams each week.[36] The red brick buildings of the school were dominated by a silo-like tower 150 feet high and containing 240,000 gallons of water. The challenges of submarine school included a requirement that each candidate make a simulated underwater escape from a depth of one hundred feet, and successfully completing the exercise was a huge confidence builder. James Wilkes recalled, "I wanted to shout, 'I did it!'" adding "The escape elated me and filled me with confidence."[37] With the increased demand for trained men during the war, a secondary submarine school was set up at San Diego.

Following the completion of submarine school, many men were sent for several months of further specialist training including schools in diesel engines, batteries, and radio. Training continued once men were assigned to a submarine. While each crewman was a specialist, he also needed to understand the workings of every department of the boat in order to "qualify." This process could take another year, and once these men passed an examination by the officers, they were entitled to wear embroidered dolphins on the right sleeves of their uniforms. With a successful war patrol under their belt, they were further entitled to wear a silver combat pin above their left breast pocket.[38] According to naval historian Ronald Spector, qualified submariners represented "an elite within an elite," a final step in the evolution of highly skilled and disciplined "technician-fighters."[39]

Submariners received higher pay, better food, and improved chances of promotion compared to other military branches. One of the indicators of submariners' special status was a more relaxed attitude toward rank and discipline. It was frequently claimed that the submarine service was more democratic than any other branch of the military. The officers were familiar not only with the names of each man on board, but in many cases they knew the names of their hometowns and girlfriends.[40] Dick Gamby, a crewman on USS *Spadefish*, declared, "We lived like a close family."[41] Norm Wehner professed that even without higher pay and better food he was attracted to submarines because "I found such a sense of 'family' serving on the boats."[42] Like all families, the submarine service was not without rancor. For the most part, however, the men, who had been screened for temperament as well as for abilities, met a higher standard than most other troops who passed through Australia during the war.

CHAPTER 11

WAR OF ATTRITION

Despite the fears of a naval bombardment or air attack on Fremantle in March 1944, by this stage of the war the Japanese had largely lost the initiative. From late 1943 on Japanese forces contracted behind a perimeter that included Malaya, western New Guinea, the Caroline Islands, and the Marianas. Employing Admiral Nimitz's "island hopping" strategy in the Central Pacific, U.S. troops invaded Kwajelein in the Marshall Islands in January 1944. The following month carrier planes bombed the Japanese naval stronghold at Truk in the Caroline Islands, and in March MacArthur's forces captured the Admiralty Islands north of New Guinea in his drive back to the Philippines. It was no longer a question of if the Allies would win the war, but when.

Fremantle submarines continued to accelerate the war of attrition against Japanese shipping, with fifty-six submarines leaving for patrols from the port during the first six months of 1944. Although there were only two patrols from Fremantle in March amid fears of a Japanese naval action, the following month fourteen submarines mounted war patrols, mainly in the Celebes and South China Sea. Overall, an average of nine submarines went on patrol each month during this period, and postwar assessments indicate that they sunk seventy-five ships with a combined tonnage of 318,324. Not surprisingly in light of the number of submarines on patrol, April set a new record for both the number of ships sunk, twenty-seven, and combined tonnage, 92,881.[1] This figure alone exceeded the total for the first half of 1943.

This period saw some of the war's most successful submarine commanders operating from Fremantle, one of which was Reuben T. Whitaker, skipper of USS *Flasher*. In a postwar interview, Adm. Ralph Christie ranked Whitaker as one of the "stars" of the submarine service, claiming that he never missed an opportunity to sink ships.[2] Relatively small in stature and with a blond mustache, Whitaker exuded a stylish and cavalier demeanor. As commander of *Flasher*, he researched his patrol areas before he left port, looking for the areas most likely to encounter Japanese shipping. On his first day out of Fremantle, Whitaker also assembled his officers to discuss where they could be most effective in locating targets. He put most of his faith for finding enemy ships in lookouts stationed on the bridge and periscope shears; whereas many submarines kept four lookouts on duty while on the surface, *Flasher* had seven. In clear conditions, a lookout perched on the periscope shears could spot a ship up to fifteen miles away.³

On *Flasher*'s first patrol out of Fremantle, departing April 4 for the South China Sea, Whitaker and his crew claimed three ships totaling 12,000 tons. Although JANAC later reduced the tonnage, all three ships were confirmed sunk. *Flasher* returned to the South China Sea for its next patrol and this time was credited with sinking seven ships (including one sinking shared with USS *Crevalle*) and 47,900 tons. Typically JANAC reduced the tonnage, but even though they reduced the number of ships sunk to five, it was still the most successful patrol of the month.⁴

Ralph Christie ranked only one of the skippers under his command above Whitaker, and that was the commander of USS *Harder*, Samuel D. Dealey.⁵ On April 13, 1944, *Harder* was on its fourth patrol en route from Pearl Harbor to Fremantle when Adm. Ernest King issued an order raising the priority of Japanese destroyers to the second most important targets after capital ships. Previously, submariners had been discouraged from attacking destroyers both because of their presumed danger and because it was believed they could be replaced relatively easily. As the war progressed, however, the shortage of Japanese escorts became exposed and the efficacy of sinking them exploited.⁶ On the same day King issued his order, *Harder*'s crew sank the destroyer *Ikazuchi* off the Mariana Islands. In words that would become legendary, Dealey tersely described the episode in his patrol report: "Expended four torpedoes and one Jap Destroyer."⁷ This proved to be a mere curtain raiser, however, for on *Harder*'s next patrol Dealey and his men not only completed a secret mission behind enemy lines but also claimed the destruction of five Japanese destroyers.

Sam Dealey was the type of person many submariners had in mind when they said it was impossible to predict which commanders would prove successful warriors. Fellow skipper William Germershausen described Dealey as a "real quiet southern-gentleman type."⁸ Originally from Texas, Sam claimed a place in the state's history through his uncle, George Bannerman Dealey, the founder and publisher of the *Dallas Morning News* and benefactor of Dealey Plaza (later to gain notoriety with the assassination of John F. Kennedy in 1963). When Charles Lockwood first met Dealey at Pearl Harbor in May 1943, he struck him as "earnest" and "ordinary," and although Dealey's peacetime naval career

USS *Harder*, under the command of Sam Dealey, made one of the most celebrated patrols of the war from Fremantle in 1944. U.S. Naval Institute Photo Archive

was unremarkable, he became celebrated as one of America's greatest wartime submarine commanders.[9]

When *Harder* departed Fremantle for its fifth patrol on May 26, 1944, the passengers included Australian commandos Major William T. "Bill" Jinkins and Sergeant Stan W. Dodds. Jinkins had already experienced more of the war than most combatants, having served with the Australian army's Gull Force on the island of Ambon when it fell to the Japanese. After six weeks in a prisoner-of-war camp, Jinkins escaped and then made a torturous island-to-island journey to Darwin by boat. He later volunteered for the Z Special Unit, which carried out clandestine operations behind enemy lines. Created in June 1942, the Z Special Unit's commandos were often transported to their destinations by submarines.

Once at sea the Australians quickly fell into *Harder*'s routines, with Sam Dealey noting that "Major Jinkins and Sergeant Dodds were adopted 100% as members of the crew." Dealey was especially impressed by Jinkins, noting he "showed a particular adeptness in submarining."[10] Their mission was to rescue a party of commandos known as "Python" trapped behind enemy lines in British North Borneo. Some five hundred Japanese troops were devoted to tracking down the commandos, and three had already been captured, tortured, and eventually beheaded.[11]

There had already been three unsuccessful attempts by submarines to extract the remaining six men, and with the Japanese closing in on them, the stakes were high.

In addition to Jinkins and Dodds, *Harder*'s "passengers" also included Capt. Murray Jones "Tich" Tichenor, who on September 1, 1943, had assumed the role of operations officer at Fremantle.[12] He managed to get Christie's permission to accompany the war patrol, and it was by some accounts Tichenor who suggested that *Harder* be delegated the job of extracting the stranded Python commandos. A meeting between Sam Dealey and Bill Jinkins at Admiral Christie's Bend of the Road home apparently helped overcome some of Dealey's aversion to "special missions." Able to observe Dealey at close quarters, Tichenor was impressed by both his modesty and efficiency, claiming that his crew "absolutely worshiped him."[13]

As *Harder* patrolled off Borneo in Sibutu Passage on June 6, it encountered and sank the Japanese destroyer *Minatsuki*. The submarine sank a second Japanese destroyer, *Hayanami*, the following day. On the evening of June 8, *Harder* reached its scheduled rendezvous point; Jinkins and Dodds set off for shore in two Folboats (seventeen-foot-long kayak-like craft). The surviving Python men had trekked through forty miles of perilous jungle to reach the rendezvous, and as they desperately waited near midnight they recited the Lord's Prayer. Only minutes later they jubilantly recognized the light signals of Jinkins and Dodds and with some difficulty made their way back to *Harder*. One of the commandos, Stan Neil, later recalled their reception on board: "The Yanks are marvellous. Can't do too much for us. Everyone you pass hands you a carton of cigs, a toothbrush or clothes."[14]

The action of *Harder*'s patrol, however, was not yet over. The following day, June 9, *Harder* fired torpedoes at two more Japanese destroyers, claiming to sink both (one was later confirmed as *Tanikaze*.) Yet another Japanese destroyer was attacked the next day in a daring "down-the-throat" shot. The technique, which some skippers compared to playing Russian roulette, involved firing torpedoes at an oncoming ship, with the idea that if the ship turned to evade one of the torpedoes it would be hit by the other. Quickly going deep after firing the torpedoes, *Harder*'s crew believed they had sunk yet another destroyer as explosions erupted on the surface above them, although this was never confirmed.

Within the compressed period of only five days, *Harder* had seen more action than some submarines experienced during the entire war. In fact, *Harder* added further luster to the patrol by carrying out valuable reconnaissance on the afternoon of June 10 when Dealey spotted a task force of battleships and cruisers steam south from the Japanese anchorage at Tawi Tawi. The ships were too fast and too far away to attack, but he reported his observations by radio. What Dealey had witnessed were ships under Admiral Ugaki heading toward Biak, where Gen. Douglas MacArthur was mounting an offensive. MacArthur sent *Harder* a message of commendation by reply for this timely information.[15]

As events unfolded, Ugaki was recalled to join the First Mobile Fleet before reaching Biak as it became evident that the Americans were about to invade the Mariana Islands. The Japanese employed nine aircraft carriers in defense of the islands, while the U.S. force under Admiral Spruance included thirteen aircraft carriers. American submarines had already cut off troops and supplies to the Marianas before the attack on Saipan began on June 16. They further kept Spruance apprised of Japanese fleet movements as his task force covered the invasion. In what later became known as the Battle of the Philippine Sea, the greatest clash of carriers during the Second World War took place on June 19–20. The Japanese lost three of their carriers, along with hundreds of aircraft.[16]

Harder, along with USS *Hake*, contributed at least indirectly to an Allied victory; the sinking of destroyers off the Japanese Mobile Fleet base at Tawi Tawi resulted in the suspension of flight training due to the risk to their carriers. The lack of flight training in turn contributed to what was dubbed the "Great Marianas Turkey Shoot," when scores of inexperienced Japanese pilots met their death. The loss of these naval aviators and aircraft hamstrung Japan's operations for the remainder of the war. With the capture of Saipan, as well as Guam and Tinian later, the United States moved its bombers within striking distance of the Japanese home islands, while Biak was taken by MacArthur's forces on June 21.[17]

In a move reminiscent of his earlier partial patrol with USS *Bowfin*, Adm. Ralph Christie appeared determined to witness firsthand Dealey and *Harder* in action. He flew to Darwin to join the submarine when it came into port to disembark the evacuees from Borneo and take on fuel and more torpedoes. Ostensibly, Christie was determined to sink a ship transporting nickel ore, a vital commodity to the Japanese, which made a weekly trip from Pomaela in the Celebes. *Harder* arrived at Darwin on June 21 and departed the following day, with Christie taking Murray Tichenor's place on board.

The crewmembers, looking forward to another rest period in Perth, were disappointed to learn they would be heading back to sea. At least some thought Christie was merely after a submarine combat pin.[18] In any case, this time *Harder* was unable to complete its assigned task. Although the crew spotted the nickel ship in Salier Strait, Japanese air cover prevented an attack, and after twelve days *Harder* returned to base without firing a torpedo. Nevertheless, Dealey's toll on enemy destroyers gained instant recognition from his peers. Back in Perth, his fellow submarine skippers presented him with a woodcut plaque that depicted a sinking Japanese destroyer and proclaimed him the "Destroyer Killer."[19] Dealey also received a measure of public recognition rarely afforded submariners. In July 1944 Perth newspapers reported that Samuel Dealey had been awarded a Distinguished Service Cross by Gen. Douglas MacArthur for "extraordinary heroism in action."[20]

Harder's success in rescuing the Python men also had important implications for future missions. Admiral Christie, impressed by the work of Jinkins and Dodds, began routinely assigning Australian commandos to submarine patrols. Under what was called Operation Politician, the commandos were intended to assist in various capacities from limpet mining of targets in shallow water to helping interpret information from Malay-speaking sailors. Under the leadership of Bill Jinkins, there were eventually some twenty-four commandos available for assignment to American and, after January 1945, British submarines.[21]

As in Europe with the long-awaited D-day invasion of Normandy, June had proved a pivotal month in the Southwest Pacific. A further innovation adopted that month saw the first wolf pack patrol depart from Fremantle. Although "coordinated attack groups" of three American submarines had already been operating from Pearl Harbor and Midway for more than six months, it was not until June 21 that the Fremantle base joined the experiment. Skippers and their men preferred the German descriptor of "wolf pack" for these patrols, but whereas German wolf packs typically involved eight to twenty submarines, the American versions usually involved three. They mainly functioned to share information about contacts rather than make the types of mass attacks made famous by U-boats in the Atlantic. Between July 1944 and the end of the war, almost half of the U.S. war patrols in the Pacific were made as part of a coordinated attack group.[22]

Many skippers remained skeptical about the value of wolf packs. Given the ethos of individualism within the submarine service, officers resented losing some of their autonomy. There was also a fear that increased radio traffic made submarines more vulnerable to the enemy. Herman Kossler, commander of USS *Cavalla*, believed that wolf packs were weakened not only by the poor communication between submarines but also by a lack of proper training in working together.[23] By mid-1944 communications were more efficient with the introduction of short-distance VHF radio telephones, which allowed direct voice contact between submarines with less danger of being detected by enemy direction finders.[24]

Kossler still fretted, however, about the possibility of accidentally hitting a pack mate with his torpedoes during an attack.[25] It was a concern that could not be lightly dismissed. In May 1944 the USS *Lapon* fired two torpedoes at what was believed to be a Japanese I-class submarine. Only after returning to Fremantle did *Lapon*'s skipper, Lowell Stone, compare notes with the commander of *Raton*, James Davis, and realize he had narrowly missed an American submarine. In fact, three submarines, including USS *Gunnel* as well as *Lapon* and *Raton*, had converged on the anticipated position of an enemy submarine after receiving information from headquarters in Fremantle.[26]

Despite such problems, the wolf pack tactic seemed to offer some advantages. Part of the reason for the delay in introducing coordinated attack groups was that submarines emanating from Fremantle often operated in confined waters, whereas wolf packs were better suited to the open seas. The Japanese had also lacked a coherent antisubmarine doctrine.[27] Increasingly, though, the Japanese use of larger convoys with numerous escorts and frequently supported by aircraft meant that two or three submarines traveling together could be more effective, particularly with their combination of high surface speeds, sophisticated radar, and VHF radio.[28]

The first Fremantle-based pack comprised USS *Crevalle*, USS *Angler*, and USS *Flasher*. As the senior officer, Reuben Whitaker on *Flasher* was designated tactical commander, and the pack was nicknamed "Whitaker's Wolves" in his honor. He convened a meeting of the skippers and executive officers from all three boats on the morning of their departure to discuss tactics and communications while on patrol.[29] The same morning three of *Crevalle*'s crew were unceremoniously delivered to their boat by shore patrol. The submariners had only arrived back in Perth that morning on a train from Kalgoorlie, still drunk and overdue without leave. For the time being, the three men were simply sent to their bunks to sleep it off.

They were not the only ones to return to their submarines intoxicated. Whereas Whitaker and *Flasher* made a quick exit from Fremantle, the skippers of *Crevalle* and *Angler* headed to the officers club for drinks after the morning briefing. When they returned to the Fremantle wharf, with Frank Gordon Selby from USS *Puffer* in tow, they were baying like wolves.[30] At least on *Crevalle*, the first day at sea spent sailing up the coast of Western Australia was used for recuperation instead of the usual training. In fact, after two weeks of frenetic leave, many submariners welcomed the relative quiet of the ten days or so transiting to their patrol areas.

USS *Flasher* was the first to reach Exmouth Gulf, when one of the crew, M. G. Spencer Jr., electrician's mate first class, was diagnosed with acute appendicitis and taken off for an operation.[31] USS *Angler*, under the command of Franklin Grant Hess, reached the refueling barge at Exmouth Gulf on the morning of June 24 and experienced its own drama. As the submarine attempted to moor alongside the barge, the starboard propeller hit "an uncharted submerged obstruction."[32] With all four blades badly bent, *Angler* headed back to Fremantle to have the propeller replaced. *Crevalle*, under the command of Francis David Walker Jr., also faced a setback when the crew headed out to sea after refueling and discovered that the SJ radar wasn't working. The submarine returned to Exmouth Gulf to wait until the spare part needed could be flown up from Perth. Some of *Crevalle*'s married officers used the time to feverishly write letters to their wives, having fallen behind in their correspondence during leave. As one submariner cynically noted, they tried to give their spouses the impression that they had spent much of their time in port thinking of them by mailing packets of backdated letters once they reached Exmouth Gulf. With its radar repaired, *Crevalle* resumed its journey on the afternoon of June 25 and headed for Lombok Strait.[33]

Flasher commenced its patrol with a series of successful attacks, beginning on June 29, when it encountered a Singapore-bound convoy and in a night surface action claimed the sinking of two ships. On July 7 *Flasher* added the sinking of a freighter off Hon Doi and then, in the early hours of July 19, torpedoed a *Kuma*-class cruiser.[34] After having the propeller repaired at Fremantle, *Angler* made radio contact with its pack mates on July 13 and then made a rendezvous with *Flasher* on the evening of July 24, the two submarines coming alongside within hailing distance.[35] The following morning at daybreak, *Angler* spotted a convoy of ten cargo ships accompanied by an escort carrier and a host of escorts off Cape Bolinao west of Luzon, which Hess reported to *Flasher* and *Crevalle*. Whitaker would later comment that the convoy included the largest number of modern escorts he had ever seen, ranging from destroyers to patrol boats.[36] The presence of enemy aircraft made it still more difficult to approach the convoy.

Even so, on the afternoon of July 25 *Crevalle* managed to get into position to fire at a cargo ship. Unfortunately, one of the torpedomen mistakenly opened the after-trim tank vent instead of the torpedo tube vent, and the error resulted in flooding the after-torpedo room.[37] The submarines pursued the ships into the early hours of July 26, when *Flasher* radioed that it was going in for an attack from the port side. At 2:30 a.m. the crew of *Angler* witnessed "a tremendous explosion" with one of the ships "afire from stem to stern."[38] The crew of *Crevalle* also witnessed the attack, recording in the patrol report: "Tremendous explosion lighted up whole area as Flasher opened the vents in a big tanker."[39] To Whitaker, under the bright light, "The ocean appeared full of ships."[40] The same light, however, revealed *Flasher*'s position to the enemy, and Whitaker dived the submarine as shells began falling close by.

Almost two hours later *Angler* fired six torpedoes at a large freighter in a surface attack. The crew saw one torpedo hit the freighter before another ship began firing shells, forcing them to submerge.[41] After *Angler*'s attack the convoy slowed, allowing *Crevalle* to join the action. At about 4:30 a.m. it fired at ships from both the bow and stern tubes, claiming hits on two targets. Near 10:30 in the morning *Crevalle* fired torpedoes at another target, hitting it amidships and "throwing up much smoke and debris."[42] *Crevalle*, though, was quickly forced deep by two aircraft bombs and then depth charged by escorts.

One of the advantages of a wolf pack was that while the enemy concentrated its efforts on hunting one of the submarines, the others might have an opportunity to attack. *Flasher*, *Angler*, and *Crevalle* had forced the enemy ships to radically alter course and slow down, giving them further chances to score hits. For more than twenty-four hours the submarines alternately drew off the escorts as the others moved in to fire their torpedoes.[43] *Flasher* was the first to use all of its torpedoes and head back to Fremantle, devolving the role of tactical commander to Frank Walker as the remaining senior skipper.[44] On the morning of July 28, at 9:30 a.m., *Crevalle* encountered another convoy of about eight ships with four or more escorts. The crew launched six torpedoes in a down-the-throat shot from the bow tubes, but then they had to dive as the escorts moved in.[45] In this action the *Crevalle* men were able to sink only a naval auxiliary, and they paid the price with a heavy depth charging.

Angler's crew also spotted ships off Point Rena, Luzon, but with the convoy near the coast they lost contact.[46] Hess summed up the wolf pack by noting that communications were "very satisfactory" and that it demonstrated "three submarines can effectively work over a convoy caught out away from the coast."[47] *Crevalle*'s patrol report also enthusiastically endorsed the wolf pack tactic, claiming, "Two or more packs of two or three boats each could conceivably deny completely the use of certain traffic lanes to the enemy."[48] In the final tally, *Flasher* received credit for sinking six ships totaling 47,900 tons. *Crevalle* was credited with sinking 28,000 tons including three enemy freighters, and it shared credit for an army cargo ship, *Tosan Maru*, previously crippled by *Flasher*. *Angler* was credited with damaging a freighter of 8,800 tons. It proved the most productive U.S. wolf pack up to that time.[49]

During their leave in Perth, the officers of USS *Crevalle* celebrated their good fortune with a gathering at Molinari's Restaurant that included the wardrooms of several other submarines. The festivities included a food fight and a game in which the men's dates had to change sides under the table as quickly as possible. Amid breaking glassware and chairs, the submariners were ordered out. One of the *Crevalle* men, William Ruhe, professed that he only left after "I grabbed the girl I had brought to the dinner around her legs and boosted her up to the white-washed ceiling so she could place an imprint of her red lips where it was readily seen." Other officers and their dates followed suit, causing more chaos and hilarity, although Ruhe added that "as usual, all the officers chipped in to pay for the damage done and for the clean-up necessary."[50]

CHAPTER

SUPPORT AND SUPPLY

As the war progressed and an increasing number of submarines operated from Fremantle, the Americans continued to rely heavily on Australians. Some remained skeptical of Australian methods and productive capacity. Alvin Jacobson from USS *Flier*, whose father owned a brass foundry back in Michigan, contrived to visit the largest foundry he could find in Perth. He reported back to his father that "as is true with everything else here, their equipment and methods were many years behind the times."[1] Nevertheless, Australian labor was essential to the American presence, and by late 1944 some 25,000 civilians were employed by the U.S. services nationwide.[2] At Fremantle, more than two hundred civilian workers were employed at the submarine base by the U.S. Navy. The Naval Supply Depot at Dalgety's Warehouse in Queen Victoria Street alone employed about sixty civilians, more than half of the administrative staff.[3]

Because of his engineering skills, William A. Archibald was among those manpowered to work on submarine repair. A resident of Broome Street, Cottesloe, he did contract labor for the U.S. Navy from March 1944 on. In that month a huge floating dock, ARD 10, arrived at Fremantle and was placed at the eastern end of the harbor after being towed from the United States. The dock had a lifting capacity of three thousand tons, a thousand tons greater than the slipway. Archibald acted as foreman of the civilians who manned the dock until March 1945, his efforts later recognized by a U.S. Navy Meritorious Civilian Service Award.[4]

In addition to the contribution of Australian workers to manufacturing war materials and assisting the Americans with submarine maintenance, they increasingly supplied the Allies with foodstuffs. Under the Mutual Aid Agreement, popularly known as Lend-Lease, in exchange for military equipment Australia was responsible for feeding U.S. forces as well as other services. In April 1942 an Allied Supply Council was formed to coordinate various supply organizations, along with an Australian

Food Council. The following year Prime Minister Curtin announced that the production of essential foods would be regarded as a war activity.[5] During the first half of 1943 more than two hundred Liberty ships stopped at Fremantle to take on stores.[6] As the number of Americans in the Southwest Pacific continued to escalate, the Australians strained to keep pace in supplying them food and other necessities. Already in July 1942 a Women's Land Army had been formed to assist in rural industries. So acute was the need for supplies that in early 1944 some 39,000 Australian soldiers were shifted to the civilian workforce.[7]

For the submarine service, supplies of fresh food were critical. Traditionally one of the compensations for the appalling conditions submariners endured on war patrols was good food. A skilled cook was a vital cog in maintaining morale; an article published in *Life* magazine claimed it was the "wonderful food" above all else that kept up spirits during submarine patrols.[8] Some men professed that the enticement of good food inspired them to join the submarine service in the first place. After sharing a meal on USS *Plunger* as the guest of his submariner cousin, Ernie Plantz decided, "Man, this is the place for me."[9]

Certainly compared to the other armed services, submariners appeared spoiled. At a time when most meats were strictly rationed to civilians, the fare on patrols might include lobster and shrimp as well as steaks and roasts. Fresh-baked bread, cinnamon rolls, cakes, and pies were regular offerings.[10] Holidays like Thanksgiving and Christmas were celebrated with all the traditional trimmings, including not only turkey but cranberry sauce and pumpkin pie.[11] Many submarines were further equipped with ice cream machines, and while supplies lasted there were fresh strawberries and cream. There were even stories, almost certainly apocryphal, of submarines returning to Fremantle early from patrols because their ice cream mixers broke down.[12]

During their leave, many Americans developed a taste for Australian dishes. Charley Odom, who served with USS *Billfish*, "fell in love with Aussie steak and kidney pie."[13] Steak and eggs became an enormously popular dish with submarine crews. Within the U.S. forces generally, however, there was skepticism toward food supplied by Australia—what some demeaned as "goat and cabbage."[14] Provisions supplied to submarines at Fremantle were of variable quality. The skipper of USS *Sturgeon*, Bull Wright, praised the food as of "very high quality" and boasted, "We had lettuce for over four weeks."[15] On the other hand, one of the crewmen on USS *Thresher*, Wes Headington, lamented in his diary the "bad chow" on a patrol out of Fremantle and claimed that the crew was "growling pretty bad about it."[16] The crew of USS *Batfish* had a litany of complaints about the food after taking on provisions at Fremantle for their fifth patrol. Weevils were found in the rice and macaroni; canned fruits were not yet ripe, while the canned fruit juices were too bitter to be palatable. During the patrol the crew threw hundreds of pounds of beef overboard.[17]

A major problem seems to have been that much of the Australian meat provided didn't suit American tastes; most U.S. sailors had little interest in eating mutton. Stanley J. Nicholls, who served on USS *Pompon*, bitterly complained that mutton on board created "a disaster." According to Nicholls, "The smell in the boat was terrible. Our circulation system was not adequate to handle the stink."[18] Spencer Stimler, who served on USS *Pampanito*, had a similar response, claiming, "I've eaten bear meat that smelled better and certainly tasted better."[19]

Many submariners expressed a similar aversion to rabbit. With a shortage of beef that came about soon after the Americans arrived, some crews were issued cubes of frozen and pressed rabbit meat. At sea the cooks were supposed to saw off the quantities they wanted and then stew, fry, or bake it. Submarine crews, however, soon wearied of this fare. On USS *Bowfin* the crew refused to eat the rabbits ordered by the commissary officer, preferring to dine on canned Spam or corned beef instead. At a *Bowfin* reunion more than fifty years after the war, some of the men were still complaining about the rabbit. Even Australian beef was sometimes judged substandard. The Americans claimed that compared to the U.S. product, Australian beef tended to be tough, stringy, and rubbery.[20]

Despite these complaints, most submariners found that their food remained at a high standard. Measures taken by Australia included an increase in pig farming to meet the American demand for pork and the growing of sweet corn in much greater quantities in response to servicemen's tastes.[21] From the Australian point of view the main problem was that supplying the Allied war effort tended to obscure Australians' military contribution. This became even more the case as elements of the Royal Navy's Pacific Fleet became based in Australia from 1944 on. At the same time, the increasing role played by Australians in supply led some Americans to conclude they were carrying the brunt of the fighting.[22] Also at issue was the relative deprivation of civilians compared to those in the U.S. Navy. While submarines typically carried five hundred pounds of coffee for a patrol and consumed twenty to thirty gallons a day, civilians were being deprived of their staple beverage. Tea in Australia, described by one historian as "an indispensable lubricant of national life," was rationed from March 1942 on.[23] Rationing of sugar began in August 1942, followed by butter in June 1943 and meat in January 1944.

One of the things that blunted the envy of relatively deprived Australian civilians was the frequent generosity of the Americans in sharing their seeming abundance. When submarines returned to port, the flow of goods typically reversed. As they approached Fremantle, men began hoarding their cigarettes to use for trade while on leave, along with the submarine's remaining stocks of chocolate and coffee. As described by Frank Golay, an officer on USS *Puffer*, members of the crew were "scrambling like pack rats."[24] Dutch submariners also benefited from American largesse, receiving the same supplies as their U.S. counterparts, including a carton of Lucky Strike or Chesterfield cigarettes each week. They too ingratiated themselves by sharing with the locals some of their rations, including cigarettes, canned salmon, canned California fruit, and shampoo. The pilfering of food from U.S. Navy kitchens on shore was also common, with much of it ending up in the homes of hospitable Australians.[25]

One of the most contentious commodities was beer. In early 1942 the Australian government ordered a reduction in beer production by one-third, and state governments reduced liquor trading hours.[26] The comparative ease with which Americans accessed beer stocks created considerable angst. For example, submarine officers staying at the Majestic Hotel in the Perth suburb of Applecross found a carton of beer and a couple of bottles of Scotch under their beds when they arrived.[27] On the other hand, the willingness of many Americans to share their alcohol with locals greased social interaction. USS *Jack* officer James Calvert, for example, ingratiated himself with the King's Park Tennis Club by donating his beer rations to the members.[28]

CHAPTER

CRUEL MONTHS

The high of victory in the Philippine Sea and *Harder*'s legendary patrol in June 1944 was followed by a deep trough; in mid-1944 the submarine fraternity at Fremantle was shaken by the loss of three boats and their crews in quick succession. Following the loss of *Grenadier* in April 1943, only one Fremantle submarine had been lost to the enemy in the year since. USS *Grayling*, while on patrol in the waters west of Luzon in the Philippine Islands, disappeared without survivors in early September 1943, apparently rammed by a Japanese cargo ship, *Hokuan Maru*, while submerged.[1] Less than a year later, and in the space of little over a month, three more Fremantle submarines were lost: *Robalo*, *Flier*, and *Harder*.

While USS *Crevalle* waited at Exmouth Gulf on June 25, 1944, for spare radar parts to arrive before proceeding on its wolf pack patrol with *Angler* and *Flasher*, USS *Robalo* passed through on its way north to what proved to be its last patrol.[2] The details of boats lost on patrol were usually sketchy, but the fate of those on board *Robalo* is among the most contested. The family connections of its skipper, Manning Marius Kimmel, compounded the conflicting evidence on *Robalo*'s loss. Kimmel was the eldest son of Adm. Husband Kimmel, commander in chief of the Pacific Fleet and the man in charge of Pearl Harbor when the Japanese made their devastating attack on December 7. Many blamed Kimmel for the lackadaisical defense preparations at Pearl Harbor that made the attack so successful, and President Roosevelt replaced him with Adm. Chester Nimitz a short time later. A presidential order on December 17, 1941, barred Husband Kimmel from active service, and after a forced retirement on March 1, 1942, he spent the remainder of the war testifying to a succession of inquiries.[3]

Although some considered that Admiral Kimmel became a scapegoat at a time when the American public demanded answers, the assault on his father's reputation was a heavy burden for young Manning Kimmel to carry. Ralph Christie, for one, believed Manning Kimmel was inclined to recklessness because of his father's situation. He took command of

Robalo at Fremantle on March 29, 1944, departing for his first patrol as commander less than two weeks later. On the first day of reaching his patrol area, April 24, a Japanese plane attacked with two depth bombs as *Robalo* dived for safety. According to the patrol report, the detonation of the second bomb "jarred the entire boat violently and caused extensive damage."[4] Some of the more serious damage included wrecking both periscopes, the SJ radar, a 4-inch deck gun, and a sprung conning tower hatch.

Despite these defects, Kimmel elected to remain on station, making four attacks during the course of the patrol. The patrol endorsements praised his "aggressiveness and determination," and *Robalo* received credit for sinking a 7,500-ton tanker.[5] Tex McLean concluded that Kimmel "was fired with a strong determination to go out and get them."[6] Unofficially, however, McLean later claimed that they would have relieved Kimmel had anyone else been available to command *Robalo*.[7]

During *Robalo*'s next war patrol, departing Fremantle on June 22, 1944, the submarine disappeared. Directed by an Ultra message from code breakers on the night of July 2, the *Robalo* crew set off through Balabac Strait in pursuit of a *Fuso*-class battleship. Their last received message reported spotting a battleship with two escorts east of Borneo. Some blamed *Robalo*'s loss on a battery explosion, but almost certainly the submarine hit a mine while transiting on the surface near Balabac Strait.[8] As early as April 1942, Jim Coe, commander of USS *Skipjack*, had prophetically described the dangers of the area, noting, "This is a narrow bottle-neck easily stopped by mines." Coe concluded his appraisal of Balabac Strait stating "I was glad to get through this."[9]

According to various accounts, between four and six men survived the *Robalo*'s sinking and reached land either at Comiran Island or the west coast of Palawan. Some sources claimed Manning Kimmel was among the survivors. This much of the story seems credible; if *Robalo* hit a mine while surfaced, the skipper was likely to be among the men topside at the moment of disaster and therefore more likely to escape the sinking submarine. Based on recently unearthed Japanese interrogation reports, however, Kimmel was not among the four *Robalo* men able to reach Comiran Island after fourteen hours in the water. They included Electrician's Mate 3rd Class Mason Collie Poston, Signalman 3rd Class Wallace Keet Martin, Quartermaster 1st Class Floyd Laughlin, and Ens. Samuel Lombard Tucker. Tucker, a recent graduate of Harvard, had only just joined the *Robalo* crew. The men constructed a raft and drifted to Balabac Island, but on July 8 were taken prisoner by Japanese soldiers.[10]

All versions of the saga agree that any survivors from *Robalo* quickly became prisoners of the Japanese and were taken to the POW camp at

Puerto Princesa on the island of Palawan. According to one account, the *Robalo* survivors managed to drop a note from the prison that was delivered to Filipino guerrillas on the island. Different stories have it that the men were either executed or perished in a massacre at Puerto Princesa, or lost at sea while being transported to Manila on a destroyer.[11] What is certain is that none of the *Robalo* men survived the war.

Manning Kimmel's younger brother, Thomas Kincaid Kimmel, also served in submarines at Fremantle. A graduate of the Naval Academy in 1936, Thomas became the executive officer of USS *Bergall* commissioned in June 1944. *Bergall* arrived at Fremantle at the end of its first patrol but, because of the loss of the *Robalo*, Christie informed Thomas he would be confined to shore duty. Adm. Ernest King, chief of naval operations, ordered Thomas Kimmel's return to the United States soon after; to King's mind the Kimmel family had suffered enough in the war. Thomas departed Perth in November 1944 to take up a post as officer-in-charge of submarine training at Portsmouth, New Hampshire, for the remainder of the war.[12]

There were alarming similarities between the fate of *Robalo* and the loss of USS *Flier*, which departed from Fremantle on August 2, 1944, even before it was realized that *Robalo* was missing. On August 13 *Flier* received an Ultra message on the location of a Japanese convoy off the west coast of Palawan. USS *Puffer* had attacked the convoy at the western approaches of Mindoro Strait, and it appeared that crippled ships were heading southwest toward Palawan Passage.[13] Skipper John Daniel Crowley ordered *Flier*'s crew to crank up the engines, and they set off through Balabac Strait on the surface. Ralph Christie believed that Crowley, despite poor visibility and a lack of certainty about *Flier*'s position, "took a chance to intercept the enemy, transited Balabac out of the safe channel" and in forty fathoms hit a mine.[14] At a subsequent investigation of the *Flier*'s loss in September 1944, Commander Crowley conceded they had strayed slightly south of the prescribed track into waters less than fifty fathoms deep.[15]

The following month the *New York Times* erroneously reported that although the submarine was lost, there was no loss of life. The sobering truth came more than two months later when the newspaper revealed that only eight of the crew survived, describing "a story of sudden disaster at night, eighteen hours torture in the water, days of hunger and thirst in the jungles."[16] This true story required no journalistic embellishment to add drama to one of the war's most remarkable survival stories. The "sudden disaster" was apparently caused by a mine explosion at the level of the control room on the starboard side of the submarine, the force of the blast blowing some men from the conning tower onto the bridge. These men, along with those on watch topside when the explosion occurred, were the only ones able to escape the submarine before it plunged to the bottom of the sea. Crowley and others on deck were left in the water as the submarine disappeared from beneath them.

Initially thirteen *Flier* men were counted in the water. Under a menacing sky occasionally illuminated by lightning, they struck out toward land to the north. Of the eight men who survived the next eighteen hours in the water, at least a couple were trained athletes. *Flier*'s executive officer, James W. Liddell, had graduated in engineering from Northwestern University, where he played tackle on the varsity football team. At six feet two inches tall he was solidly built. Another survivor, the tall and slim motor machinist Earl Baumgart, had served as captain of his high school swim team back in Milwaukee.

Some of the other survivors, however, persevered against the odds. Skipper John Crowley was the oldest man on board at thirty-five and had a physique on the portly side. At the Naval Academy, Crowley had required extra instruction to bring his swimming up to standard; now that saved his life. Wesley Miller, who grew up on a cattle ranch, had also initially failed his swimming test in the Navy.[17] Nevertheless, he was one of the eight men to reach land. Alvin E. Jacobson later recalled that during the exhausting swim "I had to fight with myself to keep from going to sleep."[18] He constantly changed swimming strokes to keep himself awake and moving. To his surprise, he also found himself repeating the 23rd Psalm over and over. Unfortunately, Jacobson lost his pocket knife during the swim, and later on land he realized how valuable it would have been as the men constructed a lean-to and a raft and attempted to open coconuts.

Crowley and the other crewmen from *Flier* rafted between islands until they encountered a group of Filipino guerrilla fighters. Eventually they learned that the guerrillas had been searching for survivors from *Robalo*. After making their way north to Brooke's Point on the island of Palawan, the *Flier* men were put in contact with a group of recently arrived coast watchers. Using their radio equipment, they were able to arrange a rendezvous with another submarine on the night of August 30, and they returned to Australia on USS *Redfin*.

USS *Redfin* had departed Fremantle for patrol only four days after *Flier*, pulling away from its mooring at a little after 1 p.m. on August 6. Crowley and the *Redfin*'s skipper, Marshall Austin, had spent some time together while on leave. The *Redfin* crew had completed laying a minefield off the west coast of Borneo when they were directed to head for the Sulu Sea. As it happened, William Jinkins and another Australian commando, Lieutenant T. J. Barnes, were traveling with *Redfin*. After a rendezvous was established with the *Flier* men, a small native craft took them out to sea, where Jinkins and Barnes inspected the craft to make sure it was not a Japanese trap and then brought the *Flier* survivors on board *Redfin*.[19] *Redfin*'s passengers were off-loaded at Darwin, and after spending a night there the *Flier* men made a twelve-hour flight to Perth in Admiral Christie's private plane. Once there, all but Commander Crowley were sent to Kalgoorlie. According to Jacobson, "The admiral did not think it was a good idea for us to be around sailors who were going back out to sea."[20] After ten days they were flown back to Perth and then to the United States.

The loss of *Robalo* and *Flier* so close together, both temporally and geographically, raised concerns and became the subject of an investigation in Western Australia, which began on Thursday, September 14, 1944. *Flier*'s operational orders had been drawn up by Tex McLean, who after a spell in the States returned to Fremantle to command Submarine Squadron 16 and coordinate activities on the waterfront. When Murray Tichenor accompanied USS *Harder*'s famous fifth patrol, Tex McLean had moved into the role of operations officer from May 22, 1944, until late June.[21] *Flier*'s operational orders specified taking a deep water route through Balabac Strait that had been followed by *Robalo*. The Japanese were known to have mined these waters, but it was believed that if submarines remained on track they could avoid danger. In any event, the investigation conducted by Adm. Freeland Daubin found McLean's organization and the methods of briefing commanders for patrols "exceedingly thorough and excellent in all aspects." The loss of *Flier* and *Robalo* was assigned to "the hazards of war."[22]

The *Flier* men became the first, and only, American submariners to escape from a lost submarine, avoid capture by the Japanese, and make it back to the United States. When Alvin Jacobson returned home to Grand Haven, Michigan, he received a hero's welcome. He found the attention embarrassing, though, and in his mind he was not a hero but only a survivor.[23] Perhaps as remarkable as their survival, the *Flier* men remained in the submarine service and were prepared to again put their lives at risk on patrol.

Due to the vagaries of fate, a couple of men scheduled to sail with *Flier* escaped being on its final patrol. After completing USS *Puffer*'s third patrol, Ross Tidd was to be transferred to *Flier*, but his orders were changed after crewmate William Penzenik was accused of killing an Australian sailor while on leave in Fremantle. Tidd was a potential witness in the case, so he remained behind when *Flier* sailed.[24] Jim Alls, originally from Washington, D.C., also missed *Flier*'s fatal voyage. Shortly before *Flier* departed, Alls had walked into a bar just as a New Zealander launched a glass beer mug in his direction. He suffered a broken jaw, which ruled him out of active duty for the next eight weeks. Reflecting later on *Flier*'s loss, Alls stated, "Close your eyes and imagine your family wiped out. That's what it was like for me."[25]

Following the loss of *Robalo* and *Flier*, Charles Lockwood sent his commiserations to Ralph Christie, saying, "It looks as though the yellow bellies were getting smart about their mining."[26] It is likely, though, that mines had already claimed a number of American submarines. In 2009 a documentary film crew discovered the wreck of *Flier* sitting upright in 330 feet of water. For some time, local fishermen had claimed to be able to see the submarine on rare days when the waters were perfectly still. Divers found the forward escape hatch open, indicating that there were still men alive on *Flier* when it settled on the bottom of the ocean. Because *Flier*'s resting place was too far away and isolated for most relatives to visit, on August 13, 2010, a memorial ceremony was held at the Great Lakes Naval Memorial and Museum in Muskegon, Michigan, commemorating the submarine's loss sixty-five years earlier.[27]

Only three days after *Flier* departed Fremantle, USS *Harder* headed to sea along with USS *Hake*, both submarines making their sixth war patrol. When *Harder* departed Fremantle on August 5, 1944, Sam Dealey waved a wide-brimmed Australian digger hat bestowed on him by Bill Jinkins at a party celebrating the success of their Borneo rescue mission. After five stressful patrols Dealey was due for a rest, but he insisted on taking *Harder* out one more time before taking an extended break. His executive officer, Frank Curtis Lynch Jr., was spelled in anticipation of taking command once *Harder* returned, while third officer Sam Logan moved into Lynch's former post. Lynch, whose huge stature earned him the ironic nickname "Tiny," had been a football star at the Naval Academy. As he watched *Harder* pull away from Fremantle Harbour, Lynch later professed he "never felt lower in my life."[28] Some have suggested that the absence of his steadying influence on Dealey may have contributed to *Harder*'s loss.

At least some of *Harder*'s crew faced the patrol with foreboding. Bruce Teede, a teenager during the war, recalls that his father, Guy, made friends with two *Harder* crewmen, William Vernon Diamond and Ace Graham, after meeting them at the Inglewood pub. The men regularly visited the Teede home in Fourth Avenue, Mount Lawley, for dinners and Seppelts Royal Purple Para Port. They called Teede's father "Pop," and on their last visit it was obvious the submariners were worried. They told Pop they expected the patrol to be a rough one.[29] Graham would not make *Harder*'s sixth patrol, but Diamond, a radioman first class from Pensacola Heights, Florida, was among the men to go down with the submarine.

At dawn on August 24, 1944, *Harder*, along with USS *Hake*, staked out the waters off Dasol Bay south of Lingayen Gulf on the west coast of Luzon.[30] As a minesweeper moved toward the two submarines, *Hake* moved to evade it by going deep. Those on board *Hake* then heard a series of depth charges, and when they surfaced hours later there was no sign of *Harder*. As pieced together from Japanese records, *Harder* was sunk by a coastal defense vessel.[31]

Some believed that Dealey had discounted Japanese antisubmarine capabilities to the point of recklessness. Respected submarine commander Slade Cutter claimed that, statistically, skippers were most likely to lose their boats on the first or fifth patrols. On the first patrol they lacked experience, whereas by the fifth patrol they tended to become overconfident and careless.[32] Sam Dealey had in fact made his best showing on *Harder*'s fifth patrol, but that very success may have contributed to the submarine's demise on its next outing. Reuben Whitaker thought Dealey had lost respect for the enemy, with fatal consequences, and Philip Nichols also sensed Dealey was becoming a bit too cavalier about Japanese antisubmarine warfare. Given Dealey's aggressive tactics, some believed it was only a matter of time before his luck ran out.[33] Based on intercepted enemy communications, Christie wrote to Secretary of the Navy James Forrestal claiming that an enemy commander at Dasol Bay stated that "this submarine treated us with contempt and repeatedly attacked."[34]

Some submariners blamed Christie for allowing Dealey to make the patrol when they believed he was near exhaustion. Christie, however, faced the difficult dilemma of deciding when men were approaching exhaustion or keeping productive skippers at sea. Charles Lockwood had made a similar decision when he allowed renowned skipper Dudley "Mush" Morton to take USS *Wahoo* on patrol in the Sea of Japan despite Morton's evidence of fatigue.[35] Like *Harder*, *Wahoo* failed to return from patrol. In both cases, veteran submariner Slade Cutter believed the skippers' aggressive tactics eventually meant the odds were against them. "Not that they were foolhardy; they weren't, but you can only get away with the stuff they did for so long."[36] A month shy of his thirty-eighth birthday when killed, Dealey had long passed the age limit of most skippers by this time of the war. *Harder* was also old by war production standards, well past its due date for refit. Noisy machinery was only one of the factors that exposed the submarine to the dangers of detection and destruction.

Christie, like others in the submarine force, was clearly crushed by *Harder*'s loss. Writing in his diary after learning *Harder* had disappeared, Christie called it "The most ghastly, tragic news we could possibly receive."[37] In a letter of condolence to Sam Logan's widow in Owensboro, Kentucky, he described *Harder* as "our Blue Ribbon boat."[38] Christie recommended Dealey for a Medal of Honor, America's highest combat award, on the strength of his dazzling fifth patrol. Eventually, after the politics of command played out, Dealey's widow received his Medal of Honor in August 1945, one of only seven awarded to submariners during the Second World War. Dealey's memory would also be commemorated by naming a submarine rest camp in his honor at Guam, recently prized from the Japanese in the Mariana Islands.

With the loss of three boats, July and August 1944 proved the cruelest months for Fremantle submarines. Nevertheless, with twenty-five patrols from Fremantle during these months, substantial inroads were made into enemy shipping, particularly in the South China Sea. A confirmed total of thirty-three Japanese ships were sunk, totalling 143,577 tons. For reasons not entirely clear, patrols in July were significantly more productive than in August, with only a third of the patrols departing Fremantle in the latter month sinking any ships. The most successful patrol of the period was by USS *Rasher* under the command of Henry G. Munson, which on a run from Fremantle to Pearl Harbor sank five confirmed ships for a combined total of 52,600 tons.[39]

CHAPTER 14

THE BRITISH ARRIVE

With Allied success in the Mediterranean theater, British submarines began to be shifted to the Far East from mid-1943 on. By the end of the year, the depot ship *Adamant* and the Fourth Flotilla moved from Colombo to Trincomalee, joined by another depot ship and more submarines the following year. As early as April 1944, Captain Lancelot M. Shadwell, commander of the British flotilla at Ceylon, held discussions with Ralph Christie about basing British submarines at Fremantle. Adm. Ernest J. King, commander of the U.S. Fleet and chief of naval operations, agreed on the condition that the Royal Navy provide all logistical support and that the submarines, while under British administrative command, come under American operational control. It would be some months after this agreement, however, before the number of British submarines and depot ships based in the Far East made such a redeployment practical. In August 1944, with twenty-seven submarines and the arrival of a third submarine depot ship at Trincomalee, the time was right to shift a flotilla of submarines to Fremantle.[1]

On August 10 the oversized minelayer HMS *Porpoise,* which had cut its teeth in the Mediterranean running blockades with supplies to Malta, became the first British submarine to arrive at Fremantle in order to prepare for a special clandestine operation, and the Eighth Flotilla from Trincomalee soon followed. According to Edward Young, commander of HMS *Storm,* the shift to Fremantle required "some tricky staff work and precise timing."[2] The depot ship *Maidstone* sailed directly for Australia, while the eleven submarines in its charge made patrols in the Malacca Straits en route. When the *Maidstone* arrived at Fremantle Harbour on September 4, 1944, it berthed at North Wharf near its American counterparts, the tenders *Euryale* and *Griffin.* The Eighth Flotilla became the first Royal Navy unit based in Western Australia; it included the *Telemachus, Tantivy, Tantalus, Spiteful, Sea Rover, Sturdy, Stoic, Sirdar,* and *Storm,* along with the Dutch submarines *O-19* and *Zwaardvisch.*[3]

The commander of the British flotilla, Captain Shadwell, already had considerable experience working with allies; when based at Dundee earlier in the war his flotilla included French, Polish, Dutch, and Norwegian as well as British submarines. Shadwell was now, however, under the direct authority of Adm. Ralph Christie, who was initially less than impressed with the British boats, describing them as "in the most horrible condition."[4] The depot ship *Maidstone* was similarly down at heel having gone without a refit since 1938 and without air conditioning or reliable refrigeration compartments. The British flotilla depended largely on sharing the American repair facilities, and U.S. Navy personnel quickly established a reputation for generosity in assisting their ally. Despite Admiral King's insistence that the British be entirely self-supporting, the Americans on the spot were happy to provide the British with anything not requiring approval from Washington.[5] Admiral Sir Bruce Fraser, commander of the British Pacific Fleet, later commented, "I have found that the American logistical authorities in the Pacific have interpreted self sufficiency in a very liberal sense."[6]

The move of British submarines to Fremantle and integration with a U.S. task force posed some practical problems, including the necessity of adopting American radio communications and ciphers. Peter Wood, telegraphist for HMS *Trenchant*, discovered that the American submarines, equipped with typewriters, transmitted coded signals more quickly than their British counterparts. Without a typewriter, Wood found himself struggling to transcribe communications by hand.[7] Working with the Americans also required some psychological adjustments, particularly regarding the capabilities of their respective boats. Tony Miers, on visiting Fremantle as the British liaison officer in late 1943, had already acknowledged the superiority of the U.S. fleet boats, and he suggested to Admiral Claud Barry that they should adopt a similar design. Putting this view in writing, however, earned Miers a stern rebuke. Admiral Barry accused him of undermining confidence in British submarines "at a time when we are about to embark on the submarine campaign in the East." Furthermore, Barry chided, "it would be quite impossible to embark on a complete re-design and new programme at this stage of the war."[8]

After arriving at Fremantle, Edward Young observed that "for the first time we realised that the Royal Navy was now the poor relation of the American Navy, and it was an unpalatable shock."[9] Young had designed cover art for the London publisher Allen Lane before he joined the Royal Navy Volunteer Reserve after the outbreak of World War II. He was commissioned as a sublieutenant largely on the strength of his previous experience as a keen yachtsman, and in May 1940 he became the first RNVR officer to be allowed to train for submarines. In 1943 Young became the first volunteer reserve officer to be given command of a British submarine, and by the time he came to Australia he had experienced the war in both theaters after postings to Malta and Ceylon.[10] Even so, Young had to admit the primacy of the American fleet boats. After touring a U.S. submarine he confessed, "I felt downright ashamed of the conditions which my own able seamen and stokers had to live at sea."[11]

Commander Mervyn Wingfield similarly had no illusions, acknowledging the superiority of American submarines and Britain's role as a "junior partner" in the Pacific.[12] William King, assigned command of the newly constructed *Telemachus,* had once considered himself to be on the cutting edge of modernity. The more recently built T-boats were modified for service in the Far East with air conditioning, fresh-water distillers, and an extended range of 11,100 miles. As King approached Fremantle Harbour, though, he was astounded by the cruising speed of the sleek U.S. boats and, after a tour of their interior, described the British submarines as "slums" in comparison.[13] With the latest in radar and torpedo-fire-control systems, the American submarines were not only more habitable but also proved their superiority operationally for most situations. Periscope depth for a U.S. submarine was sixty feet, compared to thirty feet for British subs, making the latter more vulnerable to detection and ramming. On the other hand, the smaller British submarines demonstrated their advantages for operating in shallow and confined areas. To this extent they complemented the larger American boats and were a welcome addition to the Fremantle base.[14]

At least some British submariners took solace in the belief that they were a more disciplined force than the Americans, and in the words of able seaman Albert Gillespie, "a better fighting machine."[15] Unlike their American counterparts, significant numbers of British submariners were conscripted into the service. Whereas volunteers were bound to serve on submarines for five years, conscripts were committed to three years. For example, Arthur Hezlet, who had once aspired to be a gunnery officer, found himself drafted into the submarine service. Once there, however, he quickly perceived the advantages of submarine service, which included nearly double the pay and more opportunities for early command.[16] No less than American submariners, British submariners viewed themselves as an elite group within the navy. They were subject to the same rigorous screening and training, including the requirement of making a simulated underwater escape.

Albert Gillespie credited the submarine service with making a man of him while teaching him comradeship and discipline. Contrary to his previous experience in the Royal Navy, he found on submarines that there was little snobbery among the officers and that "we all had the feeling of being part of a team of men who had responsibility to each other."[17] Again as with the Americans, this sense of comradeship was reinforced by the relatively small size of the service, which meant that officers and men were often well acquainted with one another. On one occasion when the crew of the HMS *Stygian* encountered the HMS *Shakespeare* at sea, they feared a trap. Knowing that the commanding officers of the two submarines were friends, the *Stygian* crew requested that *Shakespeare* radio the name of their skipper's wife. The *Shakespeare* radio man could reply not only that their commanding officer's wife was Sheila but that the wife of the *Stygian*'s commander was named Stella.[18]

At Fremantle, the Americans weren't above rubbing in the relative luxury of their submarines. Ben Skeates, assigned to the tender *Maidstone* after a bout of pleurisy, quickly wearied of "their inane jokes about our toy submarines. Theirs were like battleships, with deep freezers full of chicken and ice cream."[19] When officers of USS *Whale* entertained a British commander on board, the mess steward was instructed to prepare a special five-course meal including a dessert of crepes Suzette. After their guest complimented the meal, the *Whale*'s skipper reportedly replied, "Why, these are our normal rations."[20] In addition to the relative comfort of American submarines, British submariners envied the quality of the Americans' uniforms and their free spending. Albert Gillespie complained that "the way they threw money about makes us feel like paupers."[21]

Envy did not just flow one way, however. Reportedly, some U.S. sailors resented the relatively light duties of British sailors assigned to the depot ship *Maidstone*, and they were positively amazed by the liquor stocks on British submarines.[22] Although U.S. submarines carried small amounts of "medicinal" alcohol on board, American ships had been declared officially "dry" since the nineteenth century. U.S. submariners might be dispensed a shot of brandy following a particularly vicious depth charging, but there was nothing comparable to the daily rum ration British sailors continued to enjoy until 1970. An unwritten privilege of British submariners was the issue of their rum ration, neat and undiluted at sea, and they were allowed to bottle it for future use at the end of the patrol.[23] At least some Americans also found the British officers possessed an enviable suaveness. Ernest "Zeke" Zellmer from USS *Cavalla* recalled a night at the officers club when a British naval officer cut in on a dance with his new love interest. To Zellmer, the officer upstaged not only his own dancing abilities but also his uniform; "That dazzling white uniform made my dress khaki uniform seem almost shabby."[24] Beyond touring each others' submarines, however, social interaction between the Americans and British was often limited. As one American bluntly put it, "We were interested in girls, and submarine sailors from any country did not fit the bill."[25]

As Tony Miers predicted when he visited Fremantle in late 1943, British submariners quickly became enamored with Perth. Even before their arrival, a Naval Comforts Fund raised more than £5,000 for British sailors' entertainment. Once based in Fremantle, Miers did his part to welcome submariners; according to Roy Weston, "He worked day and night to see that we got everything that we wanted and every service that he could provide."[26] Clive Taylor, an Australian who enlisted in the Royal Navy, recalled that when his submarine arrived at Fremantle, Miers was at the gangway to meet him. After ascertaining that Taylor's wife was living in New South Wales, he quickly arranged for him to call her; it was the first time in four years that they had spoken.[27]

As in the case of the Americans, one of the reasons Western Australia appeared so attractive to British submariners was the contrast to their previous experience. In Ceylon the amenities and provisions available to submariners had been limited. While submarines were based at Colombo, the most that could be hoped for was a temporary escape from the heat in the hills at Kandy sixty miles away. Skippers could take up temporary residence with a planter there, while enlisted men stayed at a large house run by the Army. Once the submarine flotilla moved to Trincomalee in December 1943, the options became even more limited.[28] As one submariner later summed it up, Trincomalee was "really just a name on the map, there's not much to Trinco."[29] Submarines returning from patrol tied up alongside their depot ship, which, as if to maximize the distance from any recreational facilities, was relegated the outermost part of the harbor. Surrounded by jungle, the base offered little by way of amenity beyond a fleet canteen and an officers club. Returning submariners spent much of their time on the depot ship *Maidstone*, where their main entertainment was to swim alongside and play water polo.[30] The most popular destination for submariners on leave was the hills of Dijatalawa, some twelve hours away and four thousand feet above sea level, where cooler weather provided the principal attraction. In fact, some men found the nights a bit too cold, and, apart from a swimming pool and golf course, recreational facilities were minimal. Enlisted men stayed at a disused Army camp taken over by the Navy with little to do beyond eat and drink. The more fortunate shared the hospitality of local tea planters, but this was a relatively lonely existence.[31]

In the words of one British officer, Trincomalee didn't "hold a candle" to Fremantle.[32] Roy Broome, who served as a leading stoker on HMS

Trenchant, quickly concluded that compared to Trincomalee, where he had done a year's service, Fremantle "was a different kettle of fish altogether." His submarine was supplied with two large milk churns and boxes of apples as soon as it arrived. To Broome, Fremantle appeared to be "heaven on earth."[33] Gordon Tait, who served as first lieutenant on HMS *Tudor*, described his first arrival at Fremantle on a clear dawn as "an unforgettable joy."[34]

One of the first things that struck British sailors arriving at Fremantle was that there were lights ashore. Heading south from Exmouth Gulf toward Fremantle, the commander of HMS *Thule,* Alastair Mars, observed that it was the first time in five and a half years that he had been out of a war zone. The sight of lights as they approached Fremantle evoked strong emotions. "From a great distance we could see the bright arc-lamps of the Stirling Highway leading to the distant constellation which was Perth. For the first time in our blood-sodden memories we were safe."[35] By this stage of the war blackouts and darkened harbors were giving way to a more normal existence. Submariners were further impressed by an abundance of fresh food and cheap beer. Mars declared the beer from Swan Brewery "the best in the world" and was equally pleased by the availability of good gin.[36] Not long after the depot ship *Maidstone* arrived at Fremantle, representatives from the Swan Brewery installed a tap in its wardroom where beer could be purchased for a penny a glass.[37]

One of the most disconcerting features, on the other hand, was the early closing of public houses. With many men not getting to shore until the late afternoon and then facing a long walk through the docks, there was little time to enjoy a drink. Many learned to circumvent this problem by carrying "plonk bags," containers they could quickly fill at a wine shop so they could continue drinking once the pubs closed. Typical of the atmosphere of cooperation, the Americans also facilitated British submariners getting into town more quickly by sharing a special train near the depot ship.[38] Peter Wood, a telegraphist from HMS *Trenchant*, was struck by what was called the "evening swill" and professed being "absolutely astonished" by the prodigious drinking. He was no less impressed on his first train ride from Fremantle to Perth by the daring feats of the ticket collector. With only the aid of a narrow running board, Wood noted, "As the train rattled merrily along, the carriage door would suddenly swing open and that dauntless man would claw his way inside. With his business done he would somehow leave the carriage, slam the door shut and claw his way to the next carriage. It was a humbling sight."[39]

Many British submariners were similarly humbled by the hospitality they received. Edward Young proclaimed, "The people of Perth, Fremantle and the surrounding districts opened their hearts and their doors to us with a generosity beyond our previous experience."[40] Hugh Mackenzie, commander of HMS *Tantalus*, echoed this sentiment, claiming, "The Australians were the most hospitable people you could ever imagine."[41] Roy Broome from HMS *Trenchant* recalled receiving so many social invitations that invariably he had to refuse some. Many of his crewmates were quickly contemplating immigration to Australia after the war.[42] When Gordon Tait first arrived at Fremantle with HMS *Tudor*, by noon two-thirds of the crew had been whisked away to the homes of Western Australians. He believed the kindness displayed by the local population toward submariners was "unique." Most of his crewmates were in their early twenties and had been away from their homes several years by this stage of the war. Under these circumstances, "To have the privilege of being a welcome guest in a West Australian house, was for many of my contemporaries, a highlight of the war."[43]

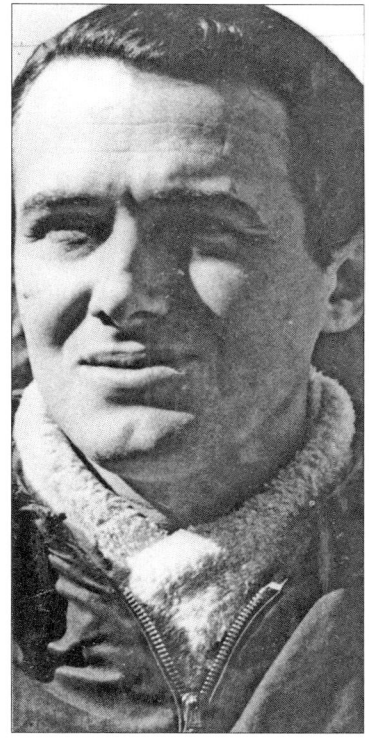

Alistair Mars, British submarine commander   Royal Navy Submarine Museum, Gosport

Edwin J. Young, who arrived at Fremantle with HMS *Trenchant*, quickly formed an opinion of Perth similar to his predecessors, declaring, "This is the best port of call since we left England. The canteen service is the very best ever and the people are sincerely hospitable."[44] Young was equally impressed by the city of Perth, comparing St. Georges Terrace to Prince's Street in Edinburgh and claiming that the cinemas were better than in his native Oxford. Delighted by the relative strength of the British pound, he declared that a meal of steak, eggs, and chips could be had for a fraction of what it cost at home. For the men of the Royal Navy, Phyllis Dean's Hostel in Irwin Street offered free meals as well as sleeping accommodation in Murray Street for those with overnight leave.[45] Phyllis

Dean, run by a Citizens Reception Committee, also organized stays with local families. According to a twenty-one-year-old submariner from the *Telemachus*, the locals practically grabbed British sailors off the dock, insisting "I'll have him, I'll look after him."[46] He ended up staying with a family in Victoria Park, who took him swimming in the Swan River on summer evenings.

Given the close identification of most Australians with Britain, those from British submarines were arguably more popular than their U.S. counterparts. A British intelligence report at the time claimed that "Australia as a whole is still grateful to the Americans but tired of them and apprehensive. As a result, the feeling in all classes is preponderantly in favour of Great Britain."[47] This sentiment was probably less true in Western Australia than in the rest of the country, but there is at least some anecdotal evidence to suggest that the British submariners were considered more favorably by the parents of young women. June Turner was eighteen years old when she began a nursing career at the children's hospital in Subiaco and recalls that after taking the tram to work "I always had to call my mother as soon as I got there because she was convinced I was going to be whisked away by the Americans."[48] She was forbidden to go out with Americans, but her parents had no qualms about June dating British submarine officers.

Rob Cairns, a young boy during the war, recalls many British submariners visiting his family's rented semidetached home in Hay Street, Subiaco. His mother's work for the Australian Red Cross meant she had contact with many visiting submariners, and most visitors seemed content with a home-cooked meal and an opportunity to talk or to play with kids. According to Cairns, "It was simple things that they were looking for, and it was simple things that seemed to please them, and that's what we gave them."[49] Some two thousand households volunteered to host visiting British submariners. In addition, there was a beachside rest camp thirty-five miles south of Fremantle set up for men on leave. Many went further afield. On one occasion, only a day after the depot ship *Adamant* arrived at Fremantle, a day trip some seventy miles inland to York to attend a race meeting was organized for the crew by the naval officer in command, Captain Howden.[50]

Submarine commander Edward Young spent two periods of leave visiting a sheep station named Borawing, about one hundred miles inland from Perth. According to Young, the owners of the property, Harold and Joan Klug, treated him and his fellow officers as though they were sons. Activities included rabbit shooting, horse riding, and watching sunsets from the veranda while drinking a beer.[51] After he arrived at Fremantle from patrol, Lieutenant Commander Reid spent time at Gingin on a stud farm hosted by the Farquar family. The Farquars' son and two daughters kept him busy horseback riding for much of his leave. He then went to York, where he stayed at the Castle Hotel owned by Basil and Mary Craig, which he summed up as a "Terrific place, terrific time, and one of the most enjoyable rests I ever had."[52]

Edwin J. Young from *Trenchant* took a train to Narrogin, describing it as a "cowboy town" with one main street, disused hitching rails, and public houses that resembled saloons. He stayed at Winigin station hosted by a Mr. and Mrs. Higham, where he and his fellows went hunting and horseback riding. These were happy times, with Mrs. Higham reminding Young of his mother and engendering a genuine feeling of home.[53] Ben Skeates stayed on a farm as well. He fell in love with Australia and began making plans to settle there after the war.[54] Some submariners even traveled interstate during their leave; Hugh Mackenzie found that the Royal Australian Air Force was happy to fly him to Adelaide to visit friends.[55] Indeed, so exhausting was their social life that British submariners began facetiously referring to their leave as the "Battle of Perth," as great a test of stamina as the battle in the Pacific.[56]

CHAPTER

ADJUSTMENTS AND SPECIAL MISSIONS

While the move to Fremantle vastly improved the quality of their leave, British submariners soon discovered that their patrols also became more arduous. From Ceylon, the British patrols had been relatively brief, generally short-leg cruises to the Straits of Malacca. With the move to Fremantle, the British submarines often had to travel more than two thousand miles just to reach their assigned areas, and patrols of six weeks or longer became common. *Tantalus'* first patrol from Western Australia, under the command of Hugh Mackenzie, was conducted in the Java Sea and South China Sea during October to December 1944 and lasted fifty-two days, at the time the longest patrol made by a British submarine during the Second World War.[1]

British submariners faced not only longer journeys to their patrol areas but also some new hazards. Whereas Lombok Strait offered a menacing prospect for U.S. submarine crews traveling to their stations, it posed an even greater danger for British and Dutch boats. The slower speeds of their submarines meant that they were usually unable to traverse the strait submerged, while on the surface they faced greater difficulties outrunning Japanese patrol craft. Encountering antisubmarine vessels, the crew of HMS *Sirdar* submerged and ran the submarine on its batteries, only to discover when they surfaced hours later that due to the strong currents they had hardly moved.[2] Most submarine skippers opted to go through the strait at night on the surface, dodging any Japanese naval craft. Captain David Syme, an Australian commando who traveled on HMS *Telemachus*, described the tension as they waited submerged off Lombok Strait to make a nighttime passage: "This was our first taste of real sub life and not one of us liked it—13 hours under water with the air getting fouler and fouler, no smoking and the light so poor we're unable to read, all showed us this was not a picnic."[3]

The run through Lombok Strait developed an unenviable reputation among the British, as explained by HMS *Trenchant*'s wireless operator

Edwin Young in his diary: "The apparent fool-hardy attempt to go through the straits instead of around the coast means a saving of everything, time, fuel, food, water, precious engines, but leaves the lives—not considered so precious—open to grave risks."[4] For those submarines successfully negotiating Lombok Strait on the way to patrol areas, there was still the daunting prospect of the return voyage. Having made it through on HMS *Stoic*'s first patrol from Fremantle, one crewman professed, "[W]e felt as though two iron portals had clanged behind us for, before we could return to the friendliness of Australian shores, we would once more have to run this gauntlet of guns, radar stations and patrols."[5] When HMS *Sirdar,* under the command of Tony Spender, attempted to pass south through the strait on its homeward journey, it encountered a tricky northerly current as well as Japanese destroyers and air patrols. After being narrowly missed by a bomb, Spender elected to return to Fremantle by taking a longer route through Ombai Strait on the north side of Timor. As a result of this diversion, the crew ran out of food and had to be restocked by an American ship at Shark Bay.[6]

Dutch sailors developed a similar aversion to Lombok Strait. On *O-19*'s first patrol out of Fremantle in October 1944 the crew attempted to traverse the strait on the surface until they started being shelled, and although the submarine submerged it was then depth charged.[7] Following the *O-19*'s difficulties, Admiral Christie ordered that the relatively slow British S-boats should avoid Lombok Strait altogether; instead they were to make for Darwin, refuel, and then pass the eastern side of Timor into the Flores Sea. Even the larger *Zwaardvisch* (Swordfish), a former British T-class submarine, encountered grave problems when attempting to negotiate Lombok Strait in December 1944 after being pinned down and depth charged by an antisubmarine ship. With wrecked periscopes, gyrocompass, and Asdic, as well as suffering hull leaks, the ship was forced to head to Darwin for temporary repairs before returning to Fremantle.[8]

The smaller British submariners were largely assigned patrols in shallower waters, such as those of the Java Sea, where the larger U.S. fleet boats found it dangerous to operate. The British, as did the Dutch, discovered few large targets because the American boats had already wiped out most of Japan's merchant shipping by this stage of the war. As a result, they focused largely on sinking smaller craft with their deck guns, often combing the coastal waters where junks and coasters tended to congregate for protection. Between September and December 1944, the British submarines based at Fremantle made only eighteen torpedo attacks claiming five enemy vessels, but during the same period sank or damaged more than sixty small craft with gunfire.[9] In fact, British submariners had appreciated the full potential of gun attacks before the Americans had, and they had already used the tactic widely in the Mediterranean and in the Straits of Malacca. Even before the war, British submariners honed their skills against pirates off Hong Kong and in hotly contested gunnery competitions; a crack crew could go from periscope depth to firing rounds in a little over twenty seconds. With quick manning hatches and rotating breastworks, the British submarines were also better equipped for gun attacks than the U.S. boats were.[10]

In the Far East, the British Admiralty approved the sinking of junks and other small craft from May 1944 on. Among those to make the transition from the Mediterranean to the Far East was Mervyn Wingfield, commander of HMS *Taurus,* who earned the nickname "Dillinger" because of his frequent gun attacks.[11] Especially in the Straits of Malacca, so-called junking became the principal activity of many submarines operating out of Ceylon. The submariners often attempted to surface amid a cluster of junks and open up with their deck guns, then dive before enemy aircraft or ships could arrive on the scene.[12] The element of surprise was crucial to a successful gun action, and a common method practiced by the British was known as "over the top," in which the hatch would be forced open while the submarine was still partially submerged and, drenched with water, the gun crew rushed to their weapons. Such tactics could be highly risky, however, and if a submariner was injured in an exchange of gunfire it could take days to get him back to base for medical treatment.[13]

The most successful submarine to arrive at Fremantle with the Eighth Flotilla in September 1944 proved to be the Dutch boat *Zwaardvisch.* The submarine's commander, H. A. W. Goossens, had relatives held by the Japanese in the Dutch East Indies and was keen to make an impression in the war. On *Zwaardvisch*'s first patrol out of Fremantle it claimed the destruction not only of junks, coastal vessels, minelayers, freighters, and a tanker but of a German U-boat. As *Zwaardvisch* patrolled off Surabaya, Admiral Christie forwarded instructions to intercept a German submarine near its position identified by code breakers as carrying technical information on radar as well as plans for a new submarine prototype for the Japanese. On the morning of October 6, 1944, as *U-168* cruised off the north coast of Java en route to Surabaya, *Zwaardvisch* torpedoed the U-boat. From among the twenty-seven U-boat survivors, the German commander, Lieutenant Helmut Pich, as well as three other officers and a wounded naval rating, were taken aboard *Zwaardvisch* and delivered twenty days later to Fremantle, where they were interrogated by the Americans. An elated Admiral Christie, along with British squadron commander Lancelot Shadwell, met Goossens at the dock when he arrived back at Fremantle and presented him with a bottle of Canadian Club whiskey. The sinking of the *U-168* proved timely because it was scheduled to join the *U-537* and *U-862* in attacking shipping off Australia. Almost seventy years later, in November 2013, what is believed to be the wreck of *U-168* along with seventeen human skeletons was discovered off the Indonesian coast.[14]

Many of the British submarine patrols from Fremantle were earmarked for carrying out cloak-and-dagger-style landings and pickups described as "special missions." Of the 182 patrols carried out by British submarines in the Far East during 1944 and 1945, 48 involved special operations.[15] In the words of one British submarine commander, these were often the types of tasks that were a "submarine's nightmare."[16] While special missions epitomized cooperation between different services and nationalities, they often involved working in shallow coastal waters, where the odds of being trapped by the enemy were greatly magnified.

Under the command of Hal Marsham, HMS *Porpoise* became the first British submarine to conduct a patrol from Fremantle. *Porpoise* departed on September 11, 1944, for what was code-named Operation Rimau. The mission followed one of the most spectacular commando successes of the war—Operation Jaywick. After sailing the wooden boat *Krait* from Exmouth Gulf in September 1943 to the vicinity of Singapore, a party of commandos paddled folboats (special canoes) into Singapore Harbor and blew up seven warships by attaching magnetic limpet mines to their hulls. The *Krait* reached Exmouth Gulf on the return voyage on Tuesday, October 19, 1943, after a round-trip journey of forty-eight days.[17] Admiral Christie was there to welcome the men back and described their exploit as "almost a single handed endeavor of extremely bold pattern."[18]

Operation Jaywick had been led by Lieutenant Colonel Ivan Lyon of the Gordon Highlanders, and Operation Rimau, again led by Lyon, sought to replicate his success with another attack on shipping in Singapore Harbor. Some have claimed that the mission was largely politically inspired, a means to impress the Americans and Asians that the British remained a force to be reckoned with in the Far East.[19] In any case, the party included twenty-three Australian Z-Force commandos. Training for the operation took place at Careening Bay on the east coast of Garden Island, about fifteen miles south of Fremantle. A submarine of the *Porpoise*'s large dimensions was needed to carry not only the commandos but some fourteen tons of stores, eleven folboats, and fifteen top-secret electrically propelled submersible canoes, known as "Sleeping Beauties," for the planned attack. The commandos were to set up a base on the small island of Merapas southeast of Singapore and then capture a junk to transport the assault team.[20]

While transporting the commandos north, the crew of HMS *Porpoise* had to let a ten-thousand-ton tanker slide by so as not to compromise its mission. They delivered the commandos to the designated area, after which the commandos commandeered a junk, the forty-ton *Mustika*, and loaded it with their equipment. *Porpoise*, having completed its assignment, set sail for the return voyage on October 1 and arrived back at Fremantle ten days later, along with the Malay captain and the eight-man crew taken from *Mustika*.[21] The next phase of the operation involved evacuating the commandos from Merapas Island more than a month later, and with *Porpoise* undergoing repairs at Fremantle, HMS *Tantalus* under Hugh McKenzie was assigned the task. After departing Fremantle on October 16, McKenzie delayed the rendezvous from November 7 until November 21, hoping to find more targets for his torpedoes and hence create more space for his intended passengers. But when *Tantalus* landed two soldiers at Merapas to contact the commandos they found nothing except their deserted camp.[22] Only later was it discovered that the commandos had been forced to scuttle *Mustika* after a firefight with a patrol craft, and that although some of the men still contrived to carry out an attack at Singapore Harbor and sink at least three ships with limpet mines, none survived. A Japanese general praised the Rimau men's "patriotism, enterprise and sublime end," but it was a sad ending not untypical of special missions.[23]

HMS *Telemachus*, under the command of William King, departed Fremantle in September 1944 for another special mission, this time instructed to land a party of eighteen men on the east coast of Malaya near Singapore. The landing party included thirteen heavily armed Chinese, four British officers, and a Royal Marine sergeant, along with some twelve tons of equipment and supplies. The party's leader, an Irishman, had run a rubber plantation before the war and volunteered to return to set up operations near his former place of employment. Once *Telemachus* reached Exmouth Gulf, the landing party practiced disembarking the submarine with inflatable rubber boats and underwent three days of intensive training before continuing north. For the landing party, unaccustomed to submarine travel, the sixteen-day transit was far from pleasant. At Lombok Strait, *Telemachus* spent seventeen hours submerged after being forced to dive by several Japanese patrol craft, with the result that many of the men suffered splitting headaches and nausea from the lack of oxygen. As they approached Singapore, one of the submarine's engines broke down and took an anxious four days to repair as the phases of the moon became less and less favorable for the landing operation.

When finally *Telemachus* reached the landing area off Malaya, it appeared inordinately busy with Japanese activity. The rubber boats were launched and the men landed with half of their stores, but they failed to make a rendezvous with the submarine the following evening to collect the remaining supplies. When King recklessly took his submarine toward the coast looking for the landing party, a Japanese ship closed on them from the south. *Telemachus* dived but hit the muddy bottom with its periscope standards still sticking out of the water. The standards apparently blended in with the backdrop of palm trees; the Japanese failed to spot them despite passing within about eight hundred yards.[24] As more Japanese patrol craft and airplanes crowded the area and with no sign of the commandos, King and his crew assumed the worst.

On the return trip to Australia, *Telemachus* suffered another engine breakdown, this time beyond the capacity of the crew to repair. The submarine limped back toward Fremantle, in King's words, "at the pace of a fast walker."[25] When they eventually arrived back in port, the crew not only received crates of fresh fruit and milk but the welcome news that the landing party remained alive and well. They had not been captured as King and his crew feared, but had failed to make the rendezvous because there were too many Japanese in the area. Back in Australia, King would also come to comprehend why the American staff officer who had issued his orders for the mission told him, "I've never in my life so disliked sending a boat on an expedition."[26] While *Telemachus* was off on its special mission, the sprawling battle of Leyte Gulf erupted; King and his crew had missed perhaps the best opportunity of the war to bag a Japanese warship.

CHAPTER

BATTLE OF LEYTE GULF

George Grider, serving as executive officer with USS *Hawkbill*, arrived at Fremantle on October 18, 1944, following a successful patrol. In Grider's words, U.S. submarines at that time "were at a staggering peak of effectiveness."[1] On the patrol from Pearl Harbor to Fremantle, *Hawkbill* claimed its first victim on the night of October 7, sinking the 8,400-ton ammunition ship *Kinugasa Maru*. The patrol report described the devastating effect of *Hawkbill*'s torpedoes: "A mushroom of white and yellow flame rose hundreds of feet into the air; tracers, rockets, and pieces of flaming debris filled the sky. This ship literally disintegrated."[2]

In Perth, Grider met with his old Naval Academy classmate Chester Nimitz Jr. There was little time to catch up, however, since Nimitz departed for the United States the same night Grider arrived in Australia. Nimitz did have time to bequeath Grider his golf clubs, and during his leave Grider played a round of golf with Adm. Ralph Christie, scoring an embarrassing round of 175.[3] Like so many submariners before him, Grider was impressed by both the amenities available for recuperation in Western Australia and the welcoming locals.

Within days of Grider's arrival at Fremantle, the naval war in the Pacific reached its climax with the Battle of Leyte Gulf (also known as the Second Battle of the Philippine Sea), the largest sea battle of the Second World War. The Australian cruisers *Australia* and *Shropshire* were among the ships that bombarded Leyte's beaches as a prelude to invasion on October 20. Later that day, Gen. Douglas MacArthur waded ashore amid cameramen and made his famous pronouncement: "People of the Philippines, I have returned."[4] After the initial landings by U.S. troops, a sprawling naval battle developed involving nearly five hundred ships and 200,000 men.[5]

The opening stages of the naval battle were fought by the submarines USS *Darter* and USS *Dace*. Although the submarines began their patrols from Brisbane, after a brief stopover at Mios Woendi they came under the control of Admiral Christie's Task Force 71 at Fremantle. *Darter* and *Dace* kept in close touch as they patrolled an area west of Palawan Island in the Philippines, and both were alerted to the movement of Japanese heavy ships from Singapore in the direction of Balabac Strait and Palawan Passage. This was the First Striking Force (also known as Force A or Center Force) of battleships and heavy cruisers under Vice Admiral Takeo Kurita, one of three Japanese battle groups converging on the Philippines. After taking on fuel at North Borneo, Kurita's ships split up and headed toward Leyte, taking a circuitous route to avoid submarines.[6] The plan to avoid submarines proved flawed, however, partly because the Japanese ships traveled at a restricted speed due to limited fuel supplies and partly because the absence of air cover further increased their vulnerability.[7]

Shortly after midnight on October 23, *Darter*, commanded by David Hayward McClintock, picked up the group of large ships on radar and moved in to attack. The submarine fired six bow torpedoes at a heavy cruiser later identified as *Atago*, Kurita's flagship. Kurita later described the sound of the torpedoes making contact as a loud "Dong!"[8] *Darter* next fired four torpedoes from its stern tubes, this time hitting the heavy cruiser *Takao*. Bladen D. Claggett, skipper of *Dace,* reacted to the sight of the burning ships by exclaiming, "What a show! What a show!"[9] Twenty minutes later Claggett had his own opportunity to attack, and he fired six torpedoes at the heavy cruiser *Maya*. What McClintock or Claggett did not realize at the time was that they had barely missed sinking one of Japan's two super-battleships, the *Yamato*. The 73,000-ton ship carried 18.1-inch guns, the largest naval artillery afloat. From *Yamato*'s bridge, Admiral Matome Ugaki watched the dawn sea erupt in explosions as the cruisers *Takao*, *Atago*, and *Maya* were hit by torpedoes, and he recorded in his diary, "How dangerous it was! Had Yamato been situated a little bit either way, she would have taken three or four torpedoes."[10] Ugaki was convinced that no less than four submarines conducted the attacks.

Atago sank in less than twenty minutes along with 380 of its crew, while *Maya* disappeared in a haze of smoke and spray following a series of explosions as its magazines blew up.[11] The *Takao,* although slowed, remained afloat and turned back toward Brunei. When *Darter* attempted to move in for the coup de grâce, it was kept at a distance by two destroyers and a floatplane. McClintock decided to rest his crew and pursue the wounded cruiser on the surface after sunset. The plan appeared sound, but it failed to take into account the dangerous waters around Palawan Island that had already claimed *Robalo* and *Flier*. According to *Darter*'s executive officer and navigator, Ernest L. Schwab, as the submarine sped on the surface near midnight, he informed McClintock that he could only calculate their position within twenty miles. McClintock reportedly replied that "reefs were no worse than depth charges."[12] Within minutes *Darter* slammed to a halt; the bow reared out of the water as it struck the half-mile-wide reef known as Bombay Shoal. Not only had overcast conditions prevented getting an accurate fix on *Darter*'s position, but the crew had also failed to take adequate account of the strong currents in plotting their course.[13]

The stranded *Darter* was a sitting duck for Japanese aircraft within easy striking distance as well as a destroyer known to be prowling the vicinity. Almost immediately McClintock ordered the destruction of codebooks and classified equipment and sent a distress call to *Dace*. *Dace* arrived on the scene two hours later, gingerly approaching *Darter* from the stern. After an aborted attempt to tow the submarine free, *Dace*'s crew began the laborious process of evacuating *Darter*'s men in two rubber boats. Near dawn McClintock, as the last man on board *Darter*, took a final turn below deck, later reporting that "I remember trying to think what would I like to take with me, and of all things, I finally ended up with an ashtray with 'Darter' engraved on it. That was my only souvenir."[14] The next step was to destroy *Darter* so it would be of no use to the enemy, but when charges were detonated there was only a muffled explosion and no visible damage. *Dace*'s crew tried firing four torpedoes at the stranded submarine, but they all exploded on the reef, and even pouring thirty rounds from the 4-inch gun seemed to do little damage other than raise a plume of oily smoke. Little wonder some submariners thought their fleet boats were virtually indestructible.

At about 6:00 a.m. a plane was spotted and *Dace* made a hurried dive, leaving ammunition on the deck. Although there was talk of returning to set more demolition charges, *Dace* received instructions to return to Fremantle, and it set off on the twelve-day transit with twice the usual number of men on board. To make the crowded conditions more habitable, Claggett tried not to submerge *Dace* for more than ten hours at a time, and men were asked to remain in their assigned compartments. Meals were cut back to two a day, and McClintock later commented, "They seemed to have nothing but mushroom soup and peanut butter, and I don't care if I never see any of either of those again."[15]

Back in Fremantle, some senior officers criticized *Darter*'s pursuit of *Takao* when McClintock lacked precise information about the submarine's position, but Admiral Christie chalked up the loss to "the fortunes of war."[16] *Darter* was one of four American submarines lost through grounding during the war, but the other three were the more primitive

S-boats, making it the only fleet boat lost in this fashion. As fate would have it, two other fleet boats—*Shark II* and *Tang*—were lost the same day in other parts of the Pacific, making October 24, 1944, "Black Tuesday," the darkest day in the U.S. submarine service's history. In *Darter*'s case, the loss was softened not only by the rescue of its entire crew but by the heavy toll it took on the enemy. Although *Takao* managed to limp to Singapore, it would never fight again. Of more immediate significance, *Darter* had made the initial contacts in what became a decisive battle, providing the first tangible evidence of the opposing fleet's size and intent. Adm. Thomas Kinkaid, commander of the Seventh Fleet, described *Darter*'s patrol as "one of the most outstanding contributions by submarines to the ultimate defeat of the Japanese Navy."[17]

October 1944 proved the high-water mark of the U.S. submarine onslaught. Over four days the Japanese lost four aircraft carriers, three battleships, ten cruisers, nine destroyers, and thousands of sailors. Apart from the toll taken on warships, sixty-eight American submarines across the Pacific claimed a total of 320,906 tons of merchant shipping that month. Following the Battle of Leyte Gulf, America's naval superiority was unassailable, and for the first time at the White House, President Roosevelt called an unscheduled press conference on October 25 to announce the victory.[18] The success of the American submarines contrasted with that of the enemy, which, although deploying sixteen submarines during the Battle of Leyte Gulf, managed to sink only one destroyer escort. In a typical denial of reality, Japanese radio propaganda claimed a great victory and broadcasts to Australia reached an all-time peak that month.[19]

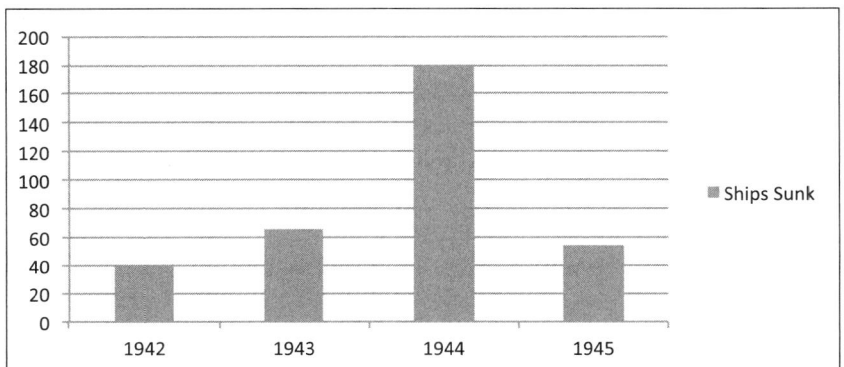

FIGURE 1: Ships sunk by U.S. submarines based at Fremantle, 1942–45

On the other hand, not all of October's events were good news for the Allies. In desperation the Japanese unleashed a new tactic in the final stages of the Battle of Leyte Gulf—kamikaze suicide airplane attacks. As explained by one Japanese officer, "Suicide attack was the only sure and reliable attack by airmen whose training had been limited because of the shortage of fuel."[20] The heavy cruiser *Australia,* supporting the Leyte invasion, was the first Allied ship to be hit by a kamikaze plane, killing thirty and wounding more than sixty other crewmen.[21] During October, Prime Minister Curtin spent nearly two weeks in Western Australia, and, typical of his visits to Perth, part of his itinerary included a visit to Admiral Christie's offices in the CML building for a briefing. Even positive news on submarine operations, however, was unable to cancel the strain the war had placed on Curtin's health, and shortly after he returned to Melbourne at the end of the month he suffered a heart attack. He would spend the next two months in a hospital.[22]

On October 31, George Grider was assigned command of USS *Flasher,* Reuben Whitaker's former command. Whitaker, after completing ten war patrols, including four with *Flasher,* returned to America, where his wealth of experience was employed at the Submarine School in New London, Connecticut.[23] As it happened, both Grider and Whitaker were from Memphis, Tennessee, and Grider continued the sterling record begun by Whitaker, which at the end of the war put *Flasher* at the top of the list for enemy tonnage sunk by a U.S. submarine. Freddy Warder, who served as a training officer at Fremantle, described *Flasher*'s crew as the best trained he had ever seen.[24]

On his first patrol in command of *Flasher,* Grider departed Fremantle in the early afternoon of November 15, stopping at Darwin a week later to refuel. The devastation caused by Japanese bombs earlier in the war was still evident, with the Darwin harbor full of sunken ships.[25] From Darwin, Grider and his crew headed for the Sulu Sea and then took a position in an area off the northwest coast of Luzon. *Flasher* received a contact from Grider's former submarine, *Hawkbill,* and he and his crew picked up a westbound convoy. The first Japanese ship sunk by *Flasher* was a destroyer, and in Grider's grim estimation this attack alone meant that they had already "justified our training, the cost of our boat and the sacrifice of our lives."[26] In fact, on December 4 *Flasher* sank two Japanese destroyers, *Kishinami* and *Iwanami,* as well as an oil tanker, the 10,000-ton *Hakko Maru*.[27] A little over two weeks later, *Flasher* sank another three Japanese tankers during an attack in the early hours of December 22. Grider had positioned *Flasher* in shallow water between the shore and a convoy and was rewarded handsomely for his daring. As described by *Flasher*'s patrol report, one of the tankers "blew up and illuminated the area like a night football game." Attacks on two more tankers added to the spectacle, covering the sea in "billowing red fire."[28] During the patrol Grider and his crew sank tankers totalling some 38,668 tons, more than on any other single patrol of the Pacific War. Back in Fremantle, Ralph Christie was ecstatic, calling the results a "wonderful Christmas present," and in his endorsement of the patrol, squadron commander Creed C. Burlingame dubbed it the "Flaming Action" patrol.[29]

The second half of 1944 was the most successful period of the war for Fremantle submarines. Over six months (July through December), U.S. submarines made eighty-three patrols from Fremantle and sank 105 ships later confirmed by JANAC. The total tonnage sunk during this period, 445,252 tons, surpassed that of any other six months and nearly tripled the tonnage sunk by submarine patrols from Fremantle during the whole of 1942.[30] Overall, the U.S. submarine force sank 603 ships during 1944, in the process decimating Japan's tanker fleet and leaving the Imperial Japanese Navy critically short of oil.[31]

CHAPTER

TRANSITIONS

Whirlwind courtships that frequently ended in marriages between submariners and Western Australian women continued apace, with a reported two U.S. Navy men requesting to marry each day. George Grider's executive officer on *Flasher*, Phil Glennon, was among those to have a local sweetheart. He had met her on a kangaroo hunt during his previous leave, and when *Flasher* returned to Fremantle they began organizing their marriage ceremony. At the wedding banquet, Grider served as a stand-in for Glennon's father. Unfortunately for the newlyweds, *Flasher*'s next patrol would terminate at Pearl Harbor instead of Fremantle, and it would be a long wait before they could see each other again. In the meantime, Glennon had to make do with a large photo of his bride over his bunk.[1] Roscoe P. Thompson from USS *Bowfin* was another submariner who faced separation soon after his marriage. He met his future wife, Cecelia Christian, while on leave at Bunbury. She was only sixteen years old at the time, so they had to wait for her seventeenth birthday and her father's permission to marry. Only six days after their wedding on September 30, 1944, Thompson departed Western Australia with USS *Raton*.[2]

The courtship and marriage of British submariners followed patterns similar to the Americans'. Alastair Mars, commander of HMS *Thule*, declared that "the attractions of the beautiful and vivacious Australian girls were compelling and resulted in many happy marriages either then or later."[3] Many sailors preferred to marry sooner rather than later; William Lawrie, a twenty-two-year-old from London who served on the depot ship *Adamant*, met his future wife his first night ashore when he attended an Anzac House dance in Fremantle.[4] Indeed, many of the British sailors who married Australian women were based on depot ships, which gave them lengthier periods to develop relationships than men on a couple of weeks' leave had. After serving as part of the crew on HMS *Porpoise*, Isaac "Gerry" Goldman joined the relief crew of the depot ship *Maidstone* and met his future wife, Miriam, at an engagement party for another sailor in November 1944.[5]

126

Among the British submariners to marry in Perth was the irascible Tony Miers. As related by David Blamey, an officer on HMS *Sturdy*, he had only recently returned to Fremantle from patrol when Miers informed him, "Tonight we have been asked to a dance in Perth, I want you to take me."[6] Blamey took Miers to the dance and was impressed by the "delightful" daughter of the hostess, Patricia Miller. Blamey danced with the young lady for just a few minutes before Miers insisted that they change partners. It wasn't long before Miers and Miller married, with Lieutenant J. A. "Tony" Spender, skipper of HMS *Sirdar*, serving in the role of best man.[7]

Already in 1944 a small number of Australian women married to U.S. submariners had arrived in America. Most of the new arrivals, according to *Life* magazine, were favorably impressed by their new home. It was mainly the little things that often made an impression; some found the bread too sweet or the butter too salty or the skirts too short.[8] Among the first brides to make it to the United States was a dress designer from Perth whose husband, WO James R. Rose, wrote his parents soon after meeting her that "I knew she was it," even though she was the first Australian woman he had dated. The wife of Chief Torpedoman Frank C. Kennaly, "Kitty," arrived unexpectedly at San Diego, apparently baffling her in-laws with her accent.[9]

In some cases, the brides of submariners had already become widows. In one of a number of fatal accidents at sea, Lt. Howard James Blind was lost when USS *Crevalle* experienced a diving accident on September 11, 1944. Due to *Crevalle*'s declining mechanical condition, there were plans to end its next patrol from Fremantle with a major refit at Mare Island in California. Eleven days out of Fremantle, after a routine dive and surface, the submarine suddenly plunged at a fifty-degree angle toward the bottom of the sea with the hatches open and men on deck, including Lieutenant Blind, officer of the deck, and lookout W. L. Fritchen. Although Fritchen was later recovered at sea, the evidence indicated that Blind managed to close the hatch to the conning tower, almost certainly saving the rest of the crew from death but sacrificing his life in the process. He was awarded a posthumous Navy Cross, given to the Australian woman he had married only shortly before leaving on patrol.[10]

With the invasion of the Philippines, the submarine base at Brisbane was scaled down, and on November 15, 1944, Admiral Christie assumed overall command of the submarines in Australia. In late 1944, while working under Adm. Ernest King in Washington, D.C., James Fife became aware of "a rather insubordinate message" from Christie to Adm.

Thomas Kinkaid.[11] After Kinkaid refused to forward a recommendation that Sam Dealey be awarded a Medal of Honor, Christie responded that his decision was "a very serious blow to the submarine service particularly in view of Harder's loss."[12] Not long after this protest, Admiral King instructed Fife to relieve Christie of his command. Although never officially confirmed, Fife connected the dots and suspected that Kinkaid requested Christie's removal.[13]

Fife received a promotion to rear admiral before departing Washington at the beginning of December 1944, and after brief stopovers at Pearl Harbor, Hollandia, and Darwin, he finally arrived at Fremantle on Christmas Eve. On Fife's arrival, Christie delayed passing over command, apparently hoping that the decision to remove him might be overturned. There was a sense of déjà vu; earlier in the war Fife had replaced Christie at Brisbane after the latter was called back to Newport, Rhode Island, to deal with torpedo problems. In his diary Christie confided, "Received about the same news I got two years ago and I don't like it any better: detachment and same relief, Fife. It disturbed my sleep."[14]

Once Christie accepted the inevitability of his transfer, he wrote to Rear Adm. Louis E. Denfeld at the Bureau of Naval Personnel asserting, "There is only one submarine command ashore for me—Portsmouth, New Hampshire."[15] Instead Christie was posted to the other side of the country to the Puget Sound Navy Yard at Bremerton, Washington. If Ernest King had any say in the placement, he may well have considered he was doing Christie a favor since from his first visit in 1930, King fell in love with the Pacific Northwest's pure air and pine forests.[16] At Bremerton, Christie successfully renewed his efforts to have Sam Dealey recognized with a Medal of Honor, this time routing the recommendation through Gen. Douglas MacArthur, who claimed that "if this young officer does not deserve the Medal of Honor, no man ever did."[17]

Christie took special pride in having fostered such good relations between submariners and the people of Western Australia. Among the testimonials received on his departure, Perth's lord mayor assured him "that the men of the American fighting services have won the admiration, respect and love of the citizens of Perth, that their behaviour whilst in our City has been exemplary."[18] His departure was further marked by a huge public event known as the Children's Christmas Party. Up to 60,000 locals turned out to the Gloucester Park racetrack to enjoy the carnival atmosphere that included pony rides, circus shows, and field sports along with copious refreshments. Christie later recalled a thank-you note from one little girl who attended: "Dear Uncle Yank Admiral. The party was great. I threw up."[19]

James Fife Jr., commander of the submarine bases at Fremantle and Subic Bay during 1945   U.S. Naval Institute Photo Archive

Like Christie, James Fife had devoted most of his naval career to the submarine service. Born in 1897, Fife attended the Submarine School at New London in 1918 and twenty years later became the school's head. When the Japanese attacked the Philippines, Fife was there as chief of staff to the Asiatic Fleet commander of submarines.[20] Fife's personality and leadership style, on the other hand, differed considerably from Christie's. Whereas Christie was gregarious, Fife was a reputed cold fish with few people skills. When serving as Charles Lockwood's chief of staff in Western Australia, by one account Lockwood assigned Fife to Albany to keep him at a distance.[21] Nevertheless, Fife's dedication to the submarine service was beyond question, and once he assumed command at Fremantle he abandoned the luxury of Bend of the Road for the relatively spartan quarters of a submarine tender.[22]

Whereas Ralph Christie exhibited some ambivalence toward the British, Fife was a self-confessed Anglophile. Before America entered the war, Fife had been sent to England as an assistant naval attaché and spent eight months as an observer with the Royal Navy. After a number of patrols on British submarines Fife developed a high regard for British crews; while less preoccupied with cleanliness than the Americans, he believed they manifested more warrior spirit. Whereas Christie had largely eschewed the invitations of Perth's exclusive Weld Club, considering it too English in tone for his taste, Fife became a not infrequent visitor at the club for tea.[23] Perhaps his ultimate accolade to the British was adopting their pronunciation of the word "submariner."[24] British submariners apparently reciprocated Fife's positive feelings toward them; at odds with most descriptions of Fife by his U.S. colleagues, the British skipper Edward Young found him "a man of great charm and impressive personality."[25] At least from Young's perspective, Fife went out of his way to treat the British as equals, personally visiting each British submarine before it departed on patrol from Fremantle.

The end of the year, December 30, 1944, brought a poignant reminder of the vagaries of war and the close relations that developed between many American submariners and Australians. When the crew of USS *Pampanito* ended their fourth war patrol at Fremantle around noon, there was an unusual reception committee there to greet them. Even though *Pampanito* had not visited Western Australia before, there was a group of men who knew some of the crew well. These were Australian former prisoners of war who had been plucked from the sea by *Pampanito*'s men after U.S. submarines sunk the Japanese transport *Rakuyo Maru*. In Western Australia the crew were reunited with twenty or so of the men they had saved from certain death.

For the rescued Australians, their ordeal had begun with the fall of Singapore in February 1942, followed by months of forced labor on the notorious Thai-Burma railway. Construction of the railway was intended in part to avoid the long sea journey to Rangoon and harassment by

Western Australians among the rescued survivors from the *Rakuyo Maru* at Saipan, 1944. National Archives of Australia, Melbourne

Allied submarines. An estimated 62,000 prisoners were employed on this enterprise, including about 13,000 Australians, resulting in the death of some 16,000 POWs from ill treatment and systematic privation.[26] Later more than 2,000 Australian and British prisoners who had survived this ordeal were herded onto two ships at Singapore destined for Japan to serve as forced labor in copper mines. As part of a convoy, the ships set sail on September 6, 1944, the same day that Paul Edward Summers, skipper of USS *Pampanito*, turned thirty-one.[27]

In the predawn hours of September 12, while traversing the South China Sea, the convoy crossed paths with a three-boat wolf pack consisting of *Pampanito*, *Growler*, and *Sealion II*. In the melee that followed most of the convoy was sunk, *Pampanito* sinking *Kachidoki Maru* with approximately 900 prisoners of war on board and *Sealion* sinking *Rakuyo Maru* with 1,317 Australians and British POWs on board.[28] On *Rakuyo Maru* the Japanese quickly evacuated the ship in lifeboats, leaving the prisoners to fend for themselves. They refused to pick up any prisoners, as did Japanese destroyers, which recovered only their countrymen. The prisoners threw rafts and any other wooden material overboard as they progressively abandoned ship. Much of the first day was spent organizing the rafts into groups and lashing them together, but by the following day many broke away as men suffered delirium and some groups struck out with the intention of reaching land. Most of the POWs, however, believed that their only chance of salvation was to be spotted by a Japanese ship.[29] After several days the Japanese did eventually pick up about 136 prisoners from *Rakuyo Maru*, but most remained in the water drifting farther and farther from the site of the sinking.

Then the inconceivable happened when four days after *Rakuyo Maru* was torpedoed, *Pampanito* surfaced to recharge its batteries nearly forty miles from where the ship went down. After sighting debris and wreckage in the water, a sharp-eyed lookout on the bridge spotted a raft shortly after 4:00 p.m. Covered in oil, the prisoners were at first unrecognizable and their shouting incomprehensible; anticipating that the men were Japanese, *Pampanito*'s crewmen carried small arms as they approached.[30] Finally, the men on *Pampanito* made out the words "Pick us up *please*," followed by excited Australian and British accents.[31] Men from the submarine dived into the sea to assist the prisoners on board, in effect risking their lives since the appearance of an aircraft or Japanese ship would result in the submarine immediately diving and leaving them behind. The last group of POWs was recovered in total darkness just after 8:00 p.m., with the submarine crew managing to rescue a total of forty-seven Australians and twenty-six British. *Pampanito* also called for assistance, and an additional eighty-six men were later recovered by *Sealion*, *Queenfish*, and *Barb*. Shocked by their emaciated and oil-covered bodies, Commander Summers recorded that the men appeared "a pitiful sight none of us will ever forget."[32] Not all of *Pampanito*'s crew felt emotionally equipped to deal with the men, with Frank Fives professing, "My stomach couldn't take it. It was terrible."[33]

On *Pampanito* the survivors' most urgent need was for water, and initially they were given wet rags to suck on in order to regulate their intake. Later they were served hot tea, soup, or broth, and gradually their diet was expanded to include beef bouillon, tomato consommé, eggnog, canned fruit, bread and butter, chicken broth, and crackers, then finally soft-boiled eggs and hash.[34] With the pharmacist's mate, Maurice L. "Doc" Demers, working round the clock treating the men, *Pampanito* made a five-day dash to Saipan, where the survivors were transferred to the tender USS *Fulton*. When the former prisoners returned to Australia, their government initially acted to suppress details of the incident from the public. The first inkling in the press came on October 13 from the *West Australian* newspaper, which had been alerted by the parents of Arthur Bancroft after they received a telegram from the Royal Australian

Navy about their son's impending return home. It was another month before the government officially revealed that Australian POWs had been rescued by U.S. submarines.[35] Far from any recrimination toward the American submariners who sank their transport, the rescued Australians from *Rakuyo Maru*, a government document reported, "cannot find adequate words of praise."[36] Landon L. Davis, an officer on *Pampanito*, claimed that the rescued men "said they were darn glad they were sunk . . . they would cheer every time they saw a torpedo hit even if it did hit their own ship, because they wanted to see the sons-of-guns go down."[37]

For many of *Pampanito*'s crewmen, the rescue operation represented their most illustrious action of the war. William Fisk, engineman second class, enthused, "It was great to see something that turned out good. That was my most satisfying war patrol."[38] Similarly, Richard Sherwood professed that "doing something positive and saving those fellows can't compare to anything else that happened while I was aboard."[39] Although the *Pampanito*'s battle flag previously displayed only Japanese flags symbolizing its "kills," a large number 73 was added in tribute to the number of POWs rescued. Partly at the *Pampanito* crew's insistence it seems, the submarine ended its next patrol at Fremantle. Somehow about a half dozen of the Australians rescued by *Pampanito* had heard word of the submarine's imminent arrival and were at the dock to greet the crew. The men included Jack Cocking, Harry Pickett, and Wally Winters, who wore the same dungarees the crew had given them after they were pulled on board. As described by PhM Maurice Demers, "The whole town was ours."[40] Some of those rescued visited the submarine with their families, while Harry Pickett hosted a group of the submariners at his home. Jack Cocking invited a number of the men to his farm, where he served them a breakfast of fried steak and eggs before taking them to a race where, against all odds, one of his horses won the Perth Handicap.[41]

There was more drama of a different kind as *Pampanito* prepared to depart Fremantle on January 17, 1945, for its fifth war patrol. With the temperature reaching a scorching 107 degrees Fahrenheit, a fire broke out on an adjacent pier at North Wharf while the crew loaded torpedoes and provisions. An aging freighter, the 13,639-ton MV *Panamanian*, was taking on a cargo of flour when a discarded cigarette ignited some Hessian sacking. When the burning material was thrown overboard it in turn ignited an oil slick and the pier, putting vessels in the harbor in grave danger. Soon ammunition on the *Panamanian*, stored for its defensive guns, began exploding. The ships in the harbor included three submarine tenders and twenty submarines (thirteen American, six British, and one Dutch), all carrying large amounts of explosives and fuel. The two

American tenders, with diesel engines, were able to get quickly under way, but the British depot ship *Maidstone*, which used steam turbines for propulsion, took forty-five minutes before raising enough steam to move. By the time tugs towed the ship to safety, flames had blistered its paintwork.[42] One of the British sailors on *Maidstone*, Sid Tiffin, concluded, "If we had gone up that day I think half of Fremantle would have gone with us."[43]

Pampanito, with food still stacked on deck, also beat a hasty retreat from the harbor. The submarine returned a couple of hours later when the blaze appeared to be under control, but the fire broke out again so the ship exited the harbor a second time.[44] The fire on board *Panamanian* was not brought under control until the following day, and one firefighter, an able seaman who fell down a hatchway, was killed in the process. *Pampanito* finally departed Fremantle for the last time on January 23, 1945, but even after the war many of the Australian ex-POWs kept in touch with members of the crew. Bob Bennett of Mason City, Iowa, a torpedoman on *Pampanito*, regularly corresponded with several Australians, and one, Frank Farmer, called Bennett every year on September 15 to say "Thank you for another year of my life."[45] Two of the men rescued, Roy Cornford and Bill McKittrick, even traveled from Australia to the United States for *Pampanito*'s fiftieth anniversary at San Francisco in 1993.

CHAPTER

TRIBULATIONS

If the *Panamanian* fire in Fremantle Harbour appeared an ill omen for the beginning of the new year, then another was the near loss of the Dutch submarine *O-19*, which had arrived at Fremantle on September 18, 1944, attached to the British Eighth Flotilla. Making its first patrol from Australia, the submarine laid a minefield off the east coast of Bawean Island on January 3, 1945, and then stalked a small freighter in the waters of the Java Sea. *O-19* managed to sink the ship, but it was then ferociously attacked by a Japanese destroyer in shallow water. With each depth charge lifting the submarine's stern, the gyro compass was knocked out and the periscope shattered. Salt water leaked into the battery compartment, while in the engine room water reached the deck plates, forcing the crew to deal simultaneously with flooding, leaking poisonous gases, and fire. The situation became so critical that the crew began breaking coding machines with a hammer. A Tokyo Rose broadcast reported that *O-19* had been sunk, and staff members in Australia initially believed the submarine was indeed lost.[1]

Finally able to surface, *O-19*'s crew discovered that the submarine could not be dived for any length of time, and in order to avoid the perils of Lombok Strait they headed back to Australia via Timor. After stopping at Darwin to assess the damage, a survey of the submarine revealed that the hydroplanes were gone and that the propellers were severely damaged. On January 17 *O-19* finally limped into Fremantle Harbour, where the Dutch crewmen received a warm reception. Siem Spruijt recalled, "I shall never forget the honour shown to us by all the American ships as we slowly sailed by and I am not ashamed to admit that I felt extremely emotional at the time."[2] For the next ten weeks *O-19* remained under repair.

While James Fife settled into his command at Fremantle, USS *Bream* experienced another near-disastrous mission. After sinking the Japanese heavy cruiser *Aoba* in the Battle of Leyte Gulf, *Bream* first arrived at Fremantle on November 22, 1944, and a few weeks later, marking the third anniversary of the attack on Pearl Harbor, James L. P. McCallum assumed command. Continuing a practice adopted following *Harder*'s dazzling fifth patrol in mid-1944, *Bream* departed Fremantle on March 7, 1945, with a complement of two Australian commandos. Lieutenant John Sachs, thirty-one years old and described by military records as five foot ten and a half inches tall and 156 pounds with dark hair, gray eyes, and a broken nose, had already distinguished himself fighting in Europe, receiving a medal for gallantry in 1941 before joining the Special Reconnaissance Department (SRD). The other commando was Cliff Perske, who at twenty-seven years old was not only younger than Sachs but shorter and heavier at five foot eight inches tall and weighing 168 pounds.

As *Bream* made its way toward Exmouth Gulf, the crew carried out attack exercises on the patrol frigates USS *Corpus Christi* and USS *Hutchinson* and practiced wolf pack tactics with the submarine USS *Rock*.[3] Once *Bream* reached its patrol area in the western portion of the Java Sea the crew used the deck guns to attack two sea trucks on March 13, sinking one and damaging the other.[4] The following day, in the early afternoon of March 14, *Bream* tracked a convoy of three small cargo ships being shepherded by an escort patrol boat. The largest of the ships was estimated to be about twenty-five hundred tons. The submarine made a torpedo attack and sank the lead cargo ship, later identified as *Keihin Maru*, and although the escort dropped a dozen depth charges *Bream* surfaced unscathed at 5:30 that evening.[5] In the meantime, the escaping ships regrouped and anchored off the southern tip of Great Maselembo Island.

That night the commandos Sachs and Perske got their chance to go into action. With the night dark, rainy, and relatively still, the conditions appeared auspicious for the men to paddle toward the convoy in their folboat and attach limpet mines to any vulnerable ships. *Bream* approached to within about 4,200 yards of the intended targets, and the commandos set off at twenty minutes before midnight. They informed *Bream*'s crew that they expected to set their limpet mines to detonate at about 4:30 a.m., after making an earlier rendezvous with the submarine. At 4:00 a.m., however, when the *Bream* men tried to contact the commandos by radio, they received no reply. Flashing a prearranged light signal from the submarine also failed to get a response, and at 9:47 in the morning *Bream* surfaced to begin searching for the commandos. About a half hour later an escort opened fire on the submarine from about 15,000 yards, but the shells fell well short of *Bream*'s position.[6]

In the early evening, *Bream*'s lookouts spotted an aircraft, and a little more than an hour later a *Chindori*-type escort moved toward them and began dropping depth charges. A total of twenty-five depth charges exploded close to the ship, causing major damage to the submarine that included leaking air banks, flooding of the forward torpedo room escape hatch, impairment to all but two of the torpedo tubes, and a series of fires throughout the boat. The submarine finally surfaced just before midnight the following day and spent much of the next twenty-four hours making repairs.[7]

The following day the *Bream* men tried to regain contact with the commandos. Using a code that apparently played on Sachs' name, a radio message was sent: "Sad Sack. We are thinking of you; will try to take care of you." A response was received a short time later in an Australian voice believed to be Cliff Perske's. The voice confirmed, "I am receiving you OK," but failed to give the authentication code. Commander McCallum reasoned that Sachs and Perske had been captured by the Japanese and forced to talk on the designated frequency, so it was decided to abandon the mission.[8] Given *Bream*'s extensive damage, the patrol was cut short and the crew arrived back at Fremantle at 6:00 p.m. on March 22 after spending only fifteen days on patrol. The disappearance of Sachs and Perske, as well as the *Bream*'s near loss, ended the practice of allowing commandos to attack targets of opportunity. In the future, commandos would be carried on submarines only for planned missions.

After the war it was discovered that Sachs and Perske were held prisoner at Surabaya before being beheaded on March 30, 1945.[9] Apparently Perske and Sachs initially told their captors that they were on a mission to blow up the engines of an Allied aircraft that had crashed in the area. Under torture, however, their true mission was disclosed, and they were executed at the Eastern Entrance Fort under authority of Captain Tamao Shinohara. According to one report, Shinohara suffered from asthma and believed he might be cured by eating a human gall bladder. After the execution, the organs of one of the prisoners, believed to be Perske, were removed for this purpose, but the remains of the men were never confirmed.[10]

The doubtful survival of submarine-borne commandos (Dutch and British as well as American) who never returned from missions preyed heavily on the minds of those associated with them. With the fates of men inserted behind enemy lines often unknown, such missions ended, as one contemporary recorded in his diary, with "just silence—a black—eery—depressing silence."[11] Despite the high rate of failure experienced by missions and the loss of many commandos, they nevertheless often served to misdirect the enemy. The Japanese frequently blamed such clandestine operations for intelligence failures, when in fact the Allies were getting most of their information from radio intercepts and cryptanalysis. As a result, the Japanese remained oblivious of what was collectively known as Ultra and failed to adequately alter their codes and procedures.[12]

James Fife was keen to move the submarine war closer to the enemy as quickly as possible. American forces captured Subic Bay on the Philippine island of Luzon at the end of January 1945, and on February 11 an advance party for setting up a submarine base arrived with the tender USS *Griffin*. USS *Pampanito* arrived at Subic Bay the following afternoon, and in mooring next to the recently arrived *Griffin* it became the first submarine to undergo refit there. Originally scheduled to return to Fremantle, the *Pampanito* men were less than happy to be rerouted to Subic Bay, where it seemed that the most memorable feature was the humidity. With fighting still going on in the vicinity, liberty for the crew extended only from noon to nightfall, and a blackout precluded screening movies on deck at night. Furthermore, *Griffin*'s lack of preparation meant that *Pampanito*'s crew had to carry out many of the repairs on their own. The redirection from Fremantle also meant *Pampanito*'s crew missed their mail; eventually forty-six bags of letters and packages caught up with them at sea on their next patrol after being transferred from USS *Sea Robin*.[13]

On March 13 the tenders USS *Athedon* and USS *Howard W. Gilmore* arrived with supplies, but with a lack of infrastructure and the onset of the rainy season the base remained a shambles. Without proper roads the base was cut off from both the local population and the rest of the U.S. Navy, and there was no shelter for parts and supplies coming from Australia.[14] Submarine crews unfortunate enough to spend their leaves there were mainly confined to the tenders, where they suffered the heat, humidity, and monotony. When the crew of USS *Cavalla* arrived on March 25, they found there was still no proper rest camp. The officers stayed on the tender, while enlisted men were put up in hastily built barracks. There were still Japanese soldiers in the area, so the men's movements were restricted.[15] Arriving at Subic Bay the following month, USS *Bullhead*'s crew found little there other than a circus tent where enlisted men could drink beer during the day and watch movies at night.[16] Fife assigned staff officer Leon Huffman, who made the trip from Australia to the Philippines in the bomb bay of a B-25, to get things started on a proper rest camp. Eventually an R&R camp was hacked out of the jungle and named in honor of James Wiggins Coe, who had been lost at sea with USS *Cisco* in 1943. When Charles Lockwood arrived on July 22, however, he was still struck by Subic Bay's "raw" appearance with Quonset huts, frame buildings, above-ground piping, and temporary roads, but little in the way of recreational facilities beyond movies and a swimming beach.[17]

Under Fife, the onslaught against Japanese shipping that peaked in 1944 continued into the early months of 1945. In January, on average, Allied submarines claimed a Japanese ship every day, amounting to

The submarine tender USS *Athedon* is waved off at Fremantle as it departs for Subic Bay, February 1945.   John Spurling

89,300 tons for the month.[18] U.S. submarines based at Fremantle made a substantial contribution to this effort, sinking twenty-seven confirmed ships during January and February for a total of 77,056 tons.[19] After March, however, the numbers of ships sunk showed a marked decline; during the last six months of the war U.S. submarines based at Fremantle sank the same number of ships, twenty-seven, as in the first two months of the year.

To some extent, however, this picture is incomplete, since in its deliberations of ships sunk JANAC excluded craft under five hundred tons. Although submarines had carried out gun attacks on small craft from early in the war, as larger targets disappeared these smaller targets sharply escalated in 1944 and then increased further in the final year of the war. Victims of gun attacks included a broad range of vessels considered too small to use a torpedo on, such as patrol boats, barges, fishing boats, junks, luggers, schooners, sea trucks, and sampans. Early in the war Charles Lockwood had advocated sinking sampans and junks off the China coast, believing they were supplying the Japanese and were therefore "fair game."[20] Other submariners rationalized attacks on small craft on the grounds that they often served as pickets, reporting the movements of Allied submarines. As explained by Delbert Mar from USS *Seawolf*, "We gunned the sampans because they radioed our position and they also fed the Empire with their fishing."[21] Still others believed gun actions were a good way to lift crew morale. On the other hand, there were those who considered gun actions not only potentially risky but immoral given that many boats attacked were manned by civilians.

Whereas a 3-inch gun was the standard weapon on submarines when the war began, they were steadily replaced by larger-bore guns. Charles Lockwood had supervised the installation of the first 5-inch gun on a submarine, USS *Gar*, while in command at Fremantle, and by 1945, as more and more attacks were made on small vessels, many submarines were carrying two 5-inch guns (one forward and one aft) as well as an assortment of smaller-caliber weapons.[22] In 1944 American submarines in the Pacific sank more than two hundred small craft and more than six hundred in 1945.

Better able to penetrate the coastal waters where junks and coasters tended to congregate for protection, and having already used gun attacks widely in the Mediterranean, British submariners initially outpaced the Americans in the destruction of shipping of less than five hundred tons. British submarines in the Far East sank nearly three hundred small craft in 1944 and almost four hundred in 1945. Taken together Allied submarines in 1945 were responsible for sinking approximately one thousand small craft, a number nearly equal the total number of Japanese merchant ships sunk by U.S. submarines, 1,113, during the entire Pacific War.[23]

CHAPTER 19

COOPERATION AT SEA

James Fife officially shifted his headquarters to Subic Bay on May 15, 1945, leaving his chief of staff, Capt. John Brown, in charge of the base at Fremantle. Having been stationed in the Philippines when the war began, Fife had in effect come full circle and in the process fulfilled his long-held ambition to make a submarine war patrol. After receiving permission from Admiral Kinkaid, Fife boarded USS *Hardhead*, under the command of Francis Greenup, at Exmouth Gulf and then patrolled the Gulf of Siam before making for the Philippines and arriving at Subic Bay.[1] The patrol had been a short one, covering only twenty-two days, but Fife wrote to Charles Lockwood that "my jaunt in the *Hardhead* was the best vacation I have had since the war started."[2]

Meanwhile the British boats of the Eighth Flotilla began moving from Fremantle to Subic Bay after being replaced by the Fourth Flotilla, which had shifted from Ceylon.[3] The depot ship *Maidstone*, under Captain Lancelot Shadwell, departed Fremantle on April 20 and, after stops at Sydney, Manus, and Leyte, arrived at Subic Bay exactly a month later on May 20. After seven years without a refit, *Maidstone* was understandably in need of repairs, while the large swells at Subic Bay made it difficult for submarines to stay alongside. The depot ship *Adamant* remained at Fremantle, so submarines could make patrols to Subic Bay and make a return trip to Western Australia with tenders at both ends of the journey.[4]

The British submariners were no more impressed with their new base than the Americans were.[5] With no alternative accommodation available, they were forced to live on their submarines during periods of leave, enduring sweltering heat. Albert Gillespie was able to get a few days leave from *Maidstone* to stay at a U.S. rest camp, but the men were forbidden from having any contact with the locals after being warned that venereal disease was endemic as a result of the Japanese occupation.[6] The British further found the delivery of mail and supplies "by no means satisfactory," and even after a store carrier arrived on July 24 with two months of supplies, *Maidstone* and its flotilla remained without fresh provisions.⁷ In large part, the British continued to depend on the Americans for both moral and material support. When *Trenchant* arrived at Subic Bay in June, for example, the film *Conspirators* was screened for the crew after dinner on their first night.⁸ In another example of the U.S. Navy's cooperative spirit, after a battery fire broke out on HMS *Seanymph* on Friday, July 13, more than a hundred American personnel were allocated to make repairs. With the men working in shifts twenty-four hours a day, *Seanymph* was again seaworthy in less than a week.⁹

Although U.S. and British submarines mainly acted independently, there were some opportunities for cooperation at sea as well as on shore. On its fifth war patrol USS *Cavalla* was assigned lifeguard duty off Hong Kong, charged with rescuing any Allied air crewmen downed during missions. With diminishing Japanese merchant vessels, submarines were increasingly employed as "lifeguards" forming a picket line along air flight paths, greatly increasing the confidence of aviators that if they had to ditch in the sea they would be recovered. On this occasion no rescues were undertaken, and *Cavalla* moved to the Java Sea in search of enemy ships. On the morning of May 21, as *Cavalla* prepared to attack a patrol boat, a submarine was spotted. Initially the submarine was believed to

USS *Cavalla* in Fremantle Harbour, 1945   Ernest "Zeke" Zellmer

be Japanese, but after it began signaling *Cavalla* with a searchlight it was identified as HMS *Terrapin*, which had departed Fremantle on May 4.

Terrapin, first commissioned in January 1944, was one of Britain's latest-model T-class submarines, adapted for service in the Far East by using the two main ballast tanks for carrying fuel. After service from Trincomalee, in April 1945 *Terrapin* followed the depot ship *Adamant* to Fremantle and joined Task Force 71. Typical of other British crews, the *Terrapin* men found Fremantle "a paradise" compared to their previous experience.[10] The downside was that their patrols became much longer and sometimes more treacherous. On patrol in the Java Sea with unreliable charts, *Terrapin*, under the command of Robert Henry Hugh Brunner, ran aground on a reef at the Arnemuiden Bank west of Batavia (today Jakarta) in the early morning of May 16. After an hour-and-a-half struggle that included jettisoning seventy tons of fuel oil and two torpedoes, *Terrapin* was able to float free.[11]

More trouble followed on May 19, when *Terrapin* fired torpedoes at an escorted tanker. In the still waters of the Java Sea, the enemy ship easily evaded *Terrapin*'s torpedoes and its escorts followed the tracks to the submarine's position. As depth charges rained down, *Terrapin* was only able to dive fifty-seven feet before it hit the muddy bottom; unable to take evasive action, *Terrapin* simply had to lie there and take a beating. Among other damage sustained during the attack, the refrigerator burst open, spilling out meat, blood, and melted ice. *Terrapin* was one of the last British submarines constructed with a riveted hull instead of welds, and as rivets began popping out, the crew frantically hammered in wooden pegs to stanch the ingress of water.

After enduring nearly eighty depth charges, *Terrapin*'s crew finally attempted to surface at dusk. The submarine could only be slowly extricated from the mud, but at about 6:00 p.m. it broke the surface with gun crews at the ready. Fortunately, the escorts were some distance away, and *Terrapin* made a run for it into the darkness. The next day the *Terrapin* men spotted what was initially taken to be the bow of an enemy destroyer and assumed their fate was sealed, but this proved to be USS *Cavalla*.[12] The British submarine, as one of the *Cavalla* crewmen put it, looked "badly beaten up," with *Terrapin*'s periscopes, sound gear, transmitters, bow planes, and torpedo tubes all wrecked.[13] Unable to dive, the submarine's top surface speed was twelve knots, while other casualties of the ordeal included the loss of its potable water supply and ventilation in the forward part of the boat.

Cavalla's crew volunteered to escort the wounded *Terrapin* back to base, with skipper Herman J. Kossler noting in the patrol report that

"My crew liked this, but I was having a hard time building up enthusiasm."[14] Kossler had good reason to be wary, because if an enemy aircraft appeared both submarines would be in jeopardy. Despite the dangers, in the words of *Terrapin* crewman Derek William Curtis, *Cavalla* escorted them like a "friendly sheepdog."[15] Manning their deck guns, the *Cavalla* men shepherded *Terrapin* through the Java Sea and then Lombok Strait, where the submarines narrowly avoided a Japanese patrol craft. Using its radar, *Cavalla* managed to lead *Terrapin* through Lombok Strait without incident.[16] *Cavalla*'s crew proved generous not only with their time but their supplies, at one stage passing over a sea bag of treats including frozen steaks, ice cream, and cigars to lift the *Terrapin* men's morale. Derek Curtis concluded that the Americans "were a great bunch."[17]

Both submarines reached Fremantle on the morning of May 27, and after entering the harbor *Cavalla* received a message from the British depot ship: "Thank you for helping our little boy across the street!"[18] Once berthed in port, the *Cavalla* crew took a closer look at the damage inflicted on *Terrapin*. As recalled by American crewman Don Haseley, they found the submarine "in very bad shape," and in fact the damage ended *Terrapin*'s fighting career.[19] That evening, after the Americans toured the boat, Derek Curtis remembered, "Things ended up in a considerable party!"[20] The British sailors shared their accumulated rum ration with the Americans, and according to the *Terrapin*'s telegraphist, G. D. Cuddon, "Within an hour there were about thirty of our crew and thirty or forty US men, all in various states of rapture."[21] With no ships sunk or aviators rescued, *Cavalla*'s fifth patrol was deemed unsuccessful for the submarine combat insignia, but it had nevertheless gone some way toward reinforcing the bonds between American and British submariners.

The supportive nature of the American-British relationship was exemplified again the following month, when HMS *Trenchant* claimed one of the most spectacular successes of the submarine war in the Pacific. On May 13, *Trenchant* departed Fremantle and proceeded north to its patrol area in company with the submarines *Taciturn* and *Thorough*. *Trenchant*'s crew and their commander, Arthur Richard "Baldy" Hezlet, had already gained some notoriety for their skills when sailing to the Far East in mid-1944. As fate would have it, *U-859* had left Kiel within a week of *Trenchant*'s departing from Scotland, and the British submarine was directed to intercept the U-boat in the waters off Penang. The *Trenchant* crew lay in wait for several days, and then almost miraculously the U-boat surfaced in front of them about a mile away. As the U-boat approached their position, *Trenchant*'s crew fired the stern tubes and one torpedo hit *U-859* amidships; the U-boat appeared to lift ten feet out of the water and then quickly sink. The *Trenchant* crew rescued eleven of the U-boat survivors, including the English-speaking engineer who was also a former Olympic skier.[22]

Hezlet had little expectation of being so fortunate again, and before departing Fremantle on May 13, Hezlet told his crew that given the relative absence of targets they should not have high hopes. As it turned out, however, *Trenchant* found an enemy ship not only worth a torpedo, but eight torpedoes. As the submarine traveled through Karimata Strait, Hezlet received a report of an enemy cruiser spotted going into Batavia to pick up troops. Hezlet requested permission to explore the area of Bangka Strait, a narrow channel between the islands of Bangka and Sumatra, where he thought the cruiser might pass through en route to Singapore. These were dangerous waters—shallow and prone to tricky currents—and to add to the danger the Dutch submarine *O-19* had laid a minefield in the area only six weeks earlier.

Thanks to a contact report from USS *Blueback* received in the early hours of June 7, the *Trenchant* men knew the cruiser was heading toward them. Once beyond the end of the Sunda Strait, the heavy cruiser, *Ashigara*, was left unescorted since it was believed that the shallow waters of Bangka Strait would deter any Allied submarines. Furthermore, a dispute between Japanese army and navy officers at Batavia meant that *Ashigara* sailed without air cover.[23] The first enemy ship *Trenchant* sighted, however, turned out to be a kamikaze-class destroyer, which charged past the submarine's port side in the middle of the night. The destroyer and submarine fired at one another from close range, but neither caused any damage. Despite this run-in, Hezlet elected to stay on station, and his persistence was rewarded the following day when *Ashigara* was spotted before noon hugging the Sumatra side of the strait and traveling at fifteen knots on a straight course. Shortly after noon Hezlet fired eight torpedoes at a range of forty-eight hundred yards, and five of the torpedoes exploded along the cruiser's side. *Ashigara*'s gunners managed to fire some rounds at *Trenchant*'s extended periscope, but within a half hour the ten-thousand-ton ship rolled on its side and sank.[24] The ship went down with an estimated five thousand Japanese troops being sent to reinforce Singapore; included was Vice Admiral Hashimoto, commander of the Fifth Cruiser Squadron. At the same time, Hezlet and his crew had eliminated a potential threat to the Australian landings taking place at Brunei. *Ashigara* proved the most significant enemy ship sunk in the Pacific during June, whether by submarine, surface ship, or aircraft.[25]

A few days later, on June 12, *Trenchant* made a rendezvous with USS *Puffer*, and as the two submarines cruised alongside one another *Puffer*'s commander shouted out his congratulations. James Fife was also keen to extend his personal congratulations to Hezlet and his crew, and he requested *Trenchant* to stop at Subic Bay before it returned to Fremantle. While serving as a U.S. observer in the Mediterranean, Fife had become friends with Hezlet early in the war.[26] On arrival at Subic Bay, Hezlet was disappointed by the apparent indifference shown by men on the British depot ship *Maidstone*. Normally a submarine completing so successful a mission would have received a "cheer ship," with lines of neatly dressed sailors shouting and waving caps from every ship in harbor, and Hezlet attributed the silence of the submariners on the *Maidstone* to a jealous Tony Miers, who was on board.[27] Fife made up for the lack of enthusiasm shown by Hezlet's countrymen; he decorated Hezlet with the American Legion of Merit at a ceremony on *Trenchant*'s deck and further rewarded the crew with good food and a film show.[28] The commander in chief of the British fleet later described *Trenchant*'s attack from shallow and enclosed waters as one of the finest submarine exploits of the war.[29]

Trenchant's crew spent six days at Subic Bay, time enough for telegraphist Peter Wood to be impressed by "the friendly ways of the Americans."[30] Because the British submariners had little in the way of appropriate clothing for an award ceremony, the Americans loaned them khaki uniforms for the occasion. A U.S. Navy landing craft later ferried the men to Manila for some time ashore, and when they returned to Subic Bay they were treated to a production of the musical *Oklahoma*. *Trenchant* departed for the patrol back to Fremantle on June 26, but there was more excitement on July 13 after the submarine stopped a schooner off the island of Celebes. When some of the submarine crew boarded the vessel to search for contraband, three Japanese soldiers below deck fired their weapons through the hatches at them. *Trenchant* quickly backed off and destroyed the schooner with gunfire, later returning to pick up some of the vessel's Sudanese crew. There was yet another close call when *Trenchant* transited Lombok Strait; after conducting a successful gun action against a submarine chaser, an incoming aircraft forced the submarine to dive. The airplane dropped a bomb near *Trenchant*, demonstrating once again the dangers of the area.[31] When *Trenchant* arrived at Fremantle on July 24, it had spent eighty-two of the previous ninety-five days at sea, one of the longest British patrols of the war.[32]

The Americans proved themselves again good allies, this time in relation to Dutch submariners, when USS *Cod* came to the rescue of *O-19*. After laying mines en route from Fremantle to Subic Bay, *O-19* encountered navigational problems in the early hours of July 8 and ran into a reef. Siem Spruijt recalled just finishing his watch when he was knocked off his feet and thrown into a bulkhead as the submarine suddenly shuddered to a stop. Another crewman, Leo Davenport, was thrown from his bunk and initially believed the submarine had been torpedoed. Instead they discovered they were stuck fast on a reef, and at low tide they could even walk on it. The crew fired the torpedoes and deck gun in an effort to lighten *O-19* and slip off, but the submarine remained stuck fast.[33]

O-19 requested the aid of a tug, but was informed that USS *Cod* would make contact.[34] *Cod*'s crew, patrolling about two hundred miles away, received a message from Task Force 71 at about 7 p.m. on July 8 directing them to make their way to Ladd Reef as quickly as possible. During the night they established radio contact with *O-19*, and *Cod*'s commander, Edwin M. Westbrook Jr., noted in his patrol report that despite the Dutch skipper's predicament, he still had his sense of humor. When Westbrook radioed that they would see them at dawn, *O-19*'s commander, J. F. Drijfhout van Hooff, replied, "We will certainly be here."[35] In a scene reminiscent of *Dace* and *Darter*, the following morning *Cod* carefully approached *O-19* and attempted to tow it off the reef. At first the rescue efforts were delayed by a terrific rain squall that obscured visibility, but even after the rain cleared the situation hardly improved. Westbrook noted, "Looks to be hopelessly stuck, but will try."[36] *O-19*'s anchor chain was wrapped around *Cod*'s conning tower, and in a nerve-racking process that brought the U.S. submarine perilously close to the reef, the next fourteen hours were spent trying to shift *O-19*. All this was with the knowledge that Japanese surface forces or aircraft might appear at any time. Finally, when *O-19* failed to budge, it was decided to evacuate the fifty-six Dutch crewmen using two rubber boats lashed together, a process that took another four hours. As Spruijt phrased it, "We abandoned our beloved sub on which we had been so very successful against the Japs and which had also shielded us with her strong body against ever so many depth charges."[37]

Once *O-19*'s crew was evacuated, the men set about trying to destroy the submarine so it could not be of use to the enemy, taking special care to destroy its radar and sonar. Demolition charges were set on board, and *Cod* fired two torpedoes into the aft of the Dutch submarine before finishing the job with sixteen rounds from its 5-inch gun. Westbrook noted in his report, "Could appreciate the [Dutch] captain's feelings as he silently watched his boat being destroyed."[38] *Cod*, along with its Dutch passengers, reached Subic Bay on the morning of July 13. From the Philippines, *O-19*'s crew initially took a ship to Manus Island, and then on July 19 flew in a Douglas Dakota aircraft to Townsville, Queensland. Two days later they flew to Sydney, and most of the crew took a train to Melbourne and then to Perth, where they received ten days survivors' leave.[39]

For USS *Cod*'s crew, their patrol was not yet over, and after taking on fuel and making minor repairs at Subic Bay, they set off for the Gulf of Siam. There the submarine searched scores of junks operating in the area, and those found to be transporting cargo valuable to the enemy were destroyed using the deck guns after first taking off their crews. Over the course of twelve days, *Cod* sank twenty-three junks and motor sampans. Operating on the surface, however, posed obvious dangers, and on two occasions the submarine was bombed by enemy aircraft and once strafed with machine-gun bullets. As *Cod* dived to avoid an attacking airplane on the morning of August 1, five of the crew were left stranded on a large junk they were inspecting at the time. When *Cod* surfaced, the junk had disappeared, leading to a frantic search to find it and the missing crewmen. Finally, after midday on August 3, *Cod* received news that the men had been recovered by USS *Blenny*, and, apparently none the worse for having spent forty-eight hours on the junk, they were transferred the same day by breeches buoy from *Blenny*. *Cod* immediately set course for Fremantle and arrived ten days later.[40]

Once back at Fremantle, *Cod*'s crewmen were invited to a "thank you" celebration by the Dutch submariners rescued from *O-19*. It was an event described by Jan van Hattam as "memorable," while his crewmate Joe Paquin recalled it as "one hell of a party."[41] *Cod*'s crew later added a champagne glass on their battle flag to commemorate the rescue of the Dutch sailors and the subsequent shared celebrations. While the two crews toasted their good fortune, news arrived of the Japanese surrender. Dutch crewman Leo Davenport returned to Britain on HMS *Trenchant* and remained forever grateful to the Americans for saving his life.[42]

CHAPTER 20

WAR'S END

For some submariners the end of the war did not come soon enough. USS *Bullhead* was lost with far more tragic results than *O-19*, taking all eighty-four men on board to the bottom of the sea. *Bullhead*'s new skipper, Edward Rowell "Skillet" Holt Jr., came from Charlotte, North Carolina, and had been keen to get a command before hostilities ended. Only recently turned thirty years of age, he became the last from his 1939 Naval Academy class to receive command of a fleet boat during the war.[1] Elated with his new responsibility, he wrote to his wife that "I couldn't have been more fortunate if I had written my own ticket."[2]

Officially launched on July 16, 1944, *Bullhead* became the fifty-seventh submarine built by the Electric Boat Company since the attack on Pearl Harbor. *Bullhead* was put into commission on December 4, 1944, by Walter T. Griffith, who had made his reputation as commander of *Bowfin*, and he skippered the submarine's first two patrols. On its first patrol, *Bullhead* had been narrowly missed by three bombs dropped from an American plane. With Griffith transferred to Admiral Lockwood's operations staff at Guam, Holt took over as skipper.[3] *Bullhead* departed Fremantle for its third war patrol on the last day of July 1945 with orders to patrol the Java Sea before heading for Subic Bay.

Bullhead's fighting career ended on August 6, the same day the atomic bomb was dropped on Hiroshima. A Japanese army aircraft caught the submarine near that most dangerous of choke points—Lombok Strait— which had become prone to increasing Japanese attacks against submarines. USS *Puffer*'s crew had only recently escaped disaster when a Japanese shore battery opened up on them off Lombok. In the case of *Bullhead*, the Japanese pilot who bombed them reported two direct hits on the submarine followed by gushing water, oil, and air bubbles. Some believed that the strait's towering mountains reduced *Bullhead*'s radar range, allowing the airplane to approach within striking distance.[4]

Holt was one of several skippers lost with their boats in 1945 while making their first patrol in command. It may have been the case, as one submariner claimed, that young skippers eager to make a record

149

contributed to Allied losses as the war's end approached.⁵ But it also indicated that in some ways Japanese antisubmarine tactics had improved, with escorts more likely to have radar and some aircraft even carrying magnetic airborne detectors (MAD), which were able to locate submerged submarines.⁶ The loss of *Bullhead* and its crew seemed especially tragic at a time when the end of the war was in sight.

The final accounting of America's war dead reflected just how dangerous the submarine service was, with 22 percent of the approximately 16,000 men who made war patrols lost at sea.⁷ In almost all of these deaths, families were left in limbo as to where and how their loved ones had died. There was no final resting place to visit, no gravesite for mourners.

For many submariners, their most anxious moments came as the war appeared to be near its end. Zeke Zellmer's former crewmates on USS *Cavalla* faced one of their closest calls on August 15, the same day they were notified that the war was over. While *Cavalla* cruised some twenty-five miles off the island of Honshu, an airplane suddenly dived out of the overcast sky and dropped a bomb as the submarine struggled to submerge. It was the first time that skipper Herman Kossler witnessed a bomb being dropped while he was on the surface. After finally getting underwater, *Cavalla*'s crew remained submerged for an hour and then transmitted a message that not all of the Japanese knew the war had ended.⁸

In Perth, many celebrated the war's end prematurely. On Friday, August 10, Edwin J. Young from HMS *Trenchant* met up at a city cinema with some new Australian friends visiting from Narrogin. During the movie's intermission, a Royal Navy officer breathlessly informed them, "it's over, they've packed up!" The cinema audience erupted into cheers. One woman grabbed Young's arm and broke down in tears; her husband had been a prisoner of the Japanese since the fall of Singapore. After a night of revelry, Young staggered back on board the submarine tender *Adamant* at 3 a.m., only to be informed the following day that the war was still on.⁹

The real celebrations came less than a week later, when a military cable received by the submarine tender USS *Holland* on August 15 announced the end of hostilities with Japan.¹⁰ The U.S. submarines in port on August 15 included *Besugo*, *Blower*, *Brill*, *Cabrilla*, *Charr*, and *Cod*; the British submarines *Stubborn*, *Tiptoe*, *Turpin*, and *Trenchant*; the Dutch submarine *O-21*. A service of thanksgiving was held on the depot ship *Adamant* that day, and then the celebrations began.¹¹ British submarine commander Alastair Mars recalled that V.J. Day in Perth

USS *Cabrilla* ship's party at the United Club, Perth, 27 August 1945
USS *Bowfin* Submarine Museum

became "V.J. week." The Swan Brewery provided complimentary barrels of beer to fuel the partying, and, for the first time in Australia, the British submarines were opened to the general public.[12]

Among those on hand for the postwar party was Edward R. Lloyd, a motor machinist's mate from USS *Cabrilla*. After two lengthy war patrols, *Cabrilla* arrived at Fremantle on August 3, when Lloyd and his fellow crewmen checked into a Perth hotel for their recreational leave little suspecting the rapid turn of events that followed. The *Cabrilla* men were still on leave when the Japanese surrendered. As Lloyd recalled, "Perth went wild, and we helped!"[13] Unfortunately, there would be a tragic postscript to the *Cabrilla* crew's celebrations. After receiving orders for their return to the United States, a final ship's party was organized in Perth for August 27. The gathering was, Edward Lloyd remembers, "a real blast," but sometime after the party broke up Henry Dewey Lauten, electrician's mate first class, wandered off alone and followed some steps down to a railroad track in the Perth goods yards, where he was run over by a train. Lauten, aged twenty-two and originally from Portland, Oregon, found his final resting place in Perth; crewmates from *Cabrilla* attended his funeral before departing for home.[14]

In Japan, Emperor Hirohito addressed his people at noon on August 15, informing his listeners that "the war-situation has developed not necessarily to Japan's advantage."[15] On September 2 the surrender ceremony was held on USS *Missouri*, under the command of Sunshine Murray, who had previously served as Lockwood's chief of staff in Fremantle. Murray first learned that *Missouri* had been selected for the ceremony from his chief yeoman, whose wife back in Santa Barbara, California, had sent him a newspaper clipping reporting that it would be the surrender ship. Admiral Sir Bruce Fraser, commander of the British Pacific Fleet and representing the United Kingdom at the surrender, supplied Murray with a mahogany table and upholstered chairs from the battleship *King George V* to be used for the ceremony.[16]

Submarines had made a major contribution to the Japanese defeat. They were largely able to cut off the enemy's supplies of raw materials from the Dutch East Indies and other parts of Southeast Asia, effectively severing the logistic lines of Japan's war machine. Fremantle-based submarines sank some 377 ships totalling 1,519,322 tons, with U.S. submarines accounting for 340 of these ships. Added to this were the scores of smaller craft also sunk that were not included in the official tally. Following the war, General Tojo ranked the destruction of Japan's merchant marine, along with America's leapfrog strategy and aircraft carrier operations, as the main factors for defeat. Even more unequivocally, the Japanese cabinet ascribed the loss of shipping as the greatest cause for losing the war. Some claim that, next to the atomic bomb, submarines were the most devastating weapon of the Pacific conflict.[17]

The Allied submarine offensive came, however, at enormous human cost. Of the forty-three U.S. submarines lost in combat in the Pacific, only eight had survivors. Of these, all but the men who escaped USS *Flier* spent much of the war in captivity. At Fukuoka Camp Number 3, a Japanese colonel climbed a stepladder and surveyed the Allied prisoners held there before informing them in clear English that "the war is over. Japan has lost the war."[18] Albert Rupp from USS *Grenadier* recalls that on hearing that the war was over, "Uncontrollable tears from my deep set eyes passed over my sunken cheeks, as I fell to my knees there in the dirt street of Camp Hell, and thanked my God."[19]

Nancy Critchlow from Easton, Maryland, whose brother Tom served on *Grenadier*, first heard he was alive and a prisoner of the Japanese seventeen months after the submarine's loss. He safely returned to America in September 1945.[20] For most of the prisoners from USS *Grenadier*, however, the war seemed far from over. Gordon "Gordy" Cox suffered from nightmares and physical disabilities and underwent a number of psychiatric labels until eventually described in 1999 as a victim of post-traumatic stress disorder. Despite sharing the diagnosis with many veterans of the Vietnam War, Cox professed, "It irritates me when I hear someone from Viet Nam complaining today that they had no parade when they came home like the World War II vets did. There were no parades for most of the soldiers and sailors that fought that war. The celebrations were over by the time we got home."[21]

Capt. James Fitzgerald from *Grenadier* received a Navy Cross for his fortitude in withstanding Japanese torture while a prisoner. He was one of a half-dozen submariners who testified at the Tokyo War Crimes Trials, which began in May 1946. The Red Cross had been unaware until August 26, 1945, of the Ofuna prison camp's existence, where so many submariners were tortured. Those Japanese put on trial by the International Military Tribunal for the Far East included thirty-three officers and enlisted men from the Ofuna camp. Based partly on Fitzgerald's testimony, three of the Japanese were sentenced to death, while the remainder received varying prison terms.[22]

It was not only former prisoners of the Japanese who continued to experience the trauma of wartime. Deen Brown, who served on USS *Trout* and USS *Gar*, recalled, "I fought the war every night for years after the war was over."[23] Kenneth Ruiz also had nightmares long after the war and suffered a lifelong aversion to sudden noises.[24] Many experienced a "survivor's guilt" bound up with the death of comrades. Some suffered physical disabilities as a result of their service, with men who worked in a submarine engine room likely to end up with permanent hearing loss.[25] Even submariners who were never formally diagnosed suffered subtle aftereffects from the war. Alvin Jacobson, one of eight men who survived the loss of USS *Flier*, developed a lifelong aversion to rice and coconuts, even though this diet had kept him alive in the Philippine Islands. After *Flier* sank, Jacobson had unsuccessfully tried to hang on to his pocket knife in the water; for the rest of his life he never went anywhere without a knife and it was the last thing he took out of his pants pocket each night.[26]

British submarine commander W. D. A. "Bill" King professed that at the end of the war he looked twenty years older than his age. "I was a wreck, physically, morally, socially, financially and in every other way."[27] King was one of only two British submarine skippers who began and finished the war in command. As it turned out, King lived longer than any other submarine commander of the Second World War. At the age of 60, he singlehandedly sailed around the world, and he died on September 21, 2012, at the age of 102.[28]

The last of the American submarines sailed from Fremantle Harbour on a Friday, the last day of August 1945. Hundreds of U.S. sailors lined the deck of the submarine tender USS *Clytie* to wave them off as a band played "Auld Lang Syne."[29] Whereas once the U.S. submarines had moored in the harbor six abreast, they were suddenly gone. The British submariners remained a while longer. As submarines returned to Fremantle from patrol, those that had been on station the longest were sent back to the United Kingdom. The more recently arrived submarines, like HMS *Turpin*, were quickly shuttled to other Australian ports on goodwill visits. *Turpin* visited Melbourne, where it was opened to thousands of visitors, then sailed to Launceston, Tasmania, before another stint at Fremantle and then Hong Kong. At Subic Bay, the Eighth Flotilla reverted to British operational control by the end of August and was dispatched to Hong Kong to join the reoccupation force.[30]

Once the Japanese surrendered, the submarine depot ship *Maidstone* became the first British ship to enter Hong Kong Harbor. After witnessing the Japanese surrender there, *Maidstone* returned to Fremantle badly in need of refit. On the way back to Australia, the tender stopped at Macassar to pick up nearly five hundred liberated prisoners of war who had survived the Battle of the Java Sea and the Battle of Sunda Strait in 1942.[31] Albert Gillespie professed, "I'll never forget the sorry sight of these men boarding the Maidstone, most of them were crying like babies." When they arrived back at Fremantle, Gillespie noted "The Dockside was crowded with old friends to welcome us back."[32] When *Maidstone* finally departed Fremantle for the last time, there were again hundreds of well-wishers at the dock. Gillespie described the ship's last departure from Fremantle as "the most moving experience I ever had." As the ship started to pull away from the dock, the crowd erupted into the song "Now Is the Hour," and Gillespie admitted, "I had a lump in my throat the size of a cannon ball." No doubt reflecting the experience of many, he concluded, "We had a good reputation in Western Australia, and I was proud to be a part of it."[33]

In the case of the British submariners, cooperation with the Americans served not only to strengthen the alliance but to help preserve ties with Australia.[34] Cooperation between the British, Americans, Australians, and Dutch was not without difficulties or jealousies. But as historian David Horner observes, "The test of a coalition is not whether all parties are completely happy, but rather whether or not the coalition works."[35] By this standard, the alliance was an undoubted success. In addition to military support, under Lend-Lease arrangements Australia had largely fed and supplied U.S. forces in the Southwest Pacific and was one of the few Allied countries to end the war without an accumulated financial debt to the United States.[36] In the case of Allied submariners, the greatest Australian contribution was to their morale, and they never forgot the open-handed hospitality received. Most of those Western Australian civilians who experienced the war reciprocated that lifelong affection. It would be difficult, if not impossible, to find a community during the war where foreign servicemen were integrated with more mutual respect and good will.

EPILOGUE

Many Allied submariners formed permanent bonds with Western Australians through marriage. Typically the couples endured lengthy separations before being reunited after the war ended. Roscoe P. Thompson, who had married Cecelia Christian in Bunbury on September 30, 1944, was reunited with his bride in New Orleans on October 6, 1945, exactly one year to the day after Roscoe departed Fremantle on patrol for the last time.[1] Zeke Zellmer and Babs Miller went through a similar period of limbo after a quick engagement and marriage on June 6, 1945. Given Zeke's initial determination not to marry until the war ended—lest he leave a widow—it seemed a momentous about-face, but with the war moving north it seemed unlikely he would have the opportunity to visit Fremantle again. Only five days after his marriage, Zeke's submarine, USS *Cavalla*, had orders to transfer to Guam, so he and Babs went through a "heart-wrenching" separation until finally reunited in May 1946 after almost a full year apart. After USS *Cavalla* sailed from Fremantle to Guam, Zeke received orders to return to the United States to help put the new submarine USS *Cusk* into commission at New London. *Cusk* would not become operational until February 1946, by which time the war had ended. In the meantime, Babs tried to arrange travel to the United States, and she eventually joined the 245 wives who departed from Fremantle in April 1946 for San Francisco on the converted troopship *Fred C. Ainsworth*. Once Babs arrived in America, she and Zeke moved into Navy housing at San Diego.[2]

Those brides and fiancées able to sail for America directly from Fremantle were a small minority; most of the women had to first cross Australia by steam train. The train from Western Australia to the eastern states earned the nickname "Perth Perambulator" because of the number of women traveling with small children in carriages on their way to America. The train journey took a grueling five days across the Nullarbor desert to reach Melbourne and Sydney, where some women had to then take another lengthy train trip north to Brisbane before departing by ship. Barbara Sheridan, who met her American husband while he was stationed

Ernest "Zeke" Zellmer and Babs Miller shop for an engagement ring in Perth, 1945. Ernest "Zeke" Zellmer

at Fremantle on the tender *Pelias*, traveled nine days by train to Brisbane before boarding the SS *Lurline*. This was no luxury cruise, because once on board she shared a cabin with six other women and their babies.[3]

Not all plans to reunite went smoothly. Tim McCoy had proposed marriage to Valma Gray before departing on USS *Grenadier*'s final voyage and the ordeal of Japanese imprisonment. Once released from Japanese captivity, Tim arrived at Camp Dealey on Guam and sent two telegrams. One was to his mother in Dallas, Texas; the other went to Valma Gray in Perth. Both women had believed Tim to be still alive because his name appeared on a list of POWs after he was sent to Fukuoka Camp Number 3, and in fact they had already begun writing to one another. When Valma replied to Tim, she told him she had never taken off the engagement ring he gave her, and the couple made plans to marry in the United States. But then Valma later wrote Tim that her mother had been diagnosed with cancer and she would have to remain in Australia; she returned the engagement ring and money Tim had sent her for the trip to America.[4]

Like McCoy, fellow *Grenadier* survivor Chuck Vervalin endured his imprisonment partly by fantasizing about a future reunion with the woman he loved. Once he was released, Chuck arranged for a fellow prisoner, an Australian named Arthur King, to personally deliver a letter to Gwen Haughey in Perth. After delivering the letter, King wrote Chuck telling him what an attractive girl she was, adding, "You Yanks have all the luck."[5] During Chuck's absence, though, Gwen Haughey had become engaged to another American sailor. Even so, she began to write to Chuck, who had returned to his home in Sodus, New York. She had second thoughts about her engagement to the other sailor, and in May 1946 she came to the United States under the War Brides Act, joining the ranks of what some called "petticoat pilgrims." She was one of more than a thousand women from Western Australia who sailed for the United States on so-called bride ships, and three days after she arrived in America the couple married in Chicago.

John Spanton, who made five war patrols out of Fremantle on *Ray* and *Becuna*, married his wife Kathleen in late 1944. Their first child was born in Western Australia, and Spanton was possibly the last American submariner to depart for the United States. In early 1946 he returned to his home in Wisconsin, with his wife and child following several months later.[6] Relatively few Americans planned to remain in Australia after the war. At the end of 1944 the Australian government reported that they had received only about fifty inquiries from American servicemen considering permanent settlement in the country.[7] Nevertheless, a handful of men from the U.S. Navy made Western Australia their home. George Ridgway, who had once led a kangaroo hunt on the family's property, later encountered veteran submariner Fred Helfers, who had married a Perth woman and taken a job in the wheat-belt town of Moora, one hundred miles north of Perth. Ed Packwood from USS *Growler* also married an Australian and elected to remain in Western Australia at the war's end. Some American Australian couples later returned to Western Australia. Although Roscoe P. Thompson and his bride were reunited in New Orleans, they eventually returned to live in Bunbury. Homer White, having once served on USS *Holland*, returned to live in Albany.[8]

After the war Bruce Teede came across three U.S. Navy men who had returned to make Perth their home. Along with Bruce and his father, Harold "Hal" Lee and Eddie Redmond, former submarine machinists, worked for Chamberlain Tractors. They both had Australian wives. Teede later worked for a short time with another ex-Navy man, Lyall Springer, at Bouchers' Industries in Osborne Park, Perth.[9] Another American to make Western Australia his home was Tom Snider, who had once served on the crew of the famed USS *Harder*, but was in the hospital when the submarine made its final fatal patrol. Snider later gained notoriety for his exploits as a salvage diver, including dives on some wartime wrecks, and he died in the early 1960s in a light aircraft crash at Giralia Station near Onslow.[10]

Whereas the brides of Americans almost all migrated to the United States, significant numbers of British submariners determined to migrate to Australia after the war. Some, like Gerry Goldman, who had served on HMS *Maidstone* and married a local woman in March 1945, opted to demobilize in Australia. Yet, not all of those who returned to Australia had Australian brides. Ben Skeates' wife, Muriel, lived in England and had twice been informed by telegram during the war that her husband was presumed dead. On the second occasion she had just given birth to their first child, but fortunately Skeates was able to contact her from Western Australia to set the record straight.[11] Having survived the false reports of his death, Skeates and his wife determined to move to Australia. After Roy Weston returned to England on HMS *Spiteful*, one of the people who had entertained him during leave in Western Australia invited him to return and join him in business. Weston was able to secure a seat on one of the last Sunderland flying boats to leave England on the route to Australia; the journey took ten days. On reaching Perth, Weston worked the next eleven years with his friend and also married an Australian woman before striking out in his own firm. He was one of an estimated one hundred British submariners who migrated to Western Australia following the war.[12]

Although in smaller numbers than the British, there were also Dutch submariners determined to make their home in Western Australia. Ary Jongejan first met his future wife, Joy, on Wednesday, April 4, 1945, soon after arriving on *O-24* from Scotland. It was a case of love at first sight, and Ary proposed marriage the same night they met. They married only a couple of weeks before the war ended.[13] It was also near the end of the war when Johannes Loep from *K-XV* met his future wife, Nancy Hebditch, on a blind date arranged by his landlady in Subiaco. Although it was virtually love at first sight for Loep, partly due to the machinations of the Dutch navy they would not marry for another two years. After a marriage ceremony at the Methodist Church in Shenton Park, Loep began civilian life working for the Midland Railway workshop in Western Australia.[14]

The presence of submarine veterans in Western Australia helped keep alive the memory of their contribution to the war in the Pacific. The Submarine Old Comrades Association sponsored the erection of a memorial on Monument Hill overlooking Fremantle. First unveiled on Trafalgar Day, October 21, 1972, a World War II heritage periscope rises out of a flagstone terrace with a plaque that declares, "To commemorate the close ties forged between the People of Fremantle and the Officers and Men of the British and Allied Submarines of the 4th and 8th Flotillas based in Fremantle during World War II."

A memorial to American submariners, consisting of a Mark XV torpedo mounted horizontally on a stone base, was already dedicated at

Monument Hill on September 18, 1967. A plaque explains that Fremantle citizens wished to recognize "the gallant submarine personnel of the United States Navy who lost their lives whilst operating from the port of Fremantle during the 1939–1945 War." Adm. Herman Kossler, wartime skipper of USS *Cavalla*, was among those attending the dedication. At the time he was visiting Australia to commission a communications station at North West Cape, and he jumped at the chance to revisit Fremantle. Kossler, like so many American submariners who spent time there during the war, held an abiding affection for Western Australia.[15]

Other commemorations of the Australian-American relationship include USS *Pampanito*, which became the first of the *Balao*-class submarines to be decommissioned on December 15, 1945. Thirty years later the National Maritime Museum Association rescued *Pampanito* from the scrap heap and in 1982 opened it to the public at Fisherman's Wharf in San Francisco, where it remains today. In 1989 the Australian government awarded the submarine an Australian Defence Force Plaque in recognition of its role in rescuing Australian prisoners of war after the sinking of *Rakuyo Maru*.[16] Yet another monument to the war years was the continuing close ties between the submarine service and Western Australians. When the World War II vintage boat USS *Archerfish* visited Fremantle in 1961, the crew was overwhelmed with social invitations, and at least four men from the submarine's crew ended up marrying women they met in Australia.[17]

The cross-cultural bonds symbolized by the marriages of Australian women to Allied submariners, along with the memorials on Monument Hill, serve as reminders of Fremantle's importance as a submarine base during the Second World War. They give little sense, however, of the desperation felt by Western Australians following the attack on Pearl Harbor and the fall of Singapore. Nor can they capture the remarkable transformation that occurred after March 1942, when the first refugee submarines retreated to Fremantle from the Philippines and Dutch East Indies. The Americans who initially arrived in Western Australia had few successes against the enemy and struggled with unreliable torpedoes. At the same time, the Dutch submarine force had been decimated while British submarines had virtually withdrawn from the Far East altogether.

Despite these unpromising beginnings, Fremantle submarines made a major contribution to the decisive defeat of Japan. Much of the turnaround from retreat to offense depended on individual courage. Many submariners came to accept the terror of being depth charged as the more or less inevitable consequences of making an attack on enemy shipping. Added to this were the hazards of being bombed on patrol not only by enemy planes but by "friendly" aircraft. Men facing danger together developed a strong sense of camaraderie, all the more so in submarines, where group survival depended on each man carrying out his job. Even in a shared foxhole one soldier might live while others died, whereas in a submarine all on board were likely to share a common fate. As one journalist described it, "There is no intimacy quite like the knowledge that the ship you share with your friends may at any moment serve also as your common coffin."[18]

Allied success also depended on cooperation at many levels. Despite the early flawed efforts of the ABDA command at the battles of the Java Sea and Sunda Strait, the Australians, British, Dutch, and Americans built an effective naval alliance. Sadly, both Prime Minister John Curtin of Australia and President Franklin D. Roosevelt would die before witnessing the ultimate success of that alliance. Australian support for the submarine base at Fremantle included protection by the military and the provision of supplies and skilled civilian labor; Australian commandos shared the hazards of many submarine missions behind enemy lines. While there were some inevitable tensions, the U.S. Navy established an effective working relationship with their British counterparts, and the bonds between submariners largely transcended nationality. Naval historian John Winton concludes that "of all the 'special relationships' established between British and American fighting men during the war, one of the closest was that between the two nations' submariners in the Far East at Fremantle and Subic Bay."[19] The generosity of the Americans in affording logistical support, both to the Dutch and British submarine forces, in particular helped foster good relations.

Regardless of their nationalities, all submariners suffered the discomforts and dangers of lengthy war patrols. The promise of leave in Western Australia made the hardships of patrols more bearable. The amenities available on shore were an important part of the recovery process, but the best tonic of all was the welcoming local population, who made returning submariners feel as though they were part of the community. Fremantle quickly established a reputation as the best leave center for submariners in the Pacific and, if not unique, was among a select number of bases where adversity fostered a special bond between civilians and foreign servicemen.

Notes

ABBREVIATIONS

BL	Battye Library, Perth, Western Australia
CBC	Clay Blair Collection, American Heritage Center, Laramie, Wyoming
FCL	Fremantle City Library, Western Australia
IWM	Imperial War Museum, London
LC	Library of Congress, Washington, D.C.
NAA	National Archives of Australia, Canberra and Melbourne
RSM	Royal Submarine Museum, Gosport, England
SFM	Submarine Force Museum, Groton, Connecticut
SM	Submarine Memorabilia, WWII Submarine War Patrol Reports, reproduced on DVD
UBSM	USS *Bowfin* Submarine Museum, Pearl Harbor, Hawaii
WAMM	Western Australian Maritime Museum, Fremantle

ACKNOWLEDGMENTS

Epigraph A. B. Bristowe, "A Visit to a Submarine," in *More Submarine Memories: Some More Lesser Known Facts from the Gatwick Submarine Archive*, ed. Keith Nethercoate-Bryant et al. (Hadley, Sussex: Gatwick Submarine Archive, 1997), 149.

INTRODUCTION

1. These figures are based on David Jones, "Submarines in the Battle for Australia," *Journal of Australian Naval History* 2, no. 2 (2005): 81; Fremantle Submarine Base, http://www.ozatwar.com/usnavy/fremantlesubmarinebase.htm; John Dowson, *Old Fremantle: Photographs 1850–1950* (Perth: University of Western Australia Press, 2003), 214.
2. Malcolm Murfett, *Naval Warfare 1919–1945: An Operational History of the Volatile War at Sea* (London: Routledge, 2009), 484.
3. Richard J. Aldrich, *The Faraway War: Personal Diaries of the Second World War in Asia and the Pacific* (London: Doubleday, 2005), 127; Christopher Thorne, *Allies of a Kind: The United States, Britain*

and the War against Japan, 1941–1945 (London: Hamish Hamilton, 1978), 154; Theodore Roscoe, *United States Submarine Operations in World War II* (Annapolis, Md.: Naval Institute Press, 1949), 51.
4. William King, *The Stick and the Stars* (London: Arrow Books, 1961), 116.
5. Quoted in Ian W. Toll, *Pacific Crucible: War at Sea in the Pacific, 1941–1942* (New York: W. W. Norton and Company, 2012), 257.
6. Dan Van der Vat, *The Pacific Campaign: World War II, The U.S.–Japanese Naval War 1941–1945* (New York: Simon & Schuster, 2006), 132–33; T. J. Cain and A. V. Sellwood, *H.M.S. Electra* (London: Futura Publications, 1959), 227; Mike Carlton, *Cruiser: The Life and Loss of HMAS Perth and Her Crew* (Sydney: William Heinemann, 2010), 354, 433, 626; Samuel Eliot Morison, *The Two-Ocean War: A Short History of the United States Navy in the Second World War* (Annapolis, Md.: Naval Institute Press, 1963), 87.
7. Gavin Long, *The Six Years War: Australia in the 1939–45 War* (Canberra: Australian War Memorial and the Australian Government Publishing Service, 1973), 136; Jeffrey Grey, *A Military History of Australia* (Cambridge: Cambridge University Press, 1999), 170.
8. Quoted in Norman Harper, *Australia and the United States: Documents and Readings in Australian History* (Melbourne: Nelson, 1986), 162.
9. Nicholas Evan Sarantakes, "One Last Crusade: The British Pacific Fleet and Its Impact on the Anglo-American Alliance," *English Historical Review* 121, no. 491 (April 2006): 437–40.

CHAPTER 1. ON THE EDGE

1. Quoted in Garry Disher, *Total War: The Home Front 1939–1945* (Melbourne: Oxford University Press, 1983), 3.
2. John Robertson, *Australia at War 1939–1945* (Melbourne: William Heinemann, 1981), 193.
3. Quoted in Libby Connors et al., *Australia's Frontline: Remembering the 1939–45 War* (St Lucia: University of Queensland Press, 1992), 31.
4. Quoted in Bob Wurth, *Australia's Greatest Peril 1942* (Sydney: Pan Macmillan, 2008), 58.
5. Quoted in John Hetherington, *Blamey: The Biography of Field-Marshal Sir Thomas Blamey* (Melbourne: F. W. Cheshire, 1954), 127.
6. Wurth, *Australia's Greatest Peril*, 149; Charles Lockwood, *Sink 'Em All: Submarine Warfare in the Pacific* (1951; repr., New York: Bantam Books, 1984), 39.

7. Michael McKernan, *All In! Australia during the Second World War* (Melbourne: Nelson, 1983), 103.
8. Malcolm Tull, *A Community Enterprise: The History of the Port of Fremantle, 1897–1997* (St. John's, Newfoundland: International Maritime Economic History Association, 1997), 140.
9. Robertson, *Australia at War*, 95.
10. Cain and Sellwood, *H.M.S. Electra*, 247.
11. *The Weekend West,* March 3–4, 2012, 18; Kevin Gomm, *Red Sun on the Kangaroo Paw* (Perth: Chargan, 2009), 21–22, 25, 43, 56; Alan Powell, *Northern Voyagers: Australia's Monsoon Coast in Maritime History* (Melbourne: Australian Scholarly Publishing, 2010), 270–71.
12. Quoted in Joanna Penglase and David Horner, eds., *When the War Came to Australia: Memories of the Second World War* (Sydney: Allen and Unwin, 1992), 97.
13. Gomm, *Red Sun on the Kangaroo Paw*, 160–63; IJN Submarine I-3, Combined Fleet, http://www.combinedfleet.com; David Stevens, *A Critical Vulnerability: The Impact of the Submarine Threat on Australia's Maritime Defence 1915–1954* (Canberra: Sea Power Centre, 2005), 185–86; Terry Jones and Steven Carruthers, *A Parting Shot: Shelling of Australia by Japanese Submarines 1942* (Narrabeen, N.S.W.: Casper, 2013), 232.
14. Gordon Baker to author, February 22, 2008; Anthony Barker and Lisa Jackson, *Fleeting Attraction: A Social History of American Servicemen in Western Australia during the Second World War* (Nedlands: University of Western Australia Press, 1996), 69.
15. Quoted in Penglase and Horner, *When the War Came to Australia*, 98.
16. Gordon Scott to author, February 20, 2008.
17. McKernan, *All In,* 99.
18. Patricia Cornish, *Western Australia in the 20th Century* (Perth: Fremantle Arts Centre Press and the West Australian, 1999), 115.
19. Phyllis May Atkinson, interview, May 29, 1985, OH8515, FCL.
20. Gordon Baker to author, February 22, 2008; Jack Emery in Bobbie Oliver, ed., *Papers in Labour History: The WAGR/Westrail Workshops at Midland, 1904–1994*, no. 25, September 2001, 23; Robert Chilcott, interview, February 1985, FCL, OH8548.
21. Wurth, *Australia's Greatest Peril*, 20, 31, 80.
22. James Fife, The Reminiscences of James Fife, Oral History Research Office, Columbia University, 250.
23. USS *Sargo* First War Patrol Report, Attacks, disc 6, SM; Anthony Newpower, *Iron Men and Tin Fish: The Race to Build a Better*

Torpedo during World War II (Westport, Conn.: Praeger Security International, 2006), 62, 64–65; Robert C. Stern, *U.S. Subs in Action* (Carrollton, Tex.: Squadron/Signal Publications, 1983), 5–6.
24. USS *Sargo* Second War Patrol Report, Major Defects, General Remarks.
25. *Times,* February 27, 1942, 4.
26. USS *Sargo* Third War Patrol Report, March 4, 1942.
27. Doug Rhymes, "The Saga of Bob Rose and Sargo's Welcome to Australia," *Polaris,* August 1982, 14; Doug Rhymes, in Edward Monroe-Jones and Michael Green, eds., *The Silent Service in World War II: The Story of the U.S. Navy Submarine Force in the Words of the Men who Lived It* (Philadelphia: Casemate, 2012), 60–62.
28. Report of Attack on U.S. Submarine by Hudson Aircraft A16-122 on 4th March 1942, Series A1196, Control Symbol 60/501/97, NAA (Canberra); USS *Sargo* Third War Patrol Report, March 4, 1942, Aircraft Sighted, Major Defects and Casualties; Roscoe, *Submarine Operations,* 80–81; Clay Blair Jr., *Silent Victory: The U.S. Submarine War against Japan* (1975; repr. ed., Annapolis, Md.: Naval Institute Press, 2001), 140–41, 169–70; Stevens, *A Critical Vulnerability,* 186.
29. Mervyn Wingfield, *Wingfield at War* (Dunbeath, Scotland: Whittles Publishing, 2012), 71.
30. Stuart Murray, interview, box 98, CBC; Stuart S. Murray, *Reminiscences of Admiral Stuart S. Murray* (Annapolis, Md.: Naval Institute Press, 1975), 151; Rhymes, "Saga of Bob Rose," 15.
31. Chester Smith, interview, box 99, CBC; Roscoe, *Submarine Operations,* 193; A. J. Killin, in Monroe-Jones and Green, *The Silent Service in World War II U.S. Navy Submarine Force in the Words of the Men who Lived* (Philadelphia: Casemate, 2012), 28–30; Maxwell Hawkins, *Torpedoes Away Sir! Our Submarine Navy in the Pacific* (New York: Henry Holt and Company, 1946), 67–68; Blair, *Silent Victory,* 190.
32. Stuart Murray, interview, CBC; Murray, *Reminiscences,* 174, 176.
33. Murray, *Reminiscences,* 177–79.
34. Newpower, *Iron Men and Tin Fish,* 109.
35. Michael W. D. White, *Australian Submarines: A History* (Canberra: Australian Government Printing Service, 1992), 166; Jean Hood, ed., *Submarine: An Anthology of First-hand Accounts of the War under the Sea, 1939–1945* (London: Conway, 2007), 62, 347; Pieter Van Ewijk, "History of the Dutch Submarine Force,"

The Submarine Review (July 1992): 79–81; Hans van der Ham, The Experiences of the Dutch Submariners Operating out of Australia during the Second World War, transcript of public lecture, March 1995, WAMM; Doug Hurst, *The Fourth Ally: The Dutch Forces in Australia during WWII* (Canberra: self-published, 2001), 45; Michael Wilson, *A Submariners' War: The Indian Ocean 1939–45* (Stroud, Gloucestershire: Tempus, 2000), 64; Mark C. Jones, "Give Credit Where Credit Is Due: The Dutch Role in the Development and Deployment of the Submarine Schnorkel," *Journal of Military History* 69, no. 4 (October 2005): 1004–5.

36. Johannes Loep, transcript of public lecture, March 1995, WAMM; Murray, *Reminiscences*, 182; Van der Ham, Experiences of the Dutch Submariners, transcript.
37. KVIII, Dutch Submarines, http://wwwdutchsubmarines.com; Van der Ham, Experiences of the Dutch Submariners, transcript.
38. Jan van Hattam, transcript of public lecture, March 1995, WAMM.
39. Jan van Hattam, transcript, WAMM; Van der Ham, Experience of the Dutch Submariners, transcript, WAMM.
40. D. H. Van Velden, "Fremantle's Forgotten Fleet: A Social History of the Royal Netherlands Navy in Western Australia, 1942–1945" (Doctorandus thesis, University of Leiden, 2000), 53, 84; Lockwood, *Sink 'Em All*, 40; Van der Ham, Experiences of a Dutch Submariner, transcript.
41. Barker and Jackson, *Fleeting Attraction*, 63; Lynne Cairns, *Secret Fleets: Fremantle's World War II Submarine Base*, 2nd ed. (Perth: Western Australian Museum, 2011), 19; Jones, "Submarines in the Battle for Australia," 62.
42. Lockwood to Vice Admiral Leary, June 4, 1942, box 56, folder 20, CBC; Lockwood, *Sink 'Em All*, 18; Mike Ostlund, *Find 'Em, Chase 'Em, Sink 'Em: The Mysterious Loss of the WWII Submarine USS Gudgeon* (Guilford, Conn.: Lyons Press, 2006), 127; Arthur Moorhead, *The Australian Blue Book* (Sydney: Blue Star, 1942), 64; Barker and Jackson, *Fleeting Attraction*, 75.
43. Hetherington, *Blamey*, 134–36.
44. Gomm, *Red Sun on the Kangaroo Paw*, 7, 92, 133; Jones and Carruthers, *A Parting Shot*, 232.
45. Robert Schultz and James Shell, *We Were Pirates: A Torpedoman's Pacific War* (Annapolis, Md.: Naval Institute Press, 2009), 98.
46. *West Australian*, July 5, 1944, 2.

CHAPTER 2. LIKE HEAVEN

1. Corwin Mendenhall, *Submarine Diary: The Silent Stalking of Japan* (Annapolis, Md.: Naval Institute Press, 1988), 53, 68.
2. James F. Calvert, *Silent Running: My Years on a World War II Attack Submarine* (New York: John Wiley and Sons, 1995), 134.
3. Hughston E. Lowder with Jack Scott, *Batfish: Ace Submarine Killer of World War II* (London: Sphere Books, 1982), 159.
4. Quoted in John Reeve and David Stevens, eds., *The Face of Naval Battle* (Sydney: Allen and Unwin, 2003), 184.
5. Wes Headington, War Diary of the USS *Thresher*, USS *Thresher* file, UBSM.
6. Gregory F. Michno, *USS Pampanito: Angel Killer* (Norman: University of Oklahoma Press, 2000), 106; Eugene B. Fluckey, *Thunder Below! The USS Barb Revolutionizes Submarine Warfare in World War II* (Urbana: University of Illinois Press, 1992), 63; Patsy Sumie Saiki, *Ganbare! An Example of Japanese Spirit* (Honolulu: Mutual Publishing, 2004), 22.
7. Quoted in Paul Stillwell, ed., *Submarine Stories: Recollections from the Diesel Boats* (Annapolis, Md.: Naval Institute Press, 2007), 125.
8. Robert Trumbull, *Silversides* (1945; repr., Chicago: O. W. Knutson and Company, 1990), 88.
9. Larry Colton, *No Ordinary Joes: The Extraordinary True Story of Four Submariners in War and Love and Life* (New York: Crown, 2010), 86.
10. Quoted in Colton, *No Ordinary Joes*, 92.
11. Trumbull, *Silversides*, 88.
12. See Glenn J. Gray, *The Warriors: Reflections on Men in Battle* (Lincoln: University of Nebraska Press, 1959), 61–62, 71.
13. Quoted in Annette Potts and Lucinda Strauss, *For the Love of a Soldier: Australian War Brides and their GIs* (Sydney: Australian Broadcasting Corporation, 1987), 31.
14. Lowder, *Batfish*, 160.
15. Mendenhall, *Submarine Diary*, 53, 90.
16. Jan van Hattam, transcript, WAMM.
17. John Field, "Submarine Trip to Japanese Waters," *Life*, June 29, 1942, 14.
18. Quoted in David Jones and Peter Nunan, *U.S. Subs Down Under: Brisbane, 1942–1945* (Annapolis, Md.: Naval Institute Press, 2005), 174.
19. Albert Rupp, *Threshold of Hell* (Long Beach, Calif.: Almar Press, 1983), 8.

20. Quoted in Mark Roberts, *Sub: An Oral History of U.S. Navy Submarines* (New York: Berkley Caliber, 2007), 181.
21. Quoted in *Weekend Australian*, January 28–29, 2006, 21.
22. Quoted in Lloyd R. "Joe" Vasey, The Strategic Importance of Fremantle 1945–95: Reflections on Submarine Warfare in WWII and in the Future, March 1995, transcript, WAMM.
23. Rupp, *Threshold of Hell*, 7.
24. Quoted in Stillwell, *Submarine Stories*, 103.
25. John Field, "West of Japan," *Life*, March 15, 1943, 96.
26. Ernest J. Zellmer to author, February 2, 2011; Don Haseley to author, March 6, 2011.
27. Quoted in Colton, *No Ordinary Joes*, 120.
28. Robert Hargis, *US Submarine Crewmen 1941–1945* (Oxford: Osprey, 2003), 41.

CHAPTER 3. WILKES

1. Reuben Whitaker, interview, box 99, CBC; Roscoe, *Submarine Operations*, 61.
2. Murray, *Reminiscences*, 179, 208; Cairns, *Secret Fleets*, 68; W. G. Winslow, *The Fleet the Gods Forgot: The U.S. Asiatic Fleet in World War II* (Annapolis, Md.: Naval Institute Press, 1982), 27.
3. Tull, *A Community Enterprise*, 140; Graham McKenzie-Smith, *Defending Fremantle, Albany and Bunbury 1939 to 1945* (Perth: Grimwade Publications, 2009), 2, 7–8.
4. Blair, *Silent Victory*, 223–24, 273, 906, 910.
5. Blair, *Silent Victory*, 906, 910.
6. Kate Darian-Smith, *On the Home Front: Melbourne in Wartime 1939–1945* (Melbourne: Oxford University Press, 1990), 205; Robertson, *Australia at War*, 112.
7. Quoted in Brian McKinlay, *Australia 1942: End of Innocence* (Sydney: Collins, 1985), 123.
8. Quoted in Monroe-Jones and Green, *Silent Service*, 67. See also David Creed, *Operations of the Fremantle Submarine Base 1942–1945* (Sydney: Naval Historical Society of Australia, 1979), 7; Cairns, *Secret Fleets*, 151.
9. Robertson, *Australia at War*, 94; Blair, *Silent Victory*, 356–57; Peter Stanley, *Invading Australia: Japan and the Battle for Australia, 1942* (Melbourne: Viking, 2008), 109, 122; Lionel Wigmore, *The Japanese Thrust* (1957; repr., Canberra: Australian War Memorial, 1968), 466–68; Long, *Six Years War*, 128, 165.

10. Quoted in Tom Trumble, *Rescue at 2100 Hours: The Untold Story of the Most Daring Escape of the Pacific War* (Melbourne: Viking, 2013), 197.
11. Quoted in Roberts, *Sub*, 17.
12. USS *Searaven* Third War Patrol Report, April 19, 1942, disc 7, SM.
13. Quoted in Roberts, *Sub*, 19.
14. In addition to Joseph McGrievy's firsthand account in Roberts, *Sub*, 8–26, and the USS *Searaven* Third War Patrol Report, see USS *Snapper* Second War Patrol Report, April 23–24, 1942, disc 5, SM; Lockwood, *Sink 'Em All*, 22–23; Roscoe, *Submarine Operations*, 103–4; Trumble, *Rescue at 2100 Hours*, especially 230–56.
15. Robertson, *Australia at War*, 113, 131; Long, *Six Years War*, 186–87.
16. F. W. Lipscomb, *The British Submarine* (London: Adam and Charles Black, 1954), 205, 208, 225, 233; Innes McCartney, *British Submarines 1939–1945* (Oxford: Osprey, 2006), 38, 41.
17. Robertson, *Australia at War*, 101, 114.
18. Stanley, *Invading Australia*, 133, 141; Grey, *Military History of Australia*, 171.
19. Murfett, *Naval Warfare*, 176, 181–82.
20. Ron Davison, "Papers, People and Propaganda," in *On the Homefront: Western Australia and World War II*, ed. Jenny Gregory (Perth: University of Western Australia Press, 1996), 195.

CHAPTER 4. LOCKWOOD

1. Lockwood Diary, December 8, 1941, box 56, folder 21, CBC.
2. Lockwood to Captain W. A. Heard, January 30, 1942, box 56, folder 20, CBC.
3. Charles Lockwood, *Down to the Sea in Subs: My Life in the U.S. Navy* (New York: W.W. Norton and Company, 1967), 11, 14, 192; Blair, *Silent Victory*, 66; Roscoe, *Submarine Operations*, 144–45; James Scot, *The War Below: The Story of Three Submarines that Battled Japan* (New York: Simon & Schuster, 2013), 33.
4. Lockwood to Miss L. D. Zigler, April 4, 1942, box 56, folder 20, CBC.
5. Quoted in Thomas Parrish, *The Submarine: A History* (London: Viking Penguin, 2004), 347.
6. Lockwood, *Down to the Sea in Subs*, 272.
7. Lockwood, *Down to the Sea in Subs*, 271.
8. Lockwood Diary, May 3, 1942, box 56, folder 21, CBC.

9. Steven L. Carruthers, *Japanese Submarine Raiders 1942: A Maritime Mystery* (Narrabeen, N.S.W.: Casper Publications, 2006), 23, 151; Stanley, *Invading Australia*, 177; James Ritchie Grant, "The Vicissitudes of a Dutch Submarine in Royal Australian Navy Service," *Sea Breezes,* vol. 70 (1996), http:// www.dutchsubmarines.com/specials/special_kix_club.htm; White, *Australian Submarines*, 168, 171.
10. Quoted in White, *Australian Submarines*, 170.
11. Lockwood Diary, May 31, 1942, box 56, folder 21, CBC.
12. Long, *Six Years War*, 175.
13. Quoted in Stanley, *Invading Australia*, 181.
14. Roger Bell, Sean Brawley, and Chris Dixon, *Conflict in the Pacific 1937–1951* (Cambridge: Cambridge University Press, 2005), 14.
15. Lockwood, *Sink 'Em All*, 16–17.
16. *West Australian,* October 20, 1984.
17. Audrey Van Hattem, *Time Was* (Perth: self-published, 1998), 58–59.
18. Hurst, *Fourth Ally*, 101; Van Velden, "Fremantle's Forgotten Fleet," 69; Jan van Hattam, transcript, WAMM; YMCA Services Social Centre flyer, Les Cottman Papers, courtesy of Peter Nunan.
19. Andre Bruinhout, Recollections of Fremantle, transcript, WAMM; Jan Van Hattam, WAMM transcript.
20. YMCA flyer, Les Cottman Papers, courtesy of Peter Nunan.
21. See for example Roy Weston, transcript, WAMM.
22. Charley T. Odom, interview, Center for the Study of War and Society, University of Tennessee, Knoxville, 10; Jim Vander Moere, "Remembrances," August 12, 1997, http://www.webenet./~ftoon/memory/crewmemory.html#moere.
23. Murray, *Reminiscences*, 208.
24. Quoted in Ostlund, *Find 'Em, Chase 'Em, Sink 'Em*, 225.
25. Schultz and Shell, *We Were Pirates*, 3, 113, 118.
26. Lockwood, *Sink 'Em All*, 43.
27. Anthony J. Barker, "Yanks in Western Australia: The Impact of United States Servicemen," in Gregory, *On the Homefront*, 123; Cairns, *Secret Fleets*, 127.
28. See "Australian Wives," *Life*, July 10, 1944, 44, 48; Lockwood, *Sink 'Em All*, 42–43.
29. Alastair Mars, *H.M.S. Thule Intercepts* (London: Elek Books, 1956), 22.
30. Calvert, *Silent Running*, 165, 186.

31. Quoted in Larry Bond, ed., *Crash Dive: True Stories of Submarine Combat* (New York: Tom Doherty Associates, 2010), 227.
32. Quoted in Colton, *No Ordinary Joes*, 122–23.
33. Don Keith, *War beneath the Waves: A True Story of Courage and Leadership aboard a World War II Submarine* (New York: NAL Caliber, 2010), 92.
34. Quoted in Colton, *No Ordinary Joes*, 331.
35. Lockwood to Rear Adm. R. H. English, August 1, 1942, Lockwood Papers, box 12, folder 63, LC.
36. Lockwood to Cdr. Willard J. Suits, August 3 and November 14, 1942, Lockwood Papers, box 12, folder 63, LC.
37. Quoted in Michael Bess, *Choices under Fire: Moral Dimensions of World War II* (New York: Alfred A. Knopf, 2006), 38.
38. Hosey Mays, in Stillwell, *Submarine Stories*, 160; Glenn A. Knoblock, *Black Submariners in the United States Navy, 1940–1975* (Jefferson, N.C.: McFarland, 2005), 15, 146.
39. Knoblock, *Black Submariners*, 272–73, 288–89.
40. Quoted in Knoblock, *Black Submariners*, 126.
41. Quoted in Stillwell, *Submarine Stories*, 159.
42. Knoblock, *Black Submariners*, 136.
43. Quoted in Knoblock, *Black Submariners*, 319.
44. Michno, *USS Pampanito*, 303.
45. Knoblock, *Black Submariners*, 127–28, 320.
46. Mary Anne Jebb, "'It Was Just like a Reserve in the City': Aboriginal Oral Histories of East Perth around the Power Station," in *Powering Perth: A History of the East Perth Power Station*, ed. Lenore Layman (Perth: Black Swan Press, 2012), 48; quoted in Stillwell, *Submarine Stories*, 159–60.
47. Stanley, *Invading Australia*, 170.
48. Quoted in Knoblock, *Black Submariners*, 321.

CHAPTER 5. TORPEDOES AND TRAGEDIES

1. Dan Van der Vat, *Stealth at Sea: The History of the Submarine* (London: Orion, 1994), 170; Winslow, *Fleet the Gods Forgot*, 24.
2. Robert J. Casey, *Battle Below: The War of the Submarines* (Indianapolis, Ind.: Bobbs-Merrill Company, 1975), 169.
3. Lockwood to Admiral Leary, June 23, 1942, box 56, folder 20, CBC.
4. Lockwood to Captain C. W. Styer, July 16, 1942, box 56, folder 20, CBC.
5. Allan McCann, interview, box 98, CBC.

6. See Jim Christley, *US Submarines 1941–45* (New York: Osprey, 2006), 9; Fluckey, *Thunder Below!*, 154; Robert Gannon, *Hellions of the Deep: The Development of American Torpedoes in World War II* (University Park: Pennsylvania State University Press, 1996), 43; Newpower, *Iron Men and Tin Fish*, 103.
7. US Submarine Operations—Fremantle, box 82, folder 6, CBC.
8. Mary Lee Coe Fowler, *Full Fathom Five: A Daughter's Search* (Tuscaloosa: University of Alabama Press, 2008), 180–81; Bobette Gugliotta, *Pigboat 39: An American Sub Goes to War* (Lexington: University Press of Kentucky, 1984), 18; Newpower, *Iron Men and Tin Fish*, 70–72.
9. Lockwood to Rear Adm. W. H. P. Blandy, July 11, 1942, box 56, folder 20, CBC; Blair, *Silent Victory*, 273–75; Lockwood, *Down to the Sea in Subs*, 278; Gannon, *Hellions of the Deep*, 84; Newpower, *Iron Men and Tin Fish*, 104–5; Fremantle Submarine Base, US Navy Fremantle, WA during WW2, http://www.ozatwar.com/usnavy/fremantlesubmarinebase.htm.
10. Lockwood to Rear Adm. W. H. P. Blandy, July 11, 1942, box 56, folder 20, CBC; Fowler, *Full Fathom Five*, 180–81; Newpower, *Iron Men and Tin Fish*, 106.
11. Robert P. Beynon, *The Pearl Harbor Avenger: U.S.S. Bowfin* (Deland, Fla.: Just Books, 2002), 68; Edward L. Beach, *Salt and Steel: Reflections of a Submariner* (Annapolis, Md.: Naval Institute Press, 1999), 104–5; Winslow, *Fleet the Gods Forgot*, 27; Van der Vat, *Pacific Campaign*, 247; Roscoe, *Submarine Operations*, 261.
12. See for example William Bernard Sieglaff, interview, box 99, CBC.
13. Gannon, *Hellions of the Deep*, 85.
14. Reuben Whitaker, interview, CBC; Roscoe, *Submarine Operations*, 67; Blair, *Silent Victory*, 166.
15. USS *Sturgeon* Fourth War Patrol Report, June 30, 1942, disc 5, SM.
16. Bruce Gamble, *Darkest Hour: The True Story of Lark Force at Rabaul. Australia's Worst Military Disaster of World War II* (St. Paul, Minn.: Zenith Press, 2006), 97–98, 219, 221; Wurth, *Australia's Greatest Peril*, 84, 91; Stanley, *Invading Australia*, 93–94.
17. Interviewed in *Tragedy of the Montevideo Maru*, documentary film, 2009. Gamble questions Yamaji's veracity in *Darkest Hour*, 267.
18. *Sydney Morning Herald,* October 6, 1945, 4; *Argus,* October 6, 1945, 4; November 23, 1945, 5; Jim Ridges, People of the Plaque—*Montevideo Maru,* http://www.jje.info/lostlives/exhib/potp/monte

videomaru.html; Ian Hodges, "Remembering 1942," http://www.awm.gov.au/atwar/remembering1942/montevideo.transcript.asp; Fay Anderson and Richard Trembath, *Witness to War: The History of Australian Conflict Reporting* (Melbourne: Melbourne University Press, 2011), 171; Gamble, *Darkest Hour*, 247–48.
19. *West Australian*, May 29, 2010, 25; Gamble, *Darkest Hour*, 221.
20. Doreen Beadle quoted in *Weekend West,* June 30–July 1, 2012, 21.
21. Doreen Beadle quoted in *Weekend West,* June 30–July 1, 2012, 21.
22. Lockwood to Phyllis Lockwood, July 10, 1942, box 6, folder 20, Lockwood Papers, LC.
23. Lockwood to Vice Adm. R. S. Edwards, August 19, 1942, box 56, folder 20, CBC.
24. Murray, *Reminiscences*, 1, 188; Murray, quoted in Gerald Astor, *Crisis in the Pacific: The Battles for the Philippine Islands by the Men Who Fought Them* (New York: Donald I. Fine Books, 1996), 2.
25. Evidence of Heber McLean to Proceedings of Investigation, USS *Flier*, disc 16, SM.
26. Cairns, *Secret Fleets*, 82.
27. Norvell G. Ward, *The Reminiscences of Rear Admiral Norvell G. Ward* (Annapolis, Md.: Naval Institute Press, 1996), 205.
28. Lockwood to Vice Adm. R. S. Edwards, August 19, 1942, box 56, folder 20, CBC.
29. Reuben Whitaker, interview, CBC; Heber McLean, interview, box 98, CBC; Evidence of Heber McLean to Proceedings of Investigation, USS *Flier*, disc 16, SM.
30. James O'Rourke, "Australia the Virgin," *The XXth Century* 2 (March 1942): 202.
31. Lockwood to R. H. English, November 24, 1942; Lockwood to R. S. Edwards, November 25, 1942, box 56, folder 21, CBC.
32. Lockwood to R. S. Edwards, October 1, 1942, box 56, folder 21, CBC.
33. Chris Coulthard-Clark, "The Contribution of Industry to Navy's War in the Pacific," in *The Royal Australian Navy in World War II*, ed. David Stevens (Sydney: Allen and Unwin, 1996), 64; Kenneth D. Rose, *Myth and the Greatest Generation: A Social History of Americans in World War II* (New York: Routledge, 2008), 87–88, 94–95; Aldrich, *Faraway War*, 305.
34. McKernan, *All In*, 147, 208; Long, *Six Years War*, 161, 216; Margaret Bevege, *Behind Barbed Wire: Internment in Australia during World War II* (St. Lucia: University of Queensland Press, 1993), 159; Cairns, *Secret Fleets*, 106; Richard G. Hartley, "Technologies

of Power," in Layman, *Powering Perth*, 97, 106; Linley Batterham, "Women Munition Workers, 1943–45," in *The Workshops: A History of the Midland Government Railway Workshops*, ed. Patrick Bertola and Bobbie Oliver (Perth: University of Western Australia Press, 2006), 141; Jack Emery, "Learning a Trade: Memories of an Apprentice Turner and Iron Machinist, 1940–1945", in Oliver, *Papers in Labour History*, 19, 23.
35. Murray, *Reminiscences*, 181; Jacqui Sherriff, "Fremantle South Slipway: A Vital World War II Defence Facility," *Fremantle Studies* 2, no. 2 (2002): 106, 110; Tull, *A Community Enterprise*, 142; Cairns, *Secret Fleets*, 68.
36. Vasey, Strategic Importance of Fremantle, transcript, WAMM.
37. Jones, "Submarines in the Battle for Australia," 68.
38. Hurst, *Fourth Ally*, 69, 80; Cairns, *Secret Fleets*, 151.
39. Figures are based on Blair, *Silent Victory*, 906, 910–11, 921–23; Cairns, *Secret Fleets*, 204–12.

CHAPTER 6. CHRISTIE

1. Lockwood, *Sink 'Em All*, 68.
2. Stuart Murray, interview, CBC; Murray, *Reminiscences*, 202, 205.
3. Christie to Captain Cutts, April 28, 1942, box 1, folder 1, Christie Papers, LC.
4. Ralph Christie, interview, box 97, CBC; Newpower, *Iron Men and Tin Fish*, 27, 29; Gannon, *Hellions of the Deep*, 29, 77.
5. Lockwood to Christie, November 20, 1942, box 56, folder 21, CBC.
6. Newpower, *Iron Men and Tin Fish*, 143.
7. Reuben Whitaker, interview, CBC.
8. Christie to Adm. R. S. Edwards, August 20, 1942, box 1, folder 1, LC.
9. Christie to Vice Adm. A. S. Carpender, March 16, 1943, box 1, folder 3, LC.
10. Murray, *Reminiscences*, 179, 183.
11. Heber McLean, interview, CBC.
12. Murray, *Reminiscences*, 204–5; Chester Smith, interview, CBC.
13. Douglas A. Campbell, *Eight Survived: The Harrowing Story of the USS Flier and the Only Downed World War II Submariners to Survive and Evade Capture* (Guilford, Conn.: Lyons Press, 2010), 106.
14. Heber McLean, interview, CBC.

15. Heber McLean, interview, CBC; Tim Clayton, *Sea Wolves: The Extraordinary Story of Britain's WW2 Submariners* (London: Little, Brown, 2011), 148; Van der Vat, *Pacific Campaign*, 70; Toll, *Pacific Crucible*, 73.
16. Quoted in Steven Trent Smith, *Wolfpack: The American Submarine Strategy that Helped Defeat Japan* (Hoboken, N.J.: John Wiley and Sons, 2003), 184.
17. USS *Trout* Seventh War Patrol Report, February 14, 1943, Particulars of Attacks, disc 8, SM.
18. Lawson P. Ramage, *Reminiscences of Vice Admiral Lawson P. Ramage* (Annapolis, Md.: Naval Institute Press, 1975), 105.
19. USS *Trout* Seventh War Patrol Report, Second Endorsement, disc 8, SM.
20. Stephen L. Moore, *Battle Surface! Lawson P. "Red" Ramage and the War Patrols of the USS Parche* (Annapolis, Md.: Naval Institute Press, 2011), 7, 9–10; Blair, *Silent Victory*, 391.
21. Ramage, *Reminiscences*, 118.
22. Cairns, *Secret Fleets*, 139; John G. Mansfield Jr., *Cruisers for Breakfast: War Patrols of the U.S.S. Darter and U.S.S. Dace* (Tacoma, Wash.: Media Center Publishing, 1997), 218–19; Ernest Zellmer to author, December 21, 2010, February 2, 2011.
23. Mendenhall, *Submarine Diary*, 268–69.
24. George Grider, with Lydel Sims, *War Fish* (London: Cassell, 1959), 142.
25. Ralph Christie, interview, CBC; Homer White, memoir, file 940.5481, FCL.
26. John Bertrand, Reminiscences, transcript, WAMM; Beynon, *Pearl Harbor Avenger*, 91.
27. Thomas Dykers, interview, box 97, CBC.
28. William R. McCants, *War Patrols of the USS Flasher* (Chapel Hill: Professional Press, 1994), 119.
29. George Ridgway to author, December 13, 2011.
30. Ostlund, *Find 'Em, Chase 'Em, Sink 'Em*, 129.
31. Quoted in Barker and Jackson, *Fleeting Attraction*, 156.
32. Colton, *No Ordinary Joes*, 112.
33. King, *Stick and the Stars*, 74.

CHAPTER 7. TRAVELING NORTH

1. Figures are based on Blair, *Silent Victory*, 924–25.
2. USS *Trout* Eighth War Patrol Report, April 23, 1943, disc 8, SM.

3. USS *Trout* Eighth War Patrol Report, Second Endorsement, disc 8, SM.
4. Quoted in Blair, *Silent Victory*, 392.
5. Rupp, *Threshold of Hell*, 11.
6. Robert Goralski and Russell W. Freeburg, *Oil and War: How the Deadly Struggle for Fuel in WWII Meant Victory or Defeat* (New York: William Morrow and Company, 1987), 144–45, 193; Evan Graham, *Japan's Sea Lane Security, 1940–2004: A Matter of Life and Death?* (London: Routledge, 2006), 79; Harry Holmes, *The Last Patrol* (Annapolis, Md.: Naval Institute Press, 1994), 43–44; Larry Kimmett and Margaret Regis, *U.S. Submarines in World War II: An Illustrated History* (Seattle: Navigator Publishing, 1996), 54.
7. Blair, *Silent Victory*, 395; Arthur Hezlet, *British and Allied Submarine Operations in World War II* (Gosport: Royal Navy Submarine Museum, 2001), 218; Wilson, *A Submariners' War*, 110; Rupp, *Threshold of Hell*, 13.
8. Quoted in War Damage Report No. 58, HyperWar: US Navy in World War II, http://www.ibiblio.org/hyperwar/USN/.
9. Colton, *No Ordinary Joes*, 128–29; Rupp, *Threshold of Hell*, 8, 27; Monroe-Jones and Green, *Silent Service*, 85.
10. Quoted in Colton, *No Ordinary Joes*, 139.
11. Quoted in Rupp, *Threshold of Hell*, 1.
12. Rupp, *Threshold of Hell*, 29.
13. Rupp, *Threshold of Hell*, 73–74.
14. Stephen L. Moore, *Presumed Lost: The Incredible Ordeal of America's Submarine POWs during the Pacific War* (Annapolis, Md.: Naval Institute Press, 2009), 29, 158.
15. Holmes, *Last Patrol*, 52–54, 59–60.
16. Blair, *Silent Victory*, 284–85; Eric H. McNabb, *Pot Shot Profile 1942–1946* (Yokine, W.A.: E. N. S. McNabb, n.d.), 5.
17. Christie to Vice Adm. A. S. Carpender, April 8, 1943, box 1, folder 3, Christie Papers, LC.
18. Mendenhall, *Submarine Diary*, 46.
19. Christie to Vice Adm. A. S. Carpender, March 16, 1943, box 1, folder 3, Christie Papers, LC.
20. Lockwood to Carpender, September 8, 1942; Lockwood to Lt. Gen. Gordon Bennett, November 18, 1942, box 56, folder 21, CBC; Murray, *Reminiscences*, 198.
21. Chester Smith, interview, CBC; Ramage, *Reminiscences*, 118; USS *Trout* Ninth War Patrol Report, disc 8, SM.
22. Gomm, *Red Sun on the Kangaroo Paw*, 110, 114–15.

23. USS *Trout* Ninth War Patrol Report, Prologue; Headington, War Diary of the USS *Thresher,* USBM.
24. Christie to Lockwood, June 23, 1943, box 65, folder 6, CBC.
25. McNabb, *Pot Shot Profile*, 5; Lockwood, *Sink 'Em All*, 30.
26. Johannes Loep transcript, WAMM.
27. Wurth, *Australia's Greatest Peril*, 59; Edward Young, *Undersea Patrol* (New York: McGraw Hill, 1952),
28. Quoted in Michno, *USS Pampanito*, 297.
29. See for example Clive Taylor, A Personal Account, transcript, WAMM; E. J. Young, War Time Diary: Submarine HMS *Trenchant*, WAMM, p. 21; Arthur Richard Hezlet, interview, 12571/5, IWM.
30. Charley T. Odom, interview, 5.
31. Ramage, *Reminiscences*, 111.
32. Keith Leasure, The Odyssey of the USS *Rock* (SS 274) during WWII, USS *Rock* file, UBSM.
33. Michael Sturma, "U.S. Submarine Patrol Reports during World War II: Historical Evidence and Literary Flair," *Journal of Military History* 74, no. 2 (April 2010): 477–78.
34. Figures are based on Blair, *Silent Victory*, 924–25.

CHAPTER 8. SAILORS' WOMEN

1. Ward, *Reminiscences*, 185.
2. Quoted in Carl LaVO, *The Galloping Ghost: The Extraordinary Life of Submarine Legend Eugene Fluckey* (Annapolis, Md.: Naval Institute Press, 2007), 99.
3. Kenneth C. Ruiz with John Bruning, *The Luck of the Draw: The Memoir of a World War II Submariner* (St. Paul, Minn.: Zenith Press, 2005), 181.
4. Beach, *Salt and Steel*, 116.
5. Grider, *War Fish*, 140.
6. Christie to Lockwood, July 29, 1942, box 12, folder 63, Lockwood Papers, LC.
7. Christie to Adm. R. S. Edwards, August 20, 1942, box 1, folder 2, Christie Papers, LC.
8. Peter Schrijvers, *Bloody Pacific: American Soldiers at War with Japan* (London: Palgrave Macmillan, 2010), 153.
9. Gordon Scott to author, February 20, 2008.
10. Quoted in Cairns, *Secret Fleets*, 121.
11. Craig R. McDonald, *The USS Puffer in World War II: A History of the Submarine and Its Wartime Crew* (Jefferson, N.C.: McFarland

and Company, 2008), 245; Ron Davidson, *High Jinks at the Hot Pool: Mirror Reflects the Life of a City* (Fremantle: Fremantle Arts Centre Press, 1994), 168.
12. Peter Conole, *Protect and Serve: A History of Policing in Western Australia* (Perth: Western Australia Police Service, 2002), 241; Potts and Strauss, *Love of a Soldier*, 41; Penglase and Horner, *When the War Came to Australia*, 176.
13. Quoted in Cornish, *Western Australia*, 106.
14. Colton, *No Ordinary Joes*, 157.
15. Robyn Arrowsmith, *All the Way to the USA: Australian WWII War Brides* (Sydney: self-published, 2013), 37.
16. Quoted in Penglase and Horner, *When the War Came to Australia*, 176.
17. Headington, War Diary of the USS *Thresher*, USBM.
18. Quoted in Potts and Strauss, *Love of a Soldier*, 33.
19. Grey, *Military History of Australia*, 180; Long, *Six Years War*, 321.
20. Grider, *War Fish*, 141.
21. Davidson, *High Jinks at the Hot Pool*, 174, 179–81, 184, 200; Penglase and Horner, *When the War Came to Australia*, 174–75.
22. Don Haseley to author, March 1, 2011.
23. Ernest Zellmer to author, December 21, 2010, February 2 and 9, 2011.
24. George McPherson to author, October 22 and 24, 2010.
25. Quoted in Potts and Strauss, *Love of a Soldier*, 51.
26. Schultz and Shell, *We Were Pirates*, 169.

CHAPTER 9. HUNTER AND HUNTED

1. Stevens, *Royal Australian Navy*, 95; White, *Australian Submarines*, 168–69, 173, 175; Van der Ham, Experiences of the Dutch Submariners, transcript; Grant, "Vicissitudes of a Dutch submarine"; KIX, Dutchsubmarines; Historical war submarine found buried under sand of NSW beach, *7:30 Report*, July 1999 (transcript), http://www.abc.net.au/7:30/stories/s40419.htm.
2. Stevens, *Royal Australian Navy*, 132, 136, 148; Long, *Six Years War*, 363–64.
3. Blair, *Silent Victory*, 430–31; Lockwood, *Sink 'Em All*, 105; Roscoe, *Submarine Operations*, 258; Edwin P. Hoyt, *Bowfin: The Story of One of America's Fabled Fleet Submarines in World War II* (New York: Van Nostrand Reinhold Company, 1983), 199, 209, 217, 242;

Gannon, *Hellions of the Deep*, 89; Newpower, *Iron Men and Tin Fish*, 161.
4. Peter Padfield, *War beneath the Sea: Submarine Conflict 1939–1945* (London: Pimlico, 1997), 337; I. J. Galantin, *Take Her Deep: A Submarine against Japan in World War II* (New York: Pocket Books, 1987), 60, 99; Michno, *USS Pampanito*, 125.
5. Ralph Christie, interview, CBC.
6. Joseph F. Enright with James W. Ryan, *Shinano! The Sinking of Japan's Secret Supership* (London: The Bodley Head, 1987), 73; Carl Boyd, *American Command of the Sea: Through Carriers, Codes and the Silent Service* (Newport News, Va.: The Mariner's Museum, 1995), 21, 40, 63; Mark P. Parillo, *The Japanese Merchant Marine in World War II* (Annapolis, Md.: Naval Institute Press, 1993), 90.
7. Based on figures from Blair, *Silent Victory*, 925, 936–37.
8. USS *Bowfin* First War Patrol Report, Third Endorsement.
9. Samuel C. Grashio and Bernard Norling, *Return to Freedom: The War Memoirs of Col. Samuel C. Grashio USAF (Ret.)* (Tulsa, Okla.: MCN Press, 1982), 137.
10. Report of Special Mission, USS *Bowfin*, First War Patrol Report, disc 20, SM.
11. Edward M. Kuder with Pete Martin, "The Philippines Never Surrendered," *Saturday Evening Post*, February 10, 1945: 9–11, 57–63; February 24, 1945: 22–23, 90–93; March 3, 1945: 20, 81–84; March 10, 1945: 20, 52, 55–56, 58; John Bertrand to Edwin Hoyt, August 23, 1983, *Bowfin* Boat Book, SFM.
12. Grashio and Norling, *Return to Freedom*, 136.
13. Grashio and Norling, *Return to Freedom*, 137–38.
14. Quoted in John D. Lukacs, *Escape from Davao* (New York: Simon & Schuster, 2010), 292.
15. *Life,* February 7, 1944, 27, 111.
16. Lukacs, *Escape from Davao*, 319–20, 338.
17. Beynon, *Pearl Harbor Avenger*, 35–37; Martin Sheridan, *Overdue and Presumed Lost: The Story of the USS Bullhead* (1947; repr., Annapolis, Md.: Naval Institute Press, 2004), 45–46.
18. Quoted in Beynon, *Pearl Harbor Avenger*, 246; quoted in Blair, *Silent Victory*, 488.
19. Hoyt, *Bowfin,* 60; Beynon, *Pearl Harbor Avenger*, 87; Blair, *Silent Victory*, 489; Bart Bartholomew, The Fremantle Submarine Base, http://www.subvetpaul.com/TheFremantle.htm; Roscoe, *Submarine Operations*, 270–71.

20. Quoted in Keith, *War Beneath the Waves*, 224.
21. Alan Powell, *The Shadow's Edge: Australia's Northern War* (Melbourne: Melbourne University Press, 1988), 144.
22. Quoted in Blair, *Silent Victory*, 613.
23. Parillo, *Japanese Merchant Marine*, 110.
24. Newpower, *Iron Men and Tin Fish*, 133.
25. See Edwyn Gray, *Submarine Warriors* (1988; repr. New York: Bantam Books, 1990), 191–92; Parrish, *Submarine*, 181.
26. McDonald, *USS Puffer*, 79–80.
27. Philip Nichols, interview, box 99, CBC.
28. Ostlund, *Find 'Em, Chase 'Em, Sink 'Em*, 187.
29. Quoted in Keith, *War beneath the Waves*, 150.
30. Quoted in Blair, *Silent Victory*, 490.
31. Lockwood to Christie, September 29, 1943, box 1, folder 4, Christie Papers, LC.
32. Brian Izzard, *Gamp VC: The Wartime Story of Maverick Submariner Commander Anthony Miers* (Sparkford, Somerset: Haynes Publishing, 2009), 193, 222; Paul Chapman, *Submarine Torbay* (London: Robert Hale, 1989), 47, 148.
33. Young, *Undersea Patrol*, 200.
34. Lockwood, Memorandum for Captain Denfeld, Assistant Chief, Bureau of Navigation, box 56, folder 20, CBC.
35. Galantin, *Taker Her Deep*, 99.
36. Miers to Admiral Barry, November 11, 1943, Miers Papers, Churchill Archives Centre.
37. Lockwood to Christie, November 26, 1943, box 1, folder 5, Christie Papers, LC.
38. Miers to Admiral Barry, November 11, 1943, Miers Papers.
39. Report on patrol of *Cabrilla*, January 25, 1944, Miers Papers.
40. Roscoe, *Submarine Operations*, 272; Izzard, *Gamp VC*, 175–76; Thomas Holian, "Saviors and Suppliers: World War II Submarine Special Operations in the Philippines," *Undersea Warfare* 23 (Summer 2004):http://www.navy.mil/navydata/cno/n87/usw/issue-23/saviors.htm.
41. Miers to Admiral Barry, November 11, 1943, Miers Papers.
42. Report, 31 March 1944, Miers Papers.
43. Quoted in Izzard, *Gamp VC*, 189.
44. Anon., Submarining in the Far East—An account of a patrol from Trincomalee to Fremantle, A1989/90, RSM.

CHAPTER 10. TROUBLE IN PARADISE

1. Paul Hasluck, *The Government and People 1942–1945* (Canberra: Australian War Memorial, 1970), 56, 97, 209, 423–24; Thorne, *Allies of a Kind*, 364; McCants, *War Patrols*, 119–20; McKenzie-Smith, *Defending Fremantle*, 28–29; Long, *Six Years War*, 346–47; David Day, *Reluctant Nation: Australia and the Allied Defeat of Japan 1942–45* (Oxford: Oxford University Press, 1992), 194; Lindsay J. Peet, "The Men Who Stayed Behind," in Gregory, *On the Homefront*, 45.
2. Mary Critch, *Our Kind of War: The History of the VAD/ AAMWS* (Perth: Artlook Books Trust, 1981), 130.
3. Quoted in Day, *Reluctant Nation*, 195–96.
4. Quoted in Critch, *Our Kind of War*, 131.
5. Report re Brawl in Fremantle on 11.4.'44, Police Department, Western Australia, AN 5/3 Acc. 430 [1944] Item 1609, State Records Office of Western Australia; Conole, *Protect and Serve*, 244.
6. Field, "West of Japan," 96.
7. Ernest Zellmer to author, December 21, 2010.
8. Quoted in Campbell, *Eight Survived*, 101.
9. John E. Wallin, interview, Veterans History Project.
10. Forest J. Sterling, in Bond, *Crash Dive*, 162.
11. John Wallin, interview, Veterans History Project; Ostlund, *Find 'Em, Chase 'Em, Sink 'Em*, 397.
12. Quoted in World War II, News Clipping File, 940.5451994, FCL.
13. George McPherson to author, October 24, 2010.
14. Don Haseley to author, March 6, 2011.
15. Quoted in Michno, *USS Pampanito*, 114.
16. Schultz and Shell, *We Were Pirates*, 133.
17. Quoted in Stephen L. Moore, *War of the Wolf: Texas' Memorial Submarine World War II's Famous USS Seawolf* (Dallas: Atriad Press, 2008), 139.
18. Van Velden, "Fremantle's Forgotten Fleet," 85.
19. McDonald, *USS Puffer*, 118; Knoblock, *Black Submariners*, 108.
20. Quoted in Barker and Jackson, *Fleeting Attraction*, 198.
21. Knoblock, *Black Submariners*, 108–11; McDonald, *USS Puffer*, 117–18.
22. Moore, *War of the Wolf*, 140.
23. *West Australian*, April 14, 1942, p. 1; KXII, Dutch Submarines, http://www.dutchsubmarines.com.

24. Michno, *USS Pampanito*, 305.
25. Quoted in McDonald, *USS Puffer*, 245–46.
26. See Beryl Hackner, *Rosa: A Biography of Rosa Townsend* (Perth: University of Western Australia Press, 1994), 59; George Oliver Jones, "Jonesy's Domain," http://goliverjones.com; Schultz and Shell, *We Were Pirates*, 84–85; Wingfield, *Wingfield at War*, 89; Don Keith, *Undersea Warrior: The World War II Story of "Mush" Morton and the USS Wahoo* (New York: NALCaliber, 2011), 142.
27. Quoted in McDonald, *USS Puffer*, 173.
28. Quoted in McNabb, *Pot Shot Profile*, 7.
29. Don Haseley to author, March 6, 2011.
30. Quoted in *National Times*, February 10–15, 1975, 24.
31. Rosemary Campbell, *Heroes and Lovers: A Question of National Identity* (Sydney: Allen and Unwin, 1989), 135.
32. See, for example, Betty Goldsmith and Beryl Sandford, *The Girls They Left Behind: Life in Australia during World War II—Women Remember* (Melbourne: Penguin, 1990), 46; Connors et al., *Australia's Frontline*, 154.
33. Stephen Leal Jackson, *The Men: American Enlisted Submariners in World War II* (Indianapolis, Ind.: Dog Ear, 2010), 139.
34. "Submarine School," *Life*, March 30, 1942, 93.
35. Beach, *Salt and Steel*, 244; Beynon, *Pearl Harbor Avenger*, 51–52.
36. *Life*, March 30, 1942, 93; Lockwood, *Sink 'Em All*, 137; Roscoe, *Submarine Operations*, 88–89; LaVO, *Galloping Ghost*, 32.
37. James W. Wilkes, *Down Under: My Life as a WWII Submariner* (N.p.: Xlibris, 2007), 20.
38. Flint Whitlock and Ron Smith, *The Depths of Courage: American Submariners at War with Japan, 1941–1945* (New York: Berkley Caliber, 2007), 97; George Oliver Jones, "Jonesy's Domain," http://goliverjones.com; Ward, *Reminiscences*, 86; Jackson, *The Men*, 130.
39. Ronald H. Spector, *At War at Sea: Sailors and Naval Combat in the Twentieth Century* (New York: Viking, 2001), 113.
40. See for example Walter W. Jaffe, *Steel Shark in the Pacific: USS Pampanito SS-383* (Palo Alto, Calif.: Glencannon Press, 2001), 21; Keith, *War beneath the Waves*, 32.
41. Quoted in Stephen L. Moore, *Spadefish: On Patrol with a Top-Scoring World War II Submarine* (Dallas: Atriad Press, 2006), 68.
42. Quoted in Philip Kaplan, *Run Silent* (Annapolis, Md.: Naval Institute Press, 2002), 205.

CHAPTER 11. WAR OF ATTRITION

1. Figures are based on Blair, *Silent Victory*, 946–48.
2. Ralph Christie, interview, CBC.
3. Reuben Whitaker, interview, CBC; Steven Trent Smith, *The Rescue: A True Story of Courage and Survival in World War II* (New York: John Wiley and Sons, 2001), 188.
4. Figures are based on Blair, *Silent Victory*, 948–49.
5. Ralph Christie, interview, CBC.
6. See Lockwood, *Down to the Sea in Subs*, 299; Lockwood, *Sink 'Em All*, 180.
7. Quoted in Morison, *Two-Ocean War*, 502–3.
8. William Germershausen, interview, box 97, CBC.
9. Charles Lockwood and Hans Christian Adamson, *Through Hell and Deep Water: The Stirring Story of the Navy's Deadly Submarine, the U.S.S. Harder* (New York: Greenberg, 1956), 126–27.
10. Quoted in Alan Powell, *War by Stealth: Australians and the Allied Intelligence Bureau, 1942–1945* (Melbourne: Melbourne University Press, 1996), 173.
11. A. B. Feuer, *Commando! The M/Z Units' Secret War against Japan* (Westport, Conn.: Praeger, 1996), 38; Jack Wong Sue, *Blood on Borneo* (Perth: W.A.: Skindivers Publication, 2001), 84.
12. Evidence of Murray Tichenor, Record of Proceedings, USS *Flier*, disc 16, SM.
13. Quoted in Lockwood and Adamson, *Through Hell and Deep Water*, 277.
14. Quoted in Don Wall, *Abandoned: Australians at Sandakan, 1945* (Mona Vale, N.S.W.: D. Wall, 1990), 57.
15. Charles Lockwood and Hans Christian Adamson, *Battles of the Philippine Sea* (New York: Thomas Y. Crowell Company, 1967), 58; Ministry of Defence, *War with Japan* (London: Her Majesty's Stationery Office, 1995), vol. 4, 118.
16. Lockwood and Adamson, *Battles of the Philippine Sea*, 74; Jeffrey M. Moore, *Spies for Nimitz: Joint Military Intelligence in the Pacific War* (Annapolis, Md.: Naval Institute Press, 2004), 99; Thomas W. Zeiler, *Annihilation: A Global Military History of World War II* (Oxford: Oxford University Press, 2011), 322; Long, *Six Years War*, 359; Jürgen Rohwer, *Chronology of the War at Sea 1939–1945: The Naval History of World War Two* (London: Chatham Publishing, 2005), 325, 337.

17. David C. Evans, ed., *The Japanese Navy in World War II: In the Words of Former Japanese Naval Officers* (Annapolis, Md.: Naval Institute Press, 1986), 410; Ernest J. King and Walter Muir, *Fleet Admiral King: A Naval Record* (London: Eyre and Spottiswoode, 1953), 350; Lockwood and Adamson, *Battles of the Philippine Sea*, 130.
18. Lockwood and Adamson, *Through Hell and Deep Water*, 278; Whitlock and Smith, *Depths of Courage*, 272.
19. Lockwood and Adamson, *Through Hell and Deep Water*, 280–81; Feuer, *Commando*, 38.
20. *Daily News*, July 11, 1944, 5.
21. Politician Project, Series A3269, Control Symbol E7/A, NAA (Melbourne).
22. Smith, *Wolfpack*, 293.
23. Herman Kossler, interview, box 98–99 CBC.
24. Jonathan J. McCullough, *A Tale of Two Subs: An Untold Story of World War II, Two Sister Ships, and Extraordinary Heroism* (New York: Grand Central Publishing, 2008), 172; Boyd, *American Command of the Sea*, 36.
25. Herman Kossler, interview, CBC.
26. Vasey, Strategic Importance of Fremantle, transcript, WAMM; Creed, *Fremantle Submarine Base*, 36; Blair, *Silent Victory*, 631–32.
27. Mark P. Parillo, "The Imperial Japanese Navy in World War II," in *Reevaluating Major Naval Combatants of World War II*, ed. James J. Sadkovich (Westport, Conn.: Greenwood Press, 1990), 69.
28. See Ward, *Reminiscences*, 186; Roscoe, *Submarine Operations*, 340; Lockwood, *Sink 'Em All*, 122–23; Hezlet, *British and Allied Submarine Operations*, 345; Bernard Ireland, *Jane's Naval History of World War II* (New York: Harper Collins, 1998), 101; Holmes, *Last Patrol*, 7; Edwin P. Hoyt, *The Destroyer Killer* (New York: Pocket Books, 1989), 120; Lance E. Davis and Stanley L. Engerman, *Naval Blockade in Peace and War: An Economic History since 1750* (Cambridge: Cambridge University Press, 2012), 325; Jones and Nunan, *U.S. Subs Down Under*, 204.
29. Ship's History USS *Crevalle* (SS291), http://www.cyurban.com/~protrn/crevalle.htm; William J. Ruhe, "Wolfpack," in Bond, *Crash Dive*, 219.
30. Ruhe, "Wolfpack," 220–21.
31. USS *Flasher* Third War Patrol Report, June 22, 1944, disc 16, SM.
32. USS *Angler* Fourth War Patrol Report, June 24, 1944, disc 15, SM.

33. USS *Crevalle* Fourth War Patrol Report, June 25, 1944, disc 21, SM; Ruhe, "Wolfpack," 222–23.
34. USS *Flasher* Third War Patrol Report, June 29, July 7, July 19, 1944, First Endorsement.
35. USS *Angler* Fourth War Patrol Report, July 13 and 24, 1944.
36. McCants, *USS Flasher*, 229–30.
37. USS *Crevalle* Fourth War Patrol Report, July 25, 1944, Personnel.
38. USS *Angler* Fourth War Patrol Report, July 26, 1944.
39. USS *Crevalle* Fourth War Patrol Report, July 26, 1944.
40. USS *Flasher* Third War Patrol Report, July 26, 1944.
41. USS *Angler* Fourth War Patrol Report, July 26, 1944.
42. USS *Crevalle*, Fourth War Patrol Report, July 26, 1944.
43. Ruhe, "Wolfpack," 247–48; Ship's History USS *Crevalle* (SS 291).
44. USS *Crevalle* Fourth War Patrol Report, July 26, 1944; USS *Flasher* Third War Patrol Report, July 26, 1944.
45. USS *Crevalle* Fourth War Patrol Report, July 28, 1944.
46. USS *Angler* Fourth War Patrol Report, July 28, 1944.
47. USS *Angler* Fourth War Patrol Report, Remarks.
48. USS *Crevalle* Fourth War Patrol Report, Remarks.
49. USS *Flasher* Third War Patrol Report, Second Endorsement; USS *Crevalle* Fourth War Patrol Report, August 9, 1944, Second Endorsement; USS *Angler* Fourth War Patrol Report, Second Endorsement; McCants, *USS Flasher*, 228; Ship's History USS *Crevalle* (SS 291); Allied warships, www.uboat.net.
50. William J. Ruhe, *War in the Boats: My World War II Submarine Battles* (Washington, D.C.: Brassey's, 1994), 267–68.

CHAPTER 12. SUPPORT AND SUPPLY

1. Quoted in Campbell, *Eight Survived*, 126.
2. Potts and Strauss, *For the Love of a Soldier*, 30.
3. Hurst, *Fourth Ally*, 69; Cairns, *Secret Fleets*, 18, 75, 88.
4. Tull, *A Community Enterprise*, 142; World War II News Clippings, file 940.5451994, FCL; Jones, "Submarines in the Battle for Australia," 64; Hartley, "Technologies of Power," 97; Cairns, *Secret Fleets*, 100.
5. Potts and Strauss, *For the Love of a Soldier*, 30; Long, *Six Years War*, 216, 222, 316.
6. Tull, *A Community Enterprise*, 141.
7. McKernan, *All In*, 147, 208; Bevege, *Behind Barbed Wire*, 159; Cairns, *Secret Fleets*, 106; Long, *Six Years War*, 316.
8. Field, "West of Japan," 85.

9. Quoted in Jackson, *The Men*, 69–70.
10. Quoted in Roberts, *Sub*, 41.
11. See for example Lowder, *Batfish*, 58; *Life*, February 8, 1943, 27.
12. Trumbull, *Silversides*, 23; Knoblock, *Black Submariners*, 51; Roy Davenport, *Clean Sweep* (New York: Vantage Press, 1986), 26; Grider, *War Fish*, 194–95; Cecil Anderson, interview, August 24, 1990, OH2365/3, BL.
13. Charley T. Odom, interview, 10.
14. Max Hastings, *Retribution: The Battle for Japan, 1944–45* (New York: Alfred A. Knopf, 2008), 102.
15. USS *Sturgeon* Fourth War Patrol Report, General Remarks, disc 5, SM.
16. Headington, War Diary of the USS *Thresher*, USBM.
17. Don Keith, *In the Course of Duty: The Heroic Mission of the USS Batfish* (New York: NAL Caliber, 2005), 161; Lowder, *Batfish*, 181.
18. Quoted in Roberts, *Sub*, 41.
19. Quoted in Jaffe, *Steel Shark in the Pacific*, 114.
20. Murray, *Reminiscences*, 184; Beynon, *Pearl Harbor Avenger*, 76, 91; Ivan F. Duff, *Medical Study of the Experiences of Submariners as Recorded in 1,471 Submarine Patrol Reports in World War II* (Washington, D.C.: Bureau of Medicine and Surgery, Navy Department, 1947), 147; McCants, *USS Flasher*, 148.
21. Long, *Six Years War*, 222; Michael Bosworth, "Eating for the Nation: Food and Nutrition on the Homefront," in Gregory, *On the Homefront*, 237.
22. Thorne, *Allies of a Kind*, 645; McKernan, *All In*, 204.
23. McKernan, *All In*, 148.
24. Quoted in McDonald, *USS Puffer*, 241.
25. Johannes Loep, transcript, WAMM; Andre Bruinhout, transcript, WAMM; Barker, "Yanks in Western Australia: The Impact of United States Servicemen," 122.
26. Long, *Six Years War*, 219.
27. Cecil Anderson, interview, BL.
28. Calvert, *Silent Running*, 139–40.

CHAPTER 13. CRUEL MONTHS

1. Holmes, *Last Patrol*, 54.
2. USS *Crevalle* Fourth War Patrol Report, June 25, 1944.
3. Van der Vat, *Pacific Campaign*, 143.
4. USS *Robalo* Second War Patrol Report, April 24, 1944, disc 19, SM.

5. USS *Robalo* Second War Patrol Report, Endorsements.
6. Evidence of Heber McLean, Record of Proceedings, USS *Flier*, disc 16, SM.
7. Heber McLean, interview, CBC.
8. Stephen L. Moore, "New Light on the Last Days of the Robalo," *The Great Circle: Special Issue Submarines* 34, no. 1 (2012): 67–68, ed. Michael Sturma; Holmes, *Last Patrol*, 114; W. J. Holmes, *Undersea Victory: The Influence of Submarine Operations on the War in the Pacific* (New York: Doubleday and Company, 1966), 356.
9. Quoted in Fowler, *Full Fathom Five*, 163.
10. Moore, "Last Days of the Robalo," 70–72.
11. See Charles A. Willoughby, *The Guerrilla Resistance Movement in the Philippines: 1941–1945* (New York: Vantage Books, 1972), 159; Holmes, *Last Patrol*, 114–15.
12. Slade Cutter, *The Reminiscences of Captain Slade D. Cutter* (Annapolis, Md.: Naval Institute Press, 1985), 1; Memories of Thomas K. Kimmel, http://bergall.org/kimmel.html.
13. Record of Proceedings of an Investigation of the loss of the USS *Robalo* and the USS *Flier*.
14. Christie to Clay Blair, June 19, 1972, box 65, folder 7, CBC.
15. Evidence of John Crowley, Proceedings of an Investigation of the loss of the USS *Robalo* and the USS *Flier*.
16. *New York Times*, December 3, 1944, 31. For a full account of the *Flier*'s loss see Michael Sturma, *USS Flier: Death and Survival on a World War II Submarine* (Lexington: University of Kentucky Press, 2008).
17. Campbell, *Eight Survived*, 48, 50, 128, 174, 176.
18. Quoted in Monroe-Jones and Green, *Silent Service*, 142.
19. Feuer, *Commando*, 41.
20. Quoted in Monroe-Jones and Green, *Silent Service*, 162.
21. Evidence of Heber McLean, Proceedings of an Investigation of the loss of the USS *Robalo* and the USS *Flier*.
22. Record of Proceedings of an Investigation of the loss of the USS *Robalo* and the USS *Flier*, Finding of Facts.
23. Campbell, *Eight Survived*, 254.
24. McDonald, *USS Puffer*, 120.
25. William Croyle, "Sub's Fate Haunts Veteran: Bar Fight in WWII saved NKY Man's Life,"*Northern Kentucky News*, November 7, 2010, http://nky.cincinnati.com/.
26. Lockwood to Christie, September 3, 1944, box 65, folder 6, CBC.

27. Terry Judd, *Muskegon Chronicle*, February 9, 2010, http://www.mlive.com/news/muskegon/.
28. Quoted in Lockwood and Adamson, *Through Hell and Deep Water*, 284.
29. Bruce Teede to author, March 6–7 and May 14, 2012.
30. Kimmett and Regis, *U.S. Submarines in World War II*, 108.
31. For a detailed account of the Harder's loss see Michael Sturma, *Death at a Distance: The Loss of the Legendary USS* Harder (Annapolis, Md." Naval Institute Press, 2006), 171–80.
32. Cutter, *Reminiscences*, 52–53; Carl LaVO, *Slade Cutter: Submarine Warrior* (Annapolis, Md.: Naval Institute Press, 2003), 193.
33. Reuben Whitaker, interview, CBC; Ward, *Reminiscences*, 198.
34. Christie to Secretary of the Navy James Forrestal, July 12, 1945, box 1, folder 11, Christie Papers, LC.
35. Keith, *Undersea Warrior*, 256.
36. Cutter, *Reminiscences*, 100.
37. Quoted in Blair, *Silent Victory*, 720.
38. Christie to Mrs S. Logan, October 30, 1944, box 1, folder 10, Christie Papers, LC.
39. Figures are based on Blair, *Silent Victory*, 956–57.

CHAPTER 14. THE BRITISH ARRIVE

1. Lipscomb, *British Submarine*, 234; Powell, *Northern Voyagers*, 287–88; Hezlet, *British and Allied Submarine Operations*, 277, 316; McCartney, *British Submarines*, 42.
2. Edward Young, *One of Our Submarines* (Hertfordshire: Wordsworth Editions, 1997), 292.
3. Hezlet, *British and Allied Submarine Operations*, 317; Clayton, *Sea Wolves*, 359; Jones, "Submarines in the Battle for Australia," 77.
4. Quoted in Blair, *Silent Victory*, 742.
5. David Brown, "The Forgotten Bases: The Royal Navies in the Pacific, 1945," in Stevens, *Royal Australian Navy*, 107; Nicholas Evan Sarantakes, *Allies against the Rising Sun: The United States, the British Nations, and the Defeat of Imperial Japan* (Lawrence: University Press of Kansas, 2009), 203.
6. Quoted in Sarantakes, *Allies against the Rising Sun*, 205.
7. Peter Wood, memoir, A2007/509, RSM.
8. Admiral Barry to Miers, January 12, 1944, Miers Papers.
9. Young, *Undersea Patrol*, p. 275.

10. *The Times*, April 21, 1943, 4; Bond, *Crash Dive*, 45; Clayton, *Sea Wolves*, 49, 195.
11. Young, *One of Our Submarines*, 305.
12. Mervyn Robert George Wingfield, interview, IWM.
13. Quoted in John Parker, *The Silent Service: The Inside Story of the Royal Navy's Submarine Heroes* (London: Headline, 2001), 241.
14. King, *Stick and the Stars*, 163; Hezlet, *British and Allied Submarine Operations*, 251–52, 277, 316.
15. Albert Gillespie, Record of early life and naval career, A1986/006 RSM.
16. Clayton, *Sea Wolves*, 42–43.
17. Albert Gillespie, Record of early life, RSM.
18. Keith Nethercoate-Bryant et al., eds., *Submarine Memories: Our Time in the "Boats"* (Hadley, Sussex: Gatwick Submarine Archive, 1994), 136.
19. Quoted in Clayton, *Sea Wolves*, p. 360.
20. Quoted in Knoblock, *Black Submariners*, 50.
21. Albert Gillespie, Record of early life, RSM.
22. Homer White, memoir, FCL.
23. G. D. Cuddon, A Short History of HM Submarine Terrapin, A1983/040, RSM.
24. Ernest Zellmer to author, February 2, 2011.
25. Don Haseley to author, March 6, 2011.
26. Roy Weston, transcript, WAMM.
27. Clive Taylor, transcript, WAMM.
28. Clayton, *Sea Wolves*, 353–54; Hezlet, *British and Allied Submarine Operations*, 252.
29. Roy Weston, transcript, WAMM.
30. Roy Broome, interview, 13367/4, IWM; Brown, "The Forgotten Bases," 109; Nethercoate-Bryant et al., *More Submarine Memories*, 112, 114; Hurst, *Fourth Ally*, 113.
31. Ian Trenowden, *The Hunting Submarine: The Fighting Life of HMS Tally-Ho* (1974; repr. London: New English Library, 1976), 40, 124; Hezlet, *British and Submarine Operations*, 252, 275; Wingfield, *Wingfield at War*, 105–6.
32. Lieutenant Commander Reid, Reminiscences, transcript, WAMM.
33. Roy Broome, interview, IWM.
34. Gordon Tait, transcript, WAMM.
35. Mars, *H.M.S. Thule Intercepts*, 170.
36. Ibid., 175.

37. Roger C. Lane-Knott, transcript, WAMM.
38. Nethercoate-Bryant et al., *More Submarine Memories*, 114.
39. Peter Wood, memoir, RSM.
40. Young, *Undersea Patrol*, 273.
41. Hugh Mackenzie, interview (recorded), 11745/4, IWM.
42. Roy Broome, interview, IWM.
43. Gordon Tait, transcript, WAMM.
44. E. J. Young, War Time Diary, WAMM, 20.
45. YMCA flyer, Les Cottman Papers, courtesy of Peter Nunan.
46. Quoted in *West Australian*, October 20, 1984, News clipping file, FCL.
47. Quoted in Sarantakes, *Allies against the Rising Sun*, 201.
48. Quoted in Anne Reid, ed., *Melville Remembers: World War II City of Melville Oral History Project* (Perth: City of Melville, 1997), 45.
49. Rob Cairns, Reminiscences, transcript, WAMM.
50. J. C. Ogle to wife, June 28, 1945, Personal Letters, A1995/367/002, RSM.
51. Young, *One of Our Submarines*, 302.
52. Lieutenant Commander Reid, Reminiscences, WAMM.
53. E. J. Young, War Time Diary, WAMM, 27, 48.
54. Clayton, *Sea Wolves*, 378, 386.
55. Hugh Mackenzie, interview, IWM.
56. Ibid.; Roger C. Lane-Knott, transcript, WAMM.

CHAPTER 15. ADJUSTMENTS AND SPECIAL MISSIONS

1. Arthur Richard Hezlet, interview, IWM; Hezlet, *British and Allied Submarine Operations*, 319; David A. Thomas, *Submarine Victory: The Story of British Submarines in World War II* (London: William Kimber, 1961), 184, 203.
2. Clive Taylor, transcript, WAMM.
3. Quoted in Powell, *War by Stealth*, 132.
4. Quoted in Cairns, *Secret Fleets*, 172.
5. Anon., Submarining in the Far East, RSM.
6. Clive Taylor, transcript, WAMM; Hezlet, *British and Allied Submarine Operations*, 319; Young, *Undersea Patrol*, 285; Albert Gillespie, Record of early life, RSM.
7. Elke Scholte, interview (recorded), 14585/5, IWM.
8. Hezlet, *British and Allied Submarine Operations*, 319–20.

9. Clayton, *Sea Wolves*, 359; McCartney, *British Submarines*, 42; Thomas, *Submarine Victory*, 199–200; Hezlet, *British and Allied Submarine Operations*, 321, 346.
10. Wingfield, *Wingfield at War*, 53, 59; Richard Compton-Hall, *The Underwater War 1939–1945* (Poole, Dorset: Blandford Press, 1982), 84.
11. Clayton, *Sea Wolves*, 65, 352.
12. McCartney, *British Submarines*, 41; Hezlet, *British and Allied Submarine Operations*, 277; Trenowden, *Hunting Submarine*, 161.
13. Nethercoate-Bryant et al., *More Submarine Memories*, 21; Mars, *H.M.S. Thule Intercepts*, 185; Arthur Richard Hezlet, interview, IWM.
14. McCartney, *British Submarines*, 42; Jan van Hattam, transcript, WAMM; Blair, *Silent Victory*, 743; Van Ewijk, "History of the Dutch Submarine Force," 83; Lockwood, *Sink 'Em All*, 226; Australian War Memorial, http://www.awm.gov.au; Zwaardvis, Dutch Submarines, http://www.dutchsubmarines.com; "World War II U-Boat Found with Skeletons," ABC News, http://abcnews.go.com/International/world-war-ii-boat-found-skeletons/.
15. Wilson, *A Submariners' War*, 158.
16. King, *Stick and the Stars*, 162.
17. Ronald McKie, *The Heroes* (Sydney: Angus and Robertson, 1960), 199; Roger C. Lane-Knott, transcript, WAMM; Cairns, *Secret Fleets*, 143; Hezlet, *British and Allied Submarine Operations*, 280; Lynette Ramsay Silver, *The Heroes of Rimau* (Birchgrove, N.S.W.: Sally Milner Publishing, 1990), 102; Gomm, *Red Sun on the Kangaroo Paw*, 121.
18. Quoted in Powell, *War by Stealth*, 123.
19. G. B. Courtney, *Silent Feet: The History of "Z" Special Operations 1942–1945* (Melbourne: R. J. and S. P. Austin, 1993), 7.
20. Creed, *Fremantle Submarine Base*, 44; Powell, *War by Stealth*, 197; Parker, *Silent Service*, 251–52; Roger C. Lane-Knott, transcript, WAMM; Cairns, *Secret Fleets*, 158; Hezlet, *British and Allied Submarine Operations*, 280.
21. Thomas, *Submarine Victory*, 182; King, *Stick and the Stars*, 172; Parker, *Silent Service*, 251–52.
22. Cairns, *Secret Fleets*, 159–60; Hezlet, *British and Allied Submarine Operations*, 318; Roger C. Lane-Knott, transcript, WAMM; Hugh Mackenzie, interview, IWM.
23. Quoted in Roger C. Lane-Knott, transcript, WAMM.
24. Courtney, *Silent Feet*, 152.

25. King, *Stick and the Stars*, 172.
26. Ibid., 164.

CHAPTER 16. BATTLE OF LEYTE GULF

1. Grider, *War Fish*, 139–40.
2. USS *Hawkbill* First War Patrol Report, October 7, 1944, disc 24, SM.
3. Grider, *War Fish*, 142–44.
4. Department of Veteran Affairs, *Royal Australian Navy 1939–1945: Australians in the Pacific War* (Canberra: Department of Veteran Affairs, 2005), 22.
5. Evan Thomas, *Sea of Thunder: Four Commanders and the Last Great Naval Campaign 1941–1945* (New York: Simon & Schuster, 2006), 6; Zeiler, *Annihilation*, 362.
6. Astor, *Crisis in the Pacific*, 283.
7. Tomiji Koyanagi, "The Battle of Leyte Gulf," in Evans, ed., *The Japanese Navy in World War II*, 363.
8. Thomas, *Sea of Thunder*, 190.
9. Quoted in Astor, *Crisis in the Pacific*, 287.
10. Quoted in Aldrich, *Faraway War*, 483.
11. Astor, *Crisis in the Pacific*, 286; E. B. Potter and Chester W. Nimitz, eds., *The Great Sea War: The Story of Naval Action in World War II* (Englewood Cliffs, N.J.: Prentice Hall, 1960), 375.
12. Ernest L. Schwab, "The Saga of the 'Double Ds,'" *Naval History* 8, no. 5 (September/October 1994), 20.
13. Jones and Nunan, *U.S. Subs Down Under*, 228; Mansfield, *Cruisers for Breakfast*, 179, 182.
14. Narrative by Commander D. H. McClintock, recorded March 9, 1945, disc 13, SM.
15. Ibid.
16. USS *Darter* Fifth War Patrol Report, Second Endorsement, disc 13, SM.
17. Quoted in Roscoe, *Submarine Operations*, 399.
18. Morison, *Two-Ocean War*, 505; Thomas, *Sea of Thunder*, 322; Van der Vat, *Pacific Campaign*, 362.
19. Parillo, "The Imperial Japanese Navy," in Sadkovich, *Reevaluating Major Naval Combatants*, 64; Parillo, *Japanese Merchant Marine*, 42; Morison, *Two-Ocean War*, 496; Antony Beevor, *The Second World War* (New York: Little, Brown and Company, 2012), 632; L. D. Meo, *Japan's Radio War on Australia 1941–1945* (Melbourne: Melbourne University Press, 1968), 85; Robert Guillain,

I Saw Tokyo Burning: An Eyewitness Narrative from Pearl Harbor to Hiroshima, trans. William Byron (New York: Doubleday, 1981), 168.
20. Quoted in Scot, *War Below*, 257.
21. Long, *Six Years War*, 360.
22. Ralph Christie, interview, CBC; Wurth, *Australia's Greatest Peril*, 313–14.
23. McCants, *USS Flasher*, 286; Grider, *War Fish*, 142.
24. Quoted in McCants, *USS Flasher*, 176.
25. Grider, *War Fish*, 146–47.
26. Ibid., 154.
27. USS *Flasher* Fifth War Patrol Report, December 4, 1944, disc 16, SM; Roscoe, *Submarine Operations*, 430; Blair, *Silent Victory*, 796.
28. USS *Flasher* Fifth War Patrol Report, December 22, 1944, disc 16, SM.
29. Quoted in Blair, *Silent Victory*, 799; USS *Flasher* Fifth War Patrol Report, First Endorsement, disc 16, SM.
30. Figures are based on Blair, *Silent Victory*, 956–57, 961–62, 966.
31. Joel Holwitt, "Unrestricted Submarine Victory: The U.S. Submarine Campaign against Japan," in *Commerce Raiding: Historical Case Studies, 1755–2009*, ed. Bruce A. Elleman and S. C. M. Paine (Newport, R.I.: Naval War College Press, 2013), 234.

CHAPTER 17. TRANSITIONS

1. *Sunday Times* (Perth), July 23, 1944, 2; Grider, *War Fish*, 145, 190–91.
2. Roscoe P. Thompson to author, October 9, 2002.
3. Mars, *H.M.S. Thule Intercepts*, 175.
4. William Raymond Lawrie, interview, April 12, 1994, OH, FCL.
5. Cairns, *Secret Fleets*, 128.
6. David Blamey, Reminiscences 1941–1945, A1996/075, RSM.
7. Nethercoate-Bryant et al., *More Submarine Memories*, 67; Chapman, *Submarine Torbay*, 163; Mendenhall, *Submarine Diary*, 154, 167, 270.
8. "Australian Wives," *Life*, July 10, 1944, 43, 50.
9. Ibid., 45, 50.
10. USS *Crevalle* Fourth War Patrol Report, Personnel; USS *Crevalle* Fifth War Patrol Report, September 11, 1944, and First Endorsement; Ralph Christie, interview, CBC; Blair, *Silent Victory*, 735–36; Roscoe, *Submarine Operations*, 357; Cairns, *Secret Fleets*, 124; Smith, *The Rescue*, 291.

11. Fife, Reminiscences, 405.
12. Quoted in William Tuohy, *The Bravest Man: The Story of Richard O'Kane and U.S. Submariners in the Pacific War* (2001; repr., New York: Ballantine Books, 2006), 303.
13. Fife, Reminiscences, 406; Gerald E. Wheeler, *Kinkaid of the Seventh Fleet: A Biography of Admiral Thomas C. Kinkaid* (Washington, D.C.: Naval Historical Center, 1995), 374.
14. Quoted in Blair, *Silent Victory*, 814.
15. Christie to Rear Adm. L. E. Denfeld, December 4, 1944, Correspondence, box 1, folder 10, Christie Papers, LC.
16. King and Muir, *Fleet Admiral King*, 14.
17. Christie to Clay Blair, June 20, 1972, box 65, folder 7, CBC.
18. Lord Mayor, Perth, to Christie, January 8, 1945, Correspondence, box 1, folder 10, Christie Papers, LC.
19. Ralph Christie, interview, CBC.
20. Fife, Reminiscences, 4, 8, 15, 71; Astor, *Crisis in the Pacific*, 2.
21. Heber McLean, interview, CBC.
22. Leon Huffman, interview, box 97, CBC.
23. T. S. Louch, *The History of the Weld Club* (Perth: Weld Club, 1980), 150.
24. John Coote, *Submariner* (New York: W. W. Norton, 1991), vii; Fife, Reminiscences, 129–31.
25. Young, *Undersea Patrol*, 276; Young, *One of Our Submarines*, 305.
26. Philip Towle, Margaret Kosuge, and Yoichi Kibata, eds., *Japanese Prisoners of War* (London: Hambledon and London, 2000), 38–40, 99, 176.
27. Lockwood, *Sink 'Em All*, 216; Michno, *USS Pampanito*, 5.
28. Raymond Lamont-Brown, *Ships from Hell: Japanese War Crimes on the High Seas* (Thrupp-Stroud, Gloustershire: Sutton, 2002), 151.
29. Arthur Bancroft, interview, 23824/16, IWM.
30. Michno, *USS Pampanito*, 201–204.
31. USS *Pampanito* Third War Patrol Report, September 15, 1944, disc 25, SM.
32. USS *Pampanito* Third War Patrol Report, September 15, 1944.
33. Quoted in Michno, *USS Pampanito*, 236.
34. USS *Pampanito*, Rescue of British and Australian Prisoners-of-War, Series MP1049/5, Control Symbol 1951/2/99, NAA (Melbourne).
35. *West Australian*, October 13, 1944, 4; Bonney to Lt. Wilson, October 16, 1944, Series MP1049/5, Control Symbol 1951/2/99, NAA, Melbourne; *Argus* (Melbourne), November 18, 1944, 1.

36. Australian PW Survivors ex *Rakuyo Maru*, Series MP279/8, Control Symbol 44/431, NAA, Melbourne.
37. Landon Davis, Oral History, Naval History and Heritage Command, http://www.history.navy.mil/research/library/online-reading-room/title-list-alphabetically/r/recollections-of-uss-pampanito-rescue-of-prison-ship.html.
38. Quoted in Jaffe, *Steel Shark in the Pacific*, 108.
39. Quoted in Aldona Sendzikas, *Lucky 73: USS Pampanito's Unlikely Rescue of Allied POWs in WWII* (Gainesville: University Press of Florida, 2010), 221.
40. Quoted in Michno, *USS Pampanito*, 302.
41. Ibid., 305–6.
42. *Navy News*, November 5, 1982; Hezlet, *British and Allied Submarine Operations*, 322; Cairns, *Secret Fleets*, 168–69.
43. Quoted in Fremantle Harbour Fire, http://home.vincent.net.au/~mildura/war_years_2.htm.
44. Tull, *A Community Enterprise*, 144; David Brown, ed., *The British Pacific and the East Indies Fleets: 'The Forgotten Fleets' 50th Anniversary* (Liverpool: Brodie Publishing, 1995), 59.
45. Quoted in Michno, *USS Pampanito*, 371.

CHAPTER 18. TRIBULATIONS

1. Elke Scholte, interview, 14585/5, IWM; Dutch Submarines, http://www.dutchsubmarines.com.
2. Siem Spruijt, "3rdWar Patrol of O-19," http://www.dutchsubmarines.com/specials/special_3patrolo19.htm.
3. USS *Bream* Fifth War Patrol Report, March 7, 1945, disc 15, SM.
4. USS *Bream* Fifth War Patrol Report, March 13, 1945.
5. USS *Bream* Fifth War Patrol Report, March 14, 1945; John D. Alden and Craig R. McDonald, *United States and Allied Submarine Successes in the Pacific and Far East during World War II* (Jefferson, N.C.: McFarland, 2009), 274.
6. Special Mission Report, USS *Bream* Fifth War Patrol Report; War Crimes, Series MP 742/1, Control 336/1/1939, NAA, Melbourne.
7. USS *Bream* Fifth War Patrol Report, March 16, 1945.
8. Special Mission Report, USS *Bream* Fifth War Patrol Report.
9. Courtney, *Silent Feet*, 145; Silver, *Heroes of Rimau*, 170.
10. War Crimes, Series MP 742/1, Control 336/1/1939.
11. Alexander I. Hughes, diary, June 12, 1945, Private Papers, 2222, IWM.

12. Barbara Winter, "The Intrigue Master: Commander R. B. M. Long of Naval Intelligence," in Stevens, *Royal Australian Navy*, 146.
13. Hezlet, *British and Allied Submarine Operations*, 320; Michno, *USS Pampanito*, 329–31; Jaffe, *Steel Shark in the Pacific*, 119, 122–23.
14. Chester Smith, interview, CBC; William Hazzard, interview, box 97, CBC; Blair, *Silent Victory*, 846.
15. Zellmer to author, February 2, 2011.
16. Sheridan, *Overdue and Presumed Lost*, 99.
17. Lockwood, *Sink 'Em All*, 334–35; Leon Huffman, interview, CBC; Gugliotta, *Pigboat 39*, 212–13.
18. Murfett, *Naval Warfare*, 422.
19. Figure is based on Blair, *Silent Victory*, 971–72.
20. Lockwood Memorandum, September 10, 1942, box 56, folder 21, CBC.
21. Quoted in Moore, *War of the Wolf*, 259.
22. Lockwood to R. S. Edwards, November 25, 1942, box 56, folder 21, CBC.
23. Michael Sturma, *Surface and Destroy: The Submarine Gun War in the Pacific* (Lexington: University Press of Kentucky, 2012), 179–81.

CHAPTER 19. COOPERATION AT SEA

1. Fife, Reminiscences, 268, 415, 422; Monroe-Jones and Green, *Silent Service*, 182.
2. Quoted in Blair, *Silent Victory*, 851.
3. Stevens, *Royal Australian Navy*, 107; McCartney, *British Submarines*, 43.
4. George Harry Joseph Redman, interview, 17938/4, IWM; Thomas, *Submarine Victory*, 204; Lipscomb, *The British Submarine*, 244; Hezlet, *British and Allied Submarine Operations*, 334.
5. Clayton, *Sea Wolves*, 377.
6. Albert Gillespie, Record of early life, RSM; Alastair Mars, *British Submarines at War 1939–1945* (London: William Kimber, 1971), 224.
7. Monthly General Letter for July 1945—From Captain, 8th Submarine Flotilla, Depot Ship *Maidstone*, A1945/006, RSM.
8. E. J. Young, War Time Diary, WAMM, 34.
9. Monthly General Letter for July 1945, *Maidstone*, RSM.
10. Cuddon, History of *Terrapin*, A1983/040, RSM.
11. Hezlet, *British and Allied Submarine Operations*, 338.
12. Nethercoate-Bryant et al., *More Submarine Memories*, 115–16.

13. Don Haseley to author, March 6, 2011.
14. USS *Cavalla* Fifth War Patrol Report, May 21, 1945, disc 15, SM.
15. Quoted in Nethercoate-Bryant et al., *More Submarine Memories*, 116.
16. History of USS *Cavalla* (SS 244), disc 15, SM; Cuddon, History of *Terrapin*, RSM.
17. Quoted in Nethercoate-Bryant et al., *More Submarine Memories*, 116.
18. Quoted in History of USS *Cavalla*.
19. Don Haseley to author, March 6, 2011.
20. Quoted in Nethercoate-Bryant et al., *More Submarine Memories*, 116.
21. Cuddon, History of *Terrapin*, RSM.
22. Roy Broome, interview, IWM; Arthur Richard Hezlet, interview, IWM.
23. E. J. Young, War Time Diary, WAMM, 21; Arthur Richard Hezlet, interview, IWM; S. Woodbury Kirby, *The War Against Japan*, vol. 5: *The Surrender of Japan* (London: Her Majesty's Stationery Office, 1969), 59.
24. Arthur Richard Hezlet, interview, IWM; Clayton, *Sea Wolves*, 378–79; Thomas, *Submarine Victory*, 204; Lockwood, *Sink 'Em All*, 330–31; Roy Broome, interview, IWM; Roger C. Lane-Knott, transcript, WAMM.
25. Kirby, *War Against Japan*, vol. 5, 59; Mars, *British Submarines*, 227–29; Brown, *British Pacific*, 16, 64, 103; Compton-Hall, *Underwater War*, 112; Murfett, *Naval Warfare*, 444.
26. E. J. Young, War Time Diary, WAMM, 32; Clayton, *Sea Wolves*, 378.
27. Izzard, *Gamp VC*, 197.
28. Roy Broome, interview, IWM.
29. Roger C. Lane-Knott, transcript, WAMM.
30. Peter Wood, memoir, RSM.
31. Peter Wood, memoir, RSM; Hezlet, *British and Allied Submarine Operations*, 341.
32. Arthur Richard Hezlet, interview, IWM; Hezlet, *British and Allied Submarine Operations*, 341.
33. Siem Spruijt, "Fatal War Patrol of O 19," http://www.dutchsubmarines.com/specials/special_fatalpratrolo19.htm; Leo Charles Davenport, interview, IWM; Elke Scholte, interview, IWM.
34. Leo Charles Davenport, interview, 13945/5, IWM.

35. USS *Cod* Seventh War Patrol Report, July 8, 1945, disc 12, SM.
36. USS *Cod* Seventh War Patrol Report, July 9, 1945.
37. Spruijt, "Fatal War Patrol of O 19."
38. USS *Cod* Seventh War Patrol Report, July 10, 1945.
39. Brown, *British Pacific*, 18, 108; Leo Charles Davenport, interview, IWM; Elke Scholte, interview, IWM.
40. USS *Cod* Seventh War Patrol Report, August 3, 1945.
41. Jan van Hattam, transcript, WAMM; Joe Paquin, Reminiscences, transcript, WAMM.
42. Don Keith, *Final Patrol: True Stories of World War II Submarines* (New York: NAL Caliber, 2006), 53; Leo Charles Davenport, interview, IWM.

CHAPTER 20. WAR'S END

1. Fife, Reminiscences, 438; Blair, *Silent Victory*, 856; Sheridan, *Overdue and Presumed Lost*, 126.
2. Quoted in Sheridan, *Overdue and Presumed Lost*, 127.
3. Ibid., 4, 126; Blair, *Silent Victory*, 841.
4. McDonald, *USS Puffer*, 257; Roscoe, *Submarine Operations*, 489; Creed, *Fremantle Submarine Base*, 40; Blair, *Silent Victory*, 856.
5. McDonald, *USS Puffer*, 251–52.
6. Ministry of Defence, *War with Japan*, vol. 5, 85.
7. Van der Vat, *Pacific Campaign*, 377.
8. Herman Kossler, interview, CBC.
9. E. J. Young, War Time Diary, WAMM, 50–51.
10. The same cable fetched over $20,000 at auction in 2012; *Weekend West*, August 18–19, 2012, 46.
11. J. S. Stevens, *Never Volunteer: A Submariner's Scrapbook* (self-published, 1971), 69; Cairns, *Secret Fleets*, 175.
12. Mars, *H.M.S. Thule Intercepts*, 223; Clayton, *Sea Wolves*, 381.
13. Edward R. Lloyd to Harvey Dodson, December 16, 1994, USS *Cabrilla* File, UBSM.
14. Ibid.; On Eternal Patrol, http://www.oneternalpatrol.com.
15. Quoted in Beevor, *Second World War*, 775.
16. Murray, *Reminiscences*, 258, 277.
17. Vasey, Strategic Importance of Fremantle, transcript, WAMM; Jones, "Submarines in the Battle for Australia," 81; Morison, *Two-Ocean War*, 493; Holwitt, "Unrestricted Submarine Victory," 235; Davis and Engerman, *Naval Blockades in Peace and War*, 322.
18. Quoted in Colton, *No Ordinary Joes*, 281.

19. Rupp, *Threshold of Hell*, 176.
20. Mansfield, *Cruisers for Breakfast*, 206.
21. Quoted in Colton, *No Ordinary Joes*, 348.
22. Moore, *Presumed Lost*, 291; Blair, *Silent Victory*, 397; Colton, *No Ordinary Joes*, 361–62; Clayton, *Sea Wolves*, 382.
23. Quoted in Jackson, *The Men*, 105.
24. Ruiz, *Luck of the Draw*, 265.
25. Charley T. Odom, interview, 13.
26. R. J. Hughes, *Surviving the Flier: Based on the True Story* (Muncie, Ind.: Phoenix Flair Press, 2010), 244.
27. Quoted in Parker, *Silent Service*, 267.
28. Submariners Association, Obituary, http/www.submarinerassociation.co.uk.
29. *West Australian*, September 1, 1945, 6.
30. Stevens, *Never Volunteer*, 68; Hezlet, *British and Allied Submarine Operations*, 344.
31. Roger C. Lane-Knott, transcript, WAMM; George Harry Joseph Redman, interview, IWM.
32. Albert Gillespie, Record of early life, RSM.
33. Ibid.
34. See Sarantakes, "One Last Crusade," 433.
35. David Horner, *High Command: Australia's Struggle for an Independent War Strategy 1939–1945* (Sydney: Allen and Unwin, 1992), xxiii.
36. Penglase and Horner, *When the War Came to Australia*, 168.

EPILOGUE

1. Roscoe P. Thompson to author, October 9, 2002.
2. Ernest Zellmer to author, February 2, 2011.
3. Potts and Strauss, *For the Love of a Soldier*, 69; Arrowsmith, *All the Way to the USA*, 74, 83, 86, 88, 122.
4. Colton, *No Ordinary Joes*, 293, 318, 321.
5. Ibid., 305.
6. World War II, News Clipping file, FCL.
7. *Sydney Morning Herald*, October 28, 1944, 1.
8. George Ridgway to author, December 13, 2011; Richard J. Lanigan, *Kangaroo Express: The Epic Story of the Submarine Growler* (Laurel, Fla.: RJL Express Publications, 1998), 165; Roscoe P. Thompson to author, October 9, 2002; Cairns, *Secret Fleets*, 79.
9. Bruce Teede to author, March 6, 2012, April 22, 2012.

10. Gregory, *On the Homefront*, 115; Bruce Teede to author, April 12, 2012.
11. Clayton, *Sea Wolves*, 364.
12. Roy Weston, transcript, WAMM; World War II, News Clipping File, FCL.
13. Cairns, *Secret Fleets*, 128.
14. Johannes Loep, transcript, WAMM.
15. Herman Kossler, interview, CBC.
16. Michno, *USS Pampanito*, 370, 392.
17. Ken Henry and Don Keith, *Gallant Lady: A Biography of the USS Archerfish* (New York: Tom Doherty Associates, 2004), 278–79.
18. Paul Sample, "Submarine Warfare," *Life*, December 27, 1943, 56.
19. John Winton, *The Forgotten Fleet: The British Navy in the Pacific 1944-1945* (New York: Coward-McCann, 1970), 263.

Bibliography

ARCHIVAL SOURCES

American Heritage Center, Laramie, Wyoming

Clay Blair Collection: Papers

Charles A. Lockwood Correspondence, January—August 1942, box 56, folder 20.
Administration of the Pacific Fleet Submarine Force (Charles A. Lockwood) September–December 1942, box 56, folder 21.
Administration of the U.S. Pacific Fleet Submarine Force—Charles A. Lockwood, box 57, folder 3.
Rear Adm. Ralph Waldo Christie, box 65, folder 6.
US Submarine Operations—Fremantle, box 82, folder 6.
Fremantle 1944–1945, box 82, folder 7.
U.S. Submarine Squadron Organization War Diary, box 83, folder 3.
Australia January 1943—March 1945, box 83, folder 5.
Task Force Seventeen, July—December 1944, box 84, folder 2.

Clay Blair Collection: Recorded Interviews

Charles Herbert Andrews interview, box 96.
Creed Burlingame interview, box 96.
Ralph Christie interview, box 97.
John Coye interview, box 97.
Roy Davenport interview, box 97.
Lawrence Daspit interview, box 98.
Robert Dornin interview, box 97.
Thomas Dykers interview, box 97.
Frank Lynch interview, box 98.
Malcolm Garrison interview, box 97.
William Germershausen interview, box 97.
Elton W. Grenfell interview, box 97.
William Hazzard interview, box 97.
Leon Huffman interview, box 97.
William T. Kinsella interview, box 98.
Oliver Kirk interview, box 97.
Herman Kossler interview, box 98–99.
Mrs. Charles Lockwood interview, box 97.
Charles Loughlin interview, box 98.

Frank Lynch interview, box 98.
John McCain interview, box 98.
Allan McCann interview, box 97–98.
Heber McLean interview, box 97–98.
Stuart Murray interview, box 98.
Philip Nichols interview, box 99.
Lewis Parks interview, box 98–99.
William Post interview, box 99.
Lawson Ramage interview, box 99.
Eli Reich interview, box 99.
William Bernard Sieglaff interview, box 99.
Chester Smith interview, box 99.
Frederick Warder interview, box 99.
Reuben Whitaker interview, box 99.

Battye Library of West Australian History, Perth
Cecil Anderson interview, August 24, 1990, OH2365/3.

Center for the Study of War and Society, University of Tennessee, Knoxville
Charley T. Odom interview (transcript).

Charles Darwin University, Darwin
Rowan E. Waddy, "A Submarine Adventure in the South China Sea, 1944." Unpublished manuscript, 1992.

Churchill Archives Centre, Cambridge, England
Papers of Rear Admiral Sir Anthony Miers, 1942–1944.

Columbia University, Oral History Research Office, New York
The Reminiscences of James Fife, Oral History Memoir (transcript).

Fremantle City Library, Western Australia
Homer White, memoir, file 940.5481.
World War II, news clippings, file 940.540994.

Oral History Collection
Phyllis May Atkinson interview, May 29, 1985, OH8515.
Robert Chilcott interview, February 1985, OH8548.
William Raymond Lawrie interview, April 12, 1994, OH.
Mavis Wright interview, July 27, 1981, OH/WRI.

Imperial War Museum, London
Alexander I. Hughes, private papers, 2222.

Recorded Interviews
Arthur Bancroft interview, 23824/16.
Roy Broome interview, 13367/4.

Leo Charles Davenport interview, 13945/5.
Arthur Richard Hezlet interview, 12571/5.
Hugh Mackenzie interview, 11745/4.
George Harry Joseph Redman interview, 17938/4.
Elke Scholte interview, 14585/5.
Mervyn Robert George Wingfield interview, 9153/5.

Library of Congress, Washington, D.C.
Ralph W. Christie Papers, correspondence, 1941–1945.
Charles Lockwood Papers, correspondence and diaries.
John E. Wallin, interview (audio-visual), Veterans History Project.

National Archives of Australia (Canberra)
Report of Attack on U.S. Submarine by Hudson Aircraft A16-122 on 4th March 1942, Series A1196, control symbol 60/501/97.
War Cabinet Minute No 3849—Prisoners of war recovered from Japanese vessel torpedoed by US submarine, Series A2676, control symbol 3849 (digital copy).
War Cabinet Minute No 3912—Prisoners of war rescued from torpedoed Japanese transport, Series A2676, control symbol 3912 (digital copy).

National Archives of Australia (Melbourne)
Australian POW Far East—survivors ex-Rakuyo Maru, Series MP729/8, control symbol 44/431/73 (digital copy).
Ex Prisoners of War rescued from Japanese Transport "Rykuyo Maru," Series MP1049/5, control symbol 1951/2/72.
Politician Project, Series A3269, control symbol E7/A.
Prisoners of War rescued from torpedoed Japanese Transport, "Rykuyo Maru," Series MP1049/5, control symbol 1951/2/99.
War Crimes, Series MP 742/1, control symbol 336/1/1939.

Royal Submarine Museum, Gosport, England
Anon., Submarining in the Far East—An account of a patrol from Trincomalee to Fremantle, A1989/90.
David Blamey, reminiscences 1941–1945, A1996/075.
G. D. Cuddon, A Short History of HM Submarine Terrapin, A1983/040.
Albert Gillespie, Record of early life and naval career, A1986/006.
Monthly General Letter for July 1945—From Captain, 8th Submarine Flotilla, Depot Ship HMS Maidstone, A1945/006.
Maidstone Souvenir 1938–45, A2007/1312.
J. C. Ogle, personal letters, A1995/367/002.
Peter Wood, memoir, A2007/509.

State Records Office of Western Australia, Perth
Report re brawl in Fremantle on 11.4.'44, Police Department, Western Australia, AN 5/3 Acc. 430 [1944], item 1609.

Submarine Force Museum, Groton, Connecticut
Bowfin Boat Book.
Gar Boat Book.
Sargo Boat Book.
Skipjack Boat Book.

USS *Bowfin* Submarine Museum, Pearl Harbor, Hawaii
Georgia Jensen Blosil, "On the Loss of James Ralph Jensen," unpublished typescript, 1997.
Claude D. Elder, "Claude Elder's Stay," *Badger State Newsletter,* July/August 1996, USS *Kingfish* (SS 234) file.
Wes Headington, War Diary of the USS *Thresher*, USS *Thresher* (SS 200) file.
Keith Leasure, The Odyssey of the USS *Rock* (SS 274) during WWII, USS *Rock* (SS 274) file.
Edward R. Lloyd to Harvey Dodson, December 16, 1944, USS *Cabrilla* (SS 288) file.

U.S. Submarine War Patrol Reports
(Originally held by the U.S. National Archives and Records Administration, College Park, Maryland, the following reports and papers were accessed on DVDs produced by Submarine Memorabilia.)
USS *Angler* Fourth War Patrol Report, disc 15.
USS *Bowfin* First War Patrol Report, disc 20.
USS *Bream* Fifth War Patrol Report (with Special Mission Report), disc 15.
USS *Cavalla* Fifth War Patrol Report, disc 15.
History of USS *Cavalla* (SS 244), disc 15.
USS *Charr* First War Patrol Report, disc 24.
USS *Cod* Sixth–Seventh War Patrol Reports, disc 12.
USS *Crevalle* Fourth–Fifth War Patrol Report, disc 21.
USS *Dace* Fifth War Patrol Report, disc 16.
USS *Darter* Fourth War Patrol Report, disc 13.
Narrative by Commander D. H. McClintock, recorded March 9, 1945, disc 13.
USS *Flasher* Third, Fifth–Sixth War Patrol Reports, disc 16.
USS *Flier* First War Patrol Report, disc 16.
Record of Proceedings of an Investigation to investigate the circumstances connected with the loss of the U.S.S. *Robalo* and the loss of the U.S.S. *Flier*, USS *Flier*, disc 16.

USS *Hawkbill* First War Patrol Report, disc 24.
USS *Pampanito* Third–Fourth War Patrol Reports, disc 25.
USS *Robalo* Second War Patrol Report, disc 19.
USS *Sargo* First–Third War Patrol Reports, disc 6.
USS *Searaven* Third War Patrol Report, disc 7.
History of USS *Searaven* (SS 196), disc 7.
USS *Snapper* Second War Patrol Report, disc 5.
History of USS *Snapper* (SS 185), disc 5.
USS *Sturgeon* Fourth War Patrol Report, disc 5.
History of USS *Sturgeon* (SS 187), disc 5.
USS *Thresher,* Report of Special Mission, Ninth War Patrol, disc 8.
USS *Trout* Seventh–Ninth War Patrol Reports, disc 8.

Western Australia Maritime Museum, Fremantle
E. J. Young, War Time Diary: Submarine HMS *Trenchant*.

Transcripts of International Submarine Convention, March 1995
John Bertrand, reminiscences.
Roy Broome, reminiscences.
Andre Bruinhout, Andre's recollections of Fremantle.
Rob Cairns, reminiscences.
Hans van der Ham, The Experiences of the Dutch Submariners Operating out of Australia during the Second World War.
Jan van Hattam, untitled.
Roger C. Lane-Knott, untitled.
Johannes Loep, untitled.
Corwin Mendenhall, Retreat from Manila to Fremantle and then the advance from Fremantle to Japan.
Joe Paquin, reminiscences.
Lieutenant Commander Reid, reminiscences.
Gordon Tait, untitled.
Clive Taylor, A Personal Account.
Lloyd R. "Joe" Vasey, The Strategic Importance of Fremantle 1945–95: Reflections on Submarine Warfare in WWII and in the Future.
Roy Weston, untitled.

PERSONAL COMMUNICATIONS

Henry Albertine to author, March 5 and 13, 2011.
Gordon Baker to author, February 22, 2008.
Don Haseley to author, March 1, 5–6, 8, 2011.
Rebekah Hughes to author, November 25, 2010.
George McPherson to author, October 22 and 24, 2010.

William Price to author, March 11, 2009.
George Ridgway to author, December 13, 2011.
Gordon Scott to author, February 20, 2008.
Bruce Teede to author, March 6, May 14, 2012.
Roscoe P. Thompson to author, October 9, 2002.
Ernest J. Zellmer to author, December 3 and 21, 2010, January 13, 2011, February 2 and 9, 2011.

NEWSPAPERS AND MAGAZINES

Advertiser (Adelaide)
Argus (Melbourne)
Daily News (Perth)
Fremantle Districts Sentinel
Fremantle Gazette
Life, 1942–1945
Mercury (Hobart)
Mirror (Perth)
National Times (Canberra)
New York Times
Sound Advertiser (Perth)
Sunday Times (Perth)
Sydney Morning Herald
Times (London)
Weekend Australian (Sydney)
Weekend West (Perth)
West Australian (Perth)
Western Mail (Perth)

BOOKS AND ARTICLES

Alden, John D. "Away the Boarding Party." U.S. Naval Institute *Proceedings* 743 (January 1965): 68–75.
———. *The Fleet Submarine in the U.S. Navy: A Design and Construction History.* London: Arms and Armour Press, 1979.
Alden, John D., and Craig R. McDonald. *United States and Allied Submarine Successes in the Pacific and Far East during World War II.* Jefferson, N.C.: McFarland, 2009.
Aldrich, Richard J. *The Faraway War: Personal Diaries of the Second World War in Asia and the Pacific.* London: Doubleday, 2005.
Allen, Mark W. *Leader of the Pack: The Fleet Submarine USS Batfish in World War II.* Bloomington, Ind.: iUniverse, 2011.

Ambrose, Hugh. *The Pacific*. New York: NAL Caliber, 2010.
Anderson, Fay, and Richard Trembath. *Witness to War: The History of Australian Conflict Reporting*. Melbourne: Melbourne University Press, 2011.
Anscomb, Charles. *Submariner*. London: William Kimber, 1957.
Arrowsmith, Robyn. *All the Way to the USA: Australian WWII War Brides*. Sydney: self-published, 2013.
Astor, Gerald. *Crisis in the Pacific: The Battles for the Philippine Islands By the Men who Fought Them*. New York: Donald I. Fine Books, 1996.
Bagnasco, Erminio. *Submarines of World War Two*. London: Cassell, 1977.
Banham, Tony. *The Sinking of the* Lisbon Maru: *Britain's Forgotten Wartime Tragedy*. Hong Kong: Hong Kong University Press, 2006.
Barker, Anthony, and Lisa Jackson. *Fleeting Attraction: A Social History of American Servicemen in Western Australia during the Second World War*. Nedlands: University of Western Australia Press, 1996.
Beach, Edward L. *Salt and Steel: Reflections of a Submariner*. Annapolis, Md.: Naval Institute Press, 1999.
Beaumont, Joan. "Protecting Prisoners of War, 1939–95." In *Prisoners of War and their Captors in World War II*, edited by Bob Moore and Kent Fedorowich. Oxford: Berg, 1996.
Beevor, Antony. *The Second World War*. New York: Little, Brown and Company, 2012.
Bell, Roger, Sean Brawley, and Chris Dixon. *Conflict in the Pacific 1937–1951*. Cambridge: Cambridge University Press, 2005.
Benninghof, Mike. "The Dutch Submarine Flotilla, 1941–42." http://www.avalanchepress.com/DutchSubs.php.
Bertola, Patrick, and Bobbie Oliver, eds. *The Workshops: A History of the Midland Government Railway Workshops*. Perth: University of Western Australia Press, 2006.
Bess, Michael. *Choices under Fire: Moral Dimensions of World War II*. New York: Alfred A. Knopf, 2006.
Bevege, Margaret. *Behind Barbed Wire: Internment in Australia during World War II*. St. Lucia: University of Queensland Press, 1993.
Beynon, Robert P. *The Pearl Harbor Avenger: U.S.S. Bowfin*. Deland, Fla.: Just Books, 2002.
Bicheno, Hugh. *Midway*. London: Cassell, 2001.
Black, Jeremy. *Naval Power: A History of Warfare and the Sea from 1500*. New York: Palgrave Macmillan, 2009.

Blair, Clay, Jr. *The Atomic Submarine*. London: Odhams Press, 1955.
———. *Silent Victory: The U.S. Submarine War against Japan*. 1975. Reprint, Annapolis, Md.: Naval Institute Press, 2001.
Bond, Larry, ed. *Crash Dive: True Stories of Submarine Combat*. New York: Tom Doherty Associates, 2010.
Boyd, Carl. *American Command of the Sea: Through Carriers, Codes and the Silent Service*. Newport News, Va.: The Mariner's Museum, 1995.
Brawley, Sean, Chris Dixon, and Beatrice Trefalt. *Competing Voices from the Pacific War*. Santa Barbara, Calif.: ABC-Clio, 2009.
Brenchley, Fred, and Elizabeth. *Stoker's Submarine*. Sydney: Harper Collins, 2001.
Breuer, William B. *MacArthur's Undercover War: Spies, Saboteurs, Guerrillas and Secret Missions*. New York: John Wiley and Sons, 1995.
Bridgland, Tony. *Waves of Hate: Naval Atrocities of the Second World War*. Annapolis, Md.: Naval Institute Press, 2002.
Brown, David, ed. *The British Pacific and the East Indies Fleets: 'The Forgotten Fleets' 50th Anniversary*. Liverpool: Brodie Publishing, 1995.
Buggy, Hugh. *Pacific Victory: A Short History of Australia's Part in the War against Japan*. Canberra: Minister for Information, 1945.
Cain, T. J., and A. V. Sellwood, *H.M.S. Electra*. London: Futura Publications, 1959.
Cairns, Lynne. *Secret Fleets: Fremantle's World War II Submarine Base*. 1995. 2nd ed., Perth: Western Australian Museum, 2011.
Calvert, James F. *Silent Running: My Years on a World War II Attack Submarine*. New York: John Wiley and Sons, 1995.
Campbell, Douglas A. *Eight Survived: The Harrowing Story of the USS Flier and the Only Downed World War II Submariners to Survive and Evade Capture*. Guilford, Conn.: Lyons Press, 2010.
Campbell, Rosemary. *Heroes and Lovers: A Question of National Identity*. Sydney: Allen and Unwin, 1989.
Carlton, Mike. *Cruiser: The Life and Loss of HMAS Perth and Her Crew*. Sydney: William Heinemann, 2010.
Carruthers, Steven L. *Japanese Submarine Raiders 1942: A Maritime Mystery*. Narrabeen, N.S.W.: Casper Publications, 2006.
Casey, Robert J. *Battle Below: The War of the Submarines*. Indianapolis, Ind.: Bobbs-Merrill Company, 1975.
Chapman, Paul. *Submarine Torbay*. London: Robert Hale, 1989.
Christley, Jim. *US Submarines 1941–45*. New York: Osprey, 2006.

Clayton, Tim. *Sea Wolves: The Extraordinary Story of Britain's WW2 Submariners.* London: Little, Brown, 2011.
Colton, Larry. *No Ordinary Joes: The Extraordinary True Story of Four Submariners in War and Love and Life.* New York: Crown, 2010.
Compton-Hall, Richard. *The Underwater War 1939–1945.* Poole, Dorset: Blandford Press, 1982.
Conner, Claude C. *Nothing Friendly in the Vicinity: My Patrols on the Submarine USS Guardfish during World War II.* Annapolis, Md.: Naval Institute Press, 1999.
Connors, Libby, Lynette Finch, Kay Saunders, and Helen Taylor. *Australia's Frontline: Remembering the 1939–45 War.* St Lucia: University of Queensland Press, 1992.
Conole, Peter. *Protect and Serve: A History of Policing in Western Australia.* Perth: Western Australia Police Service, 2002.
Coote, John. *Submariner.* New York: W. W. Norton, 1991.
Cornish, Patricia. *Western Australia in the 20th Century.* Perth: Fremantle Arts Centre Press and the West Australian, 1999.
Courtney, G. B. *Silent Feet: The History of "Z" Special Operations 1942–1945.* Melbourne: R. J. and S. P. Austin, 1993.
Creed, David. *Operations of the Fremantle Submarine Base 1942–1945.* Sydney: Naval Historical Society of Australia, 1979.
Critch, Mary. *Our Kind of War: The History of the VAD/AAMWS.* Perth: Artlook Books Trust, 1981.
Croyle, William. "Sub's Fate Haunts Veteran: Bar Fight in WWII saved NKY Man's Life." *Northern Kentucky News*, November 7, 2010. http://nky.cincinnati.com/.
Cutter, Slade. *The Reminiscences of Captain Slade D. Cutter.* Annapolis, Md.: Naval Institute Press, 1985.
Darian-Smith, Kate. *On the Home Front: Melbourne in Wartime 1939–1945.* Melbourne: Oxford University Press, 1990.
Davenport, Roy M. *Clean Sweep.* New York: Vantage Press, 1986.
Davidson, Ron. *High Jinks at the Hot Pool: Mirror Reflects the Life of a City.* Fremantle: Fremantle Arts Centre Press, 1994.
Davis, Lance E., and Stanley L. Engerman. *Naval Blockades in Peace and War: An Economic History since 1750.* Cambridge: Cambridge University Press, 2012.
Day, David. *Reluctant Nation: Australia and the Allied Defeat of Japan 1942–45.* Oxford: Oxford University Press, 1992.
Delgado, James P. *Silent Killers: Submarines and Underwater Warfare.* Oxford: Osprey, 2011.

Department of Veteran Affairs. *Royal Australian Navy 1939–1945: Australians in the Pacific War*. Canberra: Department of Veteran Affairs, 2005.
De Yarmin, Ray W. "Survivor Recalls POW Ordeal." *Patrol*, September 19, 1986, 2–3.
Disher, Garry. *Total War: The Home Front 1939–1945*. Melbourne: Oxford University Press, 1983.
Dissette, Edward, and H. C. Adamson. *Guerrilla Submarines*. New York: Ballantine Books, 1972.
Dowson, John. *Old Fremantle: Photographs 1850–1950*. Perth: University of Western Australia Press, 2003.
Duff, Ivan F. *Medical Study of the Experiences of Submariners as Recorded in 1,471 Submarine Patrol Reports in World War II*. Washington, D.C.: Bureau of Medicine and Surgery, Navy Department, 1947.
Elleman, Bruce A., and C. S. M. Paine, eds. *Commerce Raiding: Historical Case Studies, 1755–2009*. Newport, R.I.: Naval War College Press, 2013.
Emden, Richard van. *The Quick and the Dead: Fallen Soldiers and Their Families in the Great War*. London: Bloomsbury, 2011.
Emery, Jack. "Learning a Trade: Memories of an Apprentice Turner and Iron Machinist, 29 January 1940–1 April 1945." *Papers in Labour History* 25 (September 2001): 10–26.
Enright, Joseph F., with James W. Ryan. *Shinano! The Sinking of Japan's Secret Supership*. London: The Bodley Head, 1987.
Evans, David C., ed. *The Japanese Navy in World War II: In the Words of Former Japanese Naval Officers*. Annapolis, Md.: Naval Institute Press, 1986.
Ewijk, Pieter van. "History of the Dutch Submarine Force." *The Submarine Review* (July 1992): 78–85.
Feuer, A. B. *Commando! The M/Z Units' Secret War against Japan*. Westport, Conn.: Praeger, 1996.
Field, John. "Submarine Trip to Japanese Waters." *Life*, June 29, 1942, 14–16.
———. "West of Japan." *Life*, March 15, 1943, 84–96.
Fluckey, Eugene B. *Thunder Below! The USS Barb Revolutionizes Submarine Warfare in World War II*. Urbana: University of Illinois Press, 1992.
Ford, Douglas. *The Pacific War: Clash of Empires in World War II*. London: Continuum, 2012.
Fortune, Gabrielle A. "Bride Ship, Brothel Ship: Conflicting Images of War Brides Arriving in New Zealand in the 1940s." In *Restag-

ing War in the Western World: Non-combatant Experiences, 1890—Today, edited by Abbenhuis Maartje and Sara Buttsworth, 61–86. New York: Palgrave Macmillan, 2009.

Fowler, Mary Lee Coe. *Full Fathom Five: A Daughter's Search*. Tuscaloosa: University of Alabama Press, 2008.

Galantin, I. J. *Take Her Deep: A Submarine against Japan in World War II*. New York: Pocket Books, 1987.

Gamble, Bruce. *Darkest Hour: The True Story of Lark Force at Rabaul. Australia's Worst Military Disaster of World War II*. St. Paul, Minn.: Zenith Press, 2006.

Gannon, Robert. *Hellions of the Deep: The Development of American Torpedoes in World War II*. University Park: Pennsylvania State University Press, 1996.

Gibney, Frank, ed. *Senso: The Japanese Remember the Pacific War*. Translated by Beth Cary. London: M. E. Sharpe, 1995.

Gillette, Robert C. "Lapon vs. Raton: From Lapon's 'Memory Bank.'" *Shipmate*, May 1992, 15–16.

Goldrick, James. "World War II: The War against Japan." In *The Royal Australian Navy*, ed. David Stevens, 127–53. Melbourne: Oxford University Press, 2001.

Goldsmith, Betty, and Beryl Sandford. *The Girls They Left Behind: Life in Australia during World War II—Women Remember*. Melbourne: Penguin, 1990.

Gomm, Kevin. *Red Sun on the Kangaroo Paw*. Perth: Chargan, 2009.

Goralski, Robert, and Russell W. Freeburg. *Oil and War: How the Deadly Struggle for Fuel in WWII Meant Victory or Defeat*. New York: William Morrow and Company, 1987.

Graham, Evan. *Japan's Sea Lane Security, 1940–2004: A Matter of Life and Death?* London: Routledge, 2006.

Grant, James Ritchie. "The Vicissitudes of a Dutch Submarine in Royal Australian Navy Service." *Sea Breezes*, vol. 70(1996.) http://www.dutchsubmarines.com/specials/special_kix_club.htm.

Grashio, Samuel C., and Bernard Norling. *Return to Freedom: The War Memoirs of Col. Samuel C. Grashio USAF (Ret.)*. Tulsa, Okla.: MCN Press, 1982.

Gray, Edwyn. *Submarine Warriors*. 1988. Reprint, New York: Bantam Books, 1990.

Gray, J. Glenn. *The Warriors: Reflections on Men in Battle*. Lincoln: University of Nebraska Press, 1959.

Gregory, Jenny, ed. *On the Homefront: Western Australia and World War II*. Perth: University of Western Australia Press, 1996.

Grey, Jeffrey. *A Military History of Australia*. Cambridge: Cambridge University Press, 1999.
Grider, George, with Lydel Sims. *War Fish*. London: Cassell, 1959.
Gugliotta, Bobette. *Pigboat 39: An American Sub Goes to War*. Lexington: University Press of Kentucky, 1984.
Guillain, Robert. *I Saw Tokyo Burning: An Eyewitness Narrative from Pearl Harbor to Hiroshima*. Translated by William Byron. New York: Doubleday, 1981.
Hackner, Beryl. *Rosa: A Biography of Rosa Townsend*. Perth: University of Western Australia Press, 1994.
Hargis, Robert. *US Submarine Crewmen 1941–45*. Oxford: Osprey, 2003.
Harper, Norman. *Australia and the United States: Documents and Readings in Australian History*. Melbourne: Nelson, 1986.
Hasluck, Paul. *The Government and the People 1942–1945*. Canberra: Australian War Memorial, 1970.
Hastings, Max. *Retribution: The Battle for Japan, 1944–45*. New York: Alfred A. Knopf, 2008.
Hattem, Audrey van. *Time Was*. Perth: self-published, 1998.
Hawkins, Maxwell. *Torpedoes Away Sir! Our Submarine Navy in the Pacific*. New York: Henry Holt and Company, 1946.
Henry, Ken, and Don Keith. *Gallant Lady: A Biography of the USS Archerfish*. New York: Tom Doherty Associates, 2004.
Hetherington, John. *Blamey: The Biography of Field-Marshal Sir Thomas Blamey*. Melbourne: F. W. Cheshire, 1954.
Hezlet, Arthur. *British and Allied Submarine Operations in World War II*. Gosport: Royal Navy Submarine Museum, 2001.
———. *The Submarine and Sea Power*. London: Peter Davies, 1967.
Hill, Thomas C. "USS *Perch* (SS 176 and 313)." *Polaris*, June 1999.
Holian, Thomas. "Saviors and Suppliers: World War II Submarine Special Operations in the Philippines." *Undersea Warfare,* issue 23 (Summer 2004). http://www.navy.mil/navydata/cno/n87/usw/issue-23/saviors.htm.
Holmes, Harry. *The Last Patrol*. Annapolis, Md.: Naval Institute Press, 1994.
Holmes, W. J. *Undersea Victory: The Influence of Submarine Operations on the War in the Pacific*. New York: Doubleday and Company, 1966.
Hood, Jean, ed. *Submarine: An Anthology of First-hand Accounts of the War under the Sea, 1939–1945*. London: Conway, 2007.

Holwitt, Joel Ira. *"Execute Against Japan": The U.S. Decision to Conduct Unrestricted Submarine Warfare.* College Station: Texas A&M University Press, 2009.
Horner, David. *High Command: Australia's Struggle for an Independent War Strategy 1939–1945.* Sydney: Allen and Unwin, 1992.
Hoyt, Edwin P. *Bowfin: The Story of One of America's Fabled Fleet Submarines in World War II.* New York: Van Nostrand Reinhold Company, 1983.
Hoyt, Edwin P. *The Destroyer Killer.* New York: Pocket Books, 1989.
Hughes, R. J. *Surviving the Flier: Based on the True Story.* Muncie, Ind.: Phoenix Flair Press, 2010.
Hull, Harry. "Guerrilla Mission under the Sea." *Naval History* (June 2000): 44–46.
Hurst, Doug. *The Fourth Ally: The Dutch Forces in Australia in WWII.* Canberra: self-published, 2001.
Ind, Allison. *Allied Intelligence Bureau: Our Secret Weapon in the War Against Japan.* New York: David McKay, 1958.
Ingham, Travis. *Rendezvous by Submarine: The Story of Charles Parsons and the Guerrilla-Soldiers in the Philippines.* Garden City, N.Y.: Doubleday, Doran and Company, 1945.
Ireland, Bernard. *Jane's Naval History of World War II.* New York: Harper Collins, 1998.
Iriye, Akira. *Power and Culture: The Japanese-American War 1941–1945.* Cambridge, Mass.: Harvard University Press, 1981.
Izzard, Brian. *Gamp VC: The Wartime Story of Maverick Submarine Commander Anthony Miers.* Sparkford, Somerset: Haynes Publishing, 2009.
Jackson, Stephen Leal. *The Men: American Enlisted Submariners in World War II.* Indianapolis, Ind.: Dog Ear, 2010.
Jaffe, Walter W. *Steel Shark in the Pacific: USS Pampanito SS-383.* Palo Alto, Calif.: Glencannon Press, 2001.
Jenkins, David. *Battle Surface: Japan's Submarine War against Australia 1942–1944.* Sydney: Random House, 1992.
Jones, David. "Submarines in the Battle for Australia." *Journal of Australian Naval History* 2, no. 2 (2005): 59–89.
Jones, David, and Peter Nunan. *U.S. Subs Down Under: Brisbane, 1942–1945.* Annapolis, Md.: Naval Institute Press, 2005.
Jones, Mark C. "Experiment at Dundee: The Royal Navy's 9th Submarine Flotilla and Multinational Naval Cooperation during World War II." *Journal of Military History* 72, no. 4 (October 2008): 1179–1212.

———. "Give Credit Where Credit Is Due: The Dutch Role in the Development and Deployment of the Submarine Schnorkel." *Journal of Military History* 69, no. 4 (October 2005): 987–1012.
Jones, Terry, and Steven Carruthers. *A Parting Shot: Shelling of Australia by Japanese Submarines 1942*. Narrabeen, N.S.W.: Casper, 2013.
Junger, Sebastian. *War*. New York: Twelve Hachette Book Group, 2010.
Kaplan, Philip. *Run Silent*. Annapolis, Md.: Naval Institute Press, 2002.
Keith, Don. *Final Patrol: True Stories of World War II Submarines*. New York: NAL Caliber, 2006.
———. *In the Course of Duty: The Heroic Mission of the USS Batfish*. New York: NAL Caliber, 2005.
———. *Undersea Warrior: The World War II Story of "Mush" Morton and the USS Wahoo*. New York: NAL Caliber, 2011.
———. *War beneath the Waves: A True Story of Courage and Leadership aboard a World War II Submarine*. New York: NAL Caliber, 2010.
Kimmett, Larry, and Margaret Regis. *U.S. Submarines in World War II: An Illustrated History*. Seattle, Wash.: Navigator Publishing, 1996.
King, Ernest J., and Walter Muir. *Fleet Admiral King: A Naval Record*. London: Eyre and Spottiswoode, 1953.
King, William. *The Stick and the Stars*. London: Arrow Books, 1961.
Kirby, S. Woodbury. *The War Against Japan*. Vol. 5: *The Surrender of Japan*. London: Her Majesty's Stationery Office, 1969.
Knoblock, Glenn A. *Black Submariners in the United States Navy, 1940–1975*. Jefferson, N.C.: McFarland, 2005.
Kuder, Edward M., with Pete Martin. "The Philippines Never Surrendered." *Saturday Evening Post,* February 10, 1945, 9–11, 57–63; February 24, 1945, 22–23, 90–93; March 3, 1945, 20, 81–84; March 10, 1945, 20, 52, 55–56, 58.
Lamont-Brown, Raymond. *Ships from Hell: Japanese War Crimes on the High Seas*. Thrupp-Stroud, Gloucestershire: Sutton, 2002.
Lanigan, Richard J. *Kangaroo Express: The Epic Story of the Submarine Growler*. Laurel, Fla.: RJL Express Publications, 1998.
LaVO, Carl. "Footprints in the Sand." U.S. Naval Institute *Proceedings* (January 1986): 85–88.
———. *The Galloping Ghost: The Extraordinary Life of Submarine Legend Eugene Fluckey*. Annapolis, Md.: Naval Institute Press, 2007.
———. *Slade Cutter: Submarine Warrior*. Annapolis, Md.: Naval Institute Press, 2003.

Lawliss, Chuck. *The Submarine Book: An Illustrated History of the Attack Submarine*. Shrewsbury, UK: Airlife, 2000.
Layman, Lenore, ed. *Powering Perth: A History of the East Perth Power Station*. Perth: Black Swan Press, 2012.
Layton, Edwin T., with Roger Pineau and John Costello. *"And I Was There": Pearl Harbor and Midway—Breaking the Secrets*. 1985. Reprint, Annapolis, Md.: Naval Institute Press, 2006.
Lebra, Joyce C. *Japan's Greater East Asia Co-Prosperity Sphere in World War II: Selected Readings and Documents*. London: Oxford University Press, 1975.
Lipscomb, F. W. *The British Submarine*. London: Adam and Charles Black, 1954.
Lockwood, Charles. *Down to the Sea in Subs: My Life in the U.S. Navy*. New York: W. W. Norton and Company, 1967.
———. *Sink 'Em All: Submarine Warfare in the Pacific*. 1951. Reprint, New York: Bantam Books, 1984.
Lockwood, Charles, and Hans Christian Adamson. *Battles of the Philippine Sea*. New York: Thomas Y. Crowell Company, 1967.
———. *Through Hell and Deep Water: The Stirring Story of the Navy's Deadly Submarine, the U.S.S. Harder*. New York: Greenberg, 1956.
Long, Gavin. *The Six Years War: Australia in the 1939–45 War*. Canberra: Australian War Memorial and the Australian Government Publishing Service, 1973.
Longstaff, Reginald. *Submarine Command: A Pictorial History*. London: Robert Hale, 1984.
Lott, Arnold S. *Most Dangerous Sea: A History of Mine Warfare*. Annapolis, Md.: Naval Institute Press, 1959.
Louch, T. S. *The History of the Weld Club*. Perth: Weld Club, 1980.
Lowder, Hughston E., with Jack Scott. *Batfish: Ace Submarine Killer of World War II*. London: Sphere Books, 1982.
Lukacs, John D. *Escape from Davao*. New York: Simon & Schuster, 2010.
Lutzow, Admiral. "Submarines in Modern War." *The XXth Century*, vol. 4 (January 1943): 34–36.
Maas, Peter. *The Terrible Hours: The Epic Rescue of Men Trapped Beneath the Sea*. New York: Harper Collins, 1999.
Mackay, Richard. *Damned Un-English Sailors: British Submariners 1901–1945*. Penzance, Cornwall: Periscope Publishing, 2009.
Maga, Tim. *Judgment at Tokyo: The Japanese War Crimes Trials*. Lexington: University Press of Kentucky, 2001.
Mansfield, John G. Jr. *Cruisers for Breakfast: War Patrols of the U.S.S. Darter and U.S.S. Dace*. Tacoma, Wash.: Media Center Publishing, 1997.

Mars, Alastair. *British Submarines at War 1939–1945*. London: William Kimber, 1971.

———. *H.M.S. Thule Intercepts*. London: Elek Books, 1956.

McCants, William R. *War Patrols of the USS Flasher*. Chapel Hill: Professional Press, 1994.

McCartney, Innes. *British Submarines 1939–1945*. Oxford: Osprey, 2006.

McCoy, Melvyn, and S. M. Mellnik (as told to Welbourn Kelley). "Prisoners of Japan." *Life*, February 7, 1944, 25–31, 96–111.

McCullough, Jonathan J. *A Tale of Two Subs: An Untold Story of World War II, Two Sister Ships, and Extraordinary Heroism*. New York: Grand Central Publishing, 2008.

McDonald, Craig R. *The USS* Puffer *in World War II: A History of the Submarine and Its Wartime Crew*. Jefferson, N.C.: McFarland and Company, 2008.

McIntyre, Darryl. *Townsville at War 1942: Life in a Garrison City*. Townsville: Townsville City Council, 1992.

McKee, Christopher. *Sober Men and True: Sailor Lives in the Royal Navy 1900–1945*. Cambridge, Mass.: Harvard University Press, 2002.

McKenzie-Smith, Graham. *Defending Fremantle, Albany and Bunbury 1939 to 1945*. Perth: Grimwade Publications, 2009.

McKernan, Michael. *All In! Australia during the Second World War*. Melbourne: Nelson, 1983.

McKie, Ronald. *The Heroes*. Sydney: Angus and Robertson, 1960.

McKinlay, Brian. *Australia 1942: End of Innocence*. Sydney: Collins, 1985.

McMahon, Peter. *Development and Sustainability in WA 1829–2020*. Murdoch: Institute for Sustainability and Technology Policy, 2009.

McNabb, Eric H. *Pot Shot Profile 1942–1946*. Yokine, W.A.: E. N. S. McNabb, n.d.

Meigs, Montgomery C. *Slide Rules and Submarines: Warfare in World War II*. 1990. Reprint, Honolulu: University Press of the Pacific, 2002.

Mendenhall, Corwin. *Submarine Diary: The Silent Stalking of Japan*. Annapolis, Md.: Naval Institute Press, 1991.

Meo, L. D. *Japan's Radio War on Australia 1941–1945*. Melbourne: Melbourne University Press, 1968.

Michno, Gregory F. *USS* Pampanito: *Angel Killer*. Norman: University of Oklahoma Press, 2000.

Ministry of Defence. *War with Japan*. London: Her Majesty's Stationery Office, 1995.

Monroe-Jones, Edward, and Michael Green, eds. *The Silent Service in World War II: The Story of the U.S. Navy Submarine Force in the Words of the Men who Lived It*. Philadelphia: Casemate, 2012.

Moore, Jeffrey M. *Spies for Nimitz: Joint Military Intelligence in the Pacific War*. Annapolis, Md.: Naval Institute Press, 2004.

Moore, Stephen L. *Battle Surface! Lawson P. "Red" Ramage and the War Patrols of the USS* Parche. Annapolis, Md.: Naval Institute Press, 2011.

———. "New Light on the Last Days of the USS Robalo." *The Great Circle: Special Issue Submarines* 34, no. 1 (2012): 65–77. Edited by Michael Sturma.

———. *Presumed Lost: The Incredible Ordeal of America's Submarine POWs during the Pacific War*. Annapolis, Md.: Naval Institute Press, 2009.

———. *Spadefish: On Patrol with a Top-Scoring World War II Submarine*. Dallas: Atriad Press, 2006.

———. *War of the Wolf: Texas' Memorial Submarine World War II's Famous USS* Seawolf. Dallas: Atriad Press, 2008.

Moorhead, Arthur. *The Australian Blue Book*. Sydney: Blue Star, 1942.

Morison, Samuel Eliot. *The Two-Ocean War: A Short History of the United States Navy in the Second World War*. Annapolis, Md.: Naval Institute Press, 1963.

Mulligan, Timothy P. "German U-boat Crews in World War II: Sociology of an Elite." *Journal of Military History* 56, no. 2 (April 1992): 261–82.

Murfett, Malcolm. *Naval Warfare 1919–1945: An Operational History of the Volatile War at Sea*. London: Routledge, 2009.

Murray, Stuart S. *The Reminiscences of Admiral Stuart S. Murray*. Annapolis, Md.: Naval Institute Press, 1974.

Nagata, Yuriko. *Unwanted Aliens: Japanese Internment in Australia*. St Lucia: University of Queensland Press, 1996.

Nethercoate-Bryant, Keith et al., eds. *More Submarine Memories: Some More Lesser Known Facts from the Gatwick Submarine Archive*. Hadley, Sussex: Gatwick Submarine Archive, 1997.

———. *Submarine Memories: Our Time in the "Boats."* Hadley, Sussex: Gatwick Submarine Archive, 1994.

Newpower, Anthony. *Iron Men and Tin Fish: The Race to Build a Better Torpedo during World War II*. Westport, Conn.: Praeger Security International, 2006.

Oliver, Bobbie, ed. *Papers in Labour History: The WAGR/Westrail Workshops at Midland, 1904–1994.* No. 25 (September 2001).
O'Rourke, James. "Australia the Virgin." *The XXth Century* 2, (March 1942): 190–202.
Ostlund, Mike. *Find 'Em, Chase 'Em, Sink 'Em: The Mysterious Loss of the WWII Submarine USS Gudgeon.* Guilford, Conn.: Lyons Press, 2006.
Padfield, Peter. *War beneath the Sea: Submarine Conflict 1939–1945.* London: Pimlico, 1997.
Parker, John. *The Silent Service: The Inside Story of the Royal Navy's Submarine Heroes.* London: Headline, 2001.
Parillo, Mark P. *The Japanese Merchant Marine in World War II.* Annapolis, Md.: Naval Institute Press, 1993.
Parrish, Thomas. *The Submarine: A History.* London: Viking Penguin, 2004.
Penglase, Joanna, and David Horner, eds. *When the War Came to Australia: Memories of the Second World War.* Sydney: Allen and Unwin, 1992.
Pfennigwerth, Ian. *The Royal Australian Navy and MacArthur.* Dural, N.S.W.: Rosenberg, 2009.
Potter, E. B., and Chester W. Nimitz, eds. *The Great Sea War: The Story of Naval Action in World War II.* Englewood Cliffs, N.J.: Prentice Hall, 1960.
Potts, Annette, and Lucinda Strauss. *For the Love of a Soldier: Australian War Brides and their GIs.* Sydney: Australian Broadcasting Corporation, 1987.
Powell, Alan. *Northern Voyagers: Australia's Monsoon Coast in Maritime History.* Melbourne: Australian Scholarly Publishing, 2010.
———. *The Shadow's Edge: Australia's Northern War.* Melbourne: Melbourne University Press, 1988.
———. *War by Stealth: Australians and the Allied Intelligence Bureau 1942–1945.* Melbourne: Melbourne University Press, 1996.
Quezon, Manuel Luis. *The Good Fight.* New York: D. Appleton-Century Company, 1946.
Quigley, Dave J., ed. *Under the Jolly Roger: British Submarines at War 1939–1945.* Portsmouth: Portsmouth Publishing, 1988.
Ramage, Lawson P. *Reminiscences of Vice Admiral Lawson P. Ramage.* Annapolis, Md.: Naval Institute Press, 1975.
Redford, Duncan. *The Submarine: A Cultural History from the Great War to Nuclear Combat.* London: I. B. Tauris, 2010.
Reeve, John, and David Stevens, eds. *The Face of Naval Battle.* Sydney: Allen and Unwin, 2003.

Reid, Anne, ed. *Melville Remembers: World War II City of Melville Oral History Project*. Perth: City of Melville, 1997.
Rhymes, Doug. "The Saga of Bob Rose and Sargo's Welcome to Australia." *Polaris*, August 1982, 14–15.
Roberts, Mark. *Sub: An Oral History of U.S. Navy Submarines*. New York: Berkley Caliber, 2007.
Robertson, John. *Australia at War 1939–1945*. Melbourne: William Heinemann, 1981.
Rohwer, Jürgen. *Chronology of the War at Sea 1939–1945: The Naval History of World War Two*. London: Chatham Publishing, 2005.
Roscoe, Theodore. *United States Submarine Operations in World War II*. Annapolis, Md.: Naval Institute Press, 1949.
Rose, Kenneth D. *Myth and the Greatest Generation: A Social History of Americans in World War II*. New York: Routledge, 2008.
Ruhe, William J. *War in the Boats: My World War II Submarine Battles*. Washington: Brassey's, 1994.
Ruiz, C. Kenneth, with John Bruning. *The Luck of the Draw: The Memoir of a World War II Submariner*. St. Paul, Minn.: Zenith Press, 2005.
Rupp, Albert. *Threshold of Hell*. Long Beach, Calif.: Almar Press, 1983.
Sadkovich, James J., ed. *Reevaluating Major Naval Combatants of World War II*. Westport, Conn.: Greenwood Press, 1990.
Saiki, Patsy Sumie. *Gambare! An Example of Japanese Spirit*. Honolulu: Mutual Publishing, 2004.
Sample, Paul. "Submarine Warfare." *Life*, December 27, 1943, 54–57.
Sarantakes, Nicholas Evan. *Allies against the Rising Sun: The United States, the British Nations, and the Defeat of Imperial Japan*. Lawrence: University Press of Kansas, 2009.
———. "One Last Crusade: The British Pacific Fleet and Its Impact on the Anglo-American Alliance." *English Historical Review* 121, no. 491 (April 2006): 429–66.
Schratz, Paul R. *Submarine Commander: A Story of World War II and Korea*. Lexington: University of Kentucky Press, 1988.
Schrijvers, Peter. *Bloody Pacific: American Soldiers at War with Japan*. London: Palgrave Macmillan, 2010.
Schultz, Robert, and James Shell. *We Were Pirates: A Torpedoman's Pacific War*. Annapolis, Md.: Naval Institute Press, 2009.
Schwab, Ernest L. "The Saga of the 'Double Ds.'" *Naval History* 8, issue 5 (September/October 1994): 19–21.
Scot, James. *The War Below: The Story of Three Submarines that Battled Japan*. New York: Simon & Schuster, 2013.

Sendzikas, Aldona. *Lucky 73: USS Pampanito's Unlikely Rescue of Allied POWs in WWII*. Gainesville: University Press of Florida, 2010.
Sheridan, Martin. *Overdue and Presumed Lost: The Story of the USS Bullhead*. 1947. Reprint, Annapolis, Md.: Naval Institute Press, 2004.
Sherriff, Jacqui. "Fremantle South Slipway: A Vital World War II Defence Facility." *Fremantle Studies* 2, no. 2 (2002): 106–19.
Silver, Lynette Ramsay. *The Heroes of Rimau*. Birchgrove, N.S.W.: Sally Milner Publishing, 1990.
Simpson, Michael, ed. *Anglo-American Naval Relations, 1919–1939*. Surrey, UK: Ashgate for the Navy Records Society, 2010.
Smith, Ron. *Torpedoman*. Self-published, 1993.
Smith, Steven Trent. *The Rescue: A True Story of Courage and Survival in World War II*. New York: John Wiley and Sons, 2001.
———. *Wolfpack: The American Submarine Strategy that Helped Defeat Japan*. Hoboken, N.J.: John Wiley and Sons, 2003.
Sobocinska, Agniezka. "'The Language of Scars': Australian Prisoners of War and the Colonial Order." *History Australia* 7, no. 3 (December 2010): 58.1–58.19.
Spector, Ronald H. *At War at Sea: Sailors and Naval Combat in the Twentieth Century*. New York: Viking, 2001.
Spruijt, Siem. "Fatal War Patrol of O-19." http://www.dutchsubmarines.com/specials/special_fatalpatrolo19.htm.
———. "3rd War Patrol of O-19." http://www.dutchsubmarines.com/specials/special_3patrolo19.htm.
Stanley, Peter. *Invading Australia: Japan and the Battle for Australia, 1942*. Melbourne: Viking, 2008.
Stern, Robert C. *U.S. Subs in Action*. Carrollton, Tex.: Squadron/Signal Publications, 1983.
Stevens, David. *A Critical Vulnerability: The Impact of the Submarine Threat on Australia's Maritime Defence 1915–1954*. Canberra: Sea Power Centre, 2005.
———, ed. *The Royal Australian Navy in World War II*. Sydney: Allen and Unwin, 1996.
Stevens, J. S. *Never Volunteer: A Submariner's Scrapbook*. Self-published, 1971.
Stevens, Peter F. *Fatal Dive: Solving the World War II Mystery of the USS Grunion*. Washington, D.C.: Regnery, 2012.
Stille, Mark. *Imperial Japanese Navy Submarines 1941–45*. Oxford: Osprey, 2007.

Stillwell, Paul, ed. *Submarine Stories: Recollections from the Diesel Boats*. Annapolis, Md.: Naval Institute Press, 2007.
Sturma, Michael. *Death at a Distance: The Loss of the Legendary USS Harder*. Annapolis, Md.: Naval Institute Press, 2006.
———. *Surface and Destroy: The Submarine Gun War in the Pacific*. Lexington: University Press of Kentucky, 2012.
———. *The USS Flier: Death and Survival on a World War II Submarine*. Lexington: University Press of Kentucky, 2008.
———. "U.S. Submarine Patrol Reports during World War II: Historical Evidence and Literary Flair." *Journal of Military History* 74, no. 2 (April 2010): 475–90.
Sue, Jack Wong. *Blood on Borneo*. Perth, W.A.: Skindivers Publication, 2001.
Thomas, David A. *Submarine Victory: The Story of British Submarines in World War II*. London: William Kimber, 1961.
Thomas, Evan. *Sea of Thunder: Four Commanders and the Last Great Naval Campaign 1941–1945*. New York: Simon & Schuster, 2006.
Thorne, Christopher. *Allies of a Kind: The United States, Britain and the War against Japan, 1941–1945*. London: Hamish Hamilton, 1978.
Toland, John. *The Rising Sun: The Decline and Fall of the Japanese Empire 1936–1945*. New York: Random House, 1970.
Toll, Ian W. *Pacific Crucible: War at Sea in the Pacific, 1941–1942*. New York: W. W. Norton and Company, 2012.
Towle, Philip, Margaret Kosuge, and Yoichi Kibata, eds. *Japanese Prisoners of War*. London: Hambledon and London, 2000.
Treadwell, Terry C. *Submarines with Wings: The Past, Present and Future of Aircraft-Carrying Submarines*. London: Conway Maritime Press, 1985.
Tregoning-Lawrence, Heather, and Robyn Siers. *We'll Meet Again: Australian Stories of Love in Wartime*. Canberra: Commonwealth of Australia, 2011.
Trenowden, Ian. *The Hunting Submarine: The Fighting Life of HMS Tally-Ho*. 1974. Reprint, London: New English Library, 1976.
Trumble, Tom. *Rescue at 2100 Hours: The Untold Story of the Most Daring Escape of the Pacific War*. Melbourne: Viking, 2013.
Trumbull, Robert. *Silversides*. 1945. Reprint, Chicago: O. W. Knutson and Company, 1990.
Tull, Malcolm. *A Community Enterprise: The History of the Port of Fremantle, 1897–1997*. St. John's, Newfoundland: International Maritime Economic History Association, 1997.

Tuohy, William. *The Bravest Man: The Story of Richard O'Kane and U.S. Submariners in the Pacific War*. 2001. Reprint, New York: Ballantine Books, 2006.
Van der Vat, Dan. *The Pacific Campaign: World War II, The U.S.–Japanese Naval War 1941–1945*. New York: Simon & Schuster, 2006.
——. *Stealth at Sea: The History of the Submarine*. London: Orion, 1994.
Van Velden, D. H. "Fremantle's Forgotten Fleet: A Social History of the Royal Netherlands Navy in Western Australia, 1942–1945." Doctorandus thesis, University of Leiden, 2000.
Wall, Don. *Abandoned: Australians at Sandakan, 1945*. Mona Vale, N.S.W.: D. Wall, 1990.
Ward, Norvell G. *The Reminiscences of Rear Admiral Norvell G. Ward*. Annapolis, Md.: Naval Institute Press, 1996.
Wheeler, Gerald E. *Kinkaid of the Seventh Fleet: A Biography of Admiral Thomas C. Kinkaid*. Washington, D.C.: Naval Historical Center, 1995.
White, Michael W. D. *Australian Submarines: A History*. Canberra: Australian Government Printing Service, 1992.
Whitlock, Flint, and Ron Smith. *The Depths of Courage: American Submariners at War with Japan, 1941–1945*. New York: Berkley Caliber, 2007.
Wigmore, Lionel. *The Japanese Thrust*. 1957. Reprint, Canberra: Australian War Memorial, 1968.
Wilkes, James W. *Down Under: My Life as a WWII Submariner*. N.p.: Xlibris, 2007.
Willoughby, Charles A. *The Guerrilla Resistance Movement in the Philippines: 1941–1945*. New York: Vantage Books, 1972.
Wilson, Michael. *A Submariners' War: The Indian Ocean 1939–45*. Stroud, Gloucestershire: Tempus, 2000.
Wingfield, Mervyn. *Wingfield at War*. Dunbeath, Scotland: Whittles Publishing, 2012.
Winslow, W. G. *The Fleet the Gods Forgot: The U.S. Asiatic Fleet in World War II*. Annapolis, Md.: Naval Institute Press, 1982.
Winton, John, ed. *The Submariners: Life in British Submarines 1901–1999*. London: Constable, 1999.
Wragg, David. *Fighting Admirals of World War II*. Annapolis, Md.: Naval Institute Press, 2009.
Wurth, Bob. *Australia's Greatest Peril 1942*. Sydney: Pan Macmillan, 2008.

Wyatt, Ray A. *A Yank Down Under: From America's Heartland to Australia's Outback*. Manhattan, Kan.: Sunflower University Press, 1999.
Yamashita, Samuel Hideo. *Leaves from an Autumn of Emergencies: Selections from the Wartime Diaries of Ordinary Japanese*. Honolulu: University of Hawai`i Press, 2003.
Yell, Susan, and Meredith Fletcher. "Airgraphs and an Airman: The Role of Airgraphs in World War II family correspondence." *History Australia* 8, no. 3 (December 2011): 117–38.
Young, Edward. *One of Our Submarines*. Hertforshire: Wordsworth Editions, 1997.
———. *Undersea Patrol*. New York: McGraw Hill, 1952.
Zeiler, Thomas W. *Annihilation: A Global Military History of World War II*. Oxford: Oxford University Press, 2011.
Zellmer, Ernest. "A Submariner in Western Australia, 1944–1945." *The Great Circle: Special Issue Submarines* 34, no. 1 (2012): 80–99. Edited by Michael Sturma.

AUDIO-VISUAL

KIX. Dutchsubmarines; Historical war submarine found buried under sand of NSW beach, *7:30 Report*, July 1999 (transcript), http://www.abc.net.au/7:30/stories/s40419.htm.
Taped tour and integrated Oral History, USS *Pampanito*, San Francisco, August 2012.
The Tragedy of the Montevideo Maru. Directed by David Napier, History Channel 2009.
The War at Sea, March of Time Television, 1951.

SELECT INTERNET SOURCES

Activities of Alex Hawkins in Z Special Unit, Grants Militaria. http://www.grantsmilitaria.com/garrett/html/z_spec.htm
Australian Submarine Heritage, World War II. http://www.mm.wa.gov.au/Museum/mhist/sub/freosubs.html
Australian War Memorial. http://www.awm.gov.au
Bartholomew, Bart. The Fremantle Submarine Base. http://www.subvetpaul.com/TheFremantle.htm
Bellinghiere, Joe. *Cavalla* Crew Interviews. http://www.brazosport.cc.tx.us/-nstevens/bell2.html
Combined Fleet. http://www.combinedfleet.com
Dutch Submarines. http://www.dutchsubmarines.com

Fremantle Harbour Fire. http://home.vincent.net.au/~mildura/war_years_2.htm
Fremantle Society. http://fremantlesociety.org.au
Fremantle Submarine Base, US Navy Fremantle, WA During WW2. http//www.ozatwar.com/usnavy/fremantlesubmarinebase.htm
Historic Naval Ships Association. http://www.hnsa.org
Hodges, Ian. Remembering 1942. http://www.awm.gov.au/atwar/remembering1942/montevideo/transcript.asp
Hughes, Rebekah. The USS *Flier* Project. http://www.ussflierproject.com/
HyperWar: US Navy in World War II. http://www.ibiblio.org/hyperwar/USN/
Jones, George Oliver. Jonesy's Domain. http://goliverjones.com
Memories of Thomas K. Kimmel. http://bergall.org/kimmel.html
On Eternal Patrol. http://www.oneternalpatrol.com
Oz at War. http//www.ozatwar.com
Ridges, Jim. People of the Plaque—Montevideo Maru. http://www.jje.info/lostlives/exhib/potp/montevideomaru.html
Ship's History USS *Crevalle* (SS 291). http:www.cyburban.com/~protrn/crevalle.htm
Submariners Association. http//www.submarinersassociation.co.uk
Uboat.net. www.uboat.net.

Index

Adamant (Great Britain), 105, 112, 126, 141, 143, 150
African American servicemembers, 34–36
aircraft: books showing profiles of enemy, 8; kamikaze suicide attacks, 124
Albany, 13–14, 34
Allied submarine force: ABDA command, 161; bond between submariners and Australian civilians, 4, 16–19, 154, 160, 161; contributions to Pacific War, 152, 154–55, 159–61; cooperation between allies, 2–4, 73, 75, 154–55, 161; hospitality offered in Western Australia, 4, 16–19, 155; language barriers and communication failures, 2; memorials to recognize contributions of, 159–60; trust between allies, 3
American-British-Dutch-Australian (ABDA) command, 2–3, 161
Anderson, Andy, 31–32
Angler, 89–92
Archerfish, 160
Ashigara (Japan), 145
Athedon, 138, 139
Australia: anti-Americanism in Eastern Australia, 80–81; arrival of MacArthur and morale in, 21–22; assistance from US for defense of, 8–9; attack on, threat of, 5–6; couples staying in after the war, 158–59; defenses to protect, adequacy of, 6; entrance into WWII, 5; financial debt after war, 154–55; food and rationing for civilians, 95–96; generosity of Americans to, 96; labor resources, government control of, 43; map of, x; movement of forces in, 26; overseas military service for men, 19, 63; population of, 6;

relationship with Britain and entrance into war, 5; skilled civilian workforce, 161; submarine assaults on coast of, 13; support for Fremantle submarine base, 3, 93–96, 154–55, 161; train journey across before ship to US, 156–57; White Australia immigration policy, 35–36
Australia (Australia), 120, 124
Australian Defence Force Plaque, 160
Australian forces, 22–23, 26. *See also* Royal Australian Air Force (RAAF); Royal Australian Navy (RAN)

Balabac Strait, 98, 99, 101, 121
Bancroft, Arthur, 132–33
Barb, 60, 132
Barry, Claude, 73, 106
Bataan, 22
Batfish, 16, 18, 94–95
Battle, John, 62
Baumgart, Earl, 100
Beach, Ned, 60
Becuna, 158
Bennett, Bob, 134
Bergall, 99
Betrand, John R., 50–51
Billfish, 58, 70–71, 94
Blamey, David, 127
Blamey, Thomas, 6, 14
Blandy, W. H. P. "Spike," 38
Blenny, 31, 148
Blueback, 145
bombing operations and friendly fire, 10–11, 53–56, 98, 146, 149–50, 160–61
Bowfin, 36, 50, 67–69, 95, 126
Bream, 135–37
Brinker, Robert M, 55–56
Brisbane, 43–44, 45, 53, 80–81, 127
Broome, Roy, 109–10, 111
Brown, Deen, 153

227

Brown, John, 141
Brubaker, Elton, 77
Bullhead, 2, 138, 149–50
Burlingame, Creed C., 125

Cabrilla, 72, 73, 150, 151
Cairns, Rob, 112
Calvert, James, 16, 33
Carpender, Arthur "Chips," 56, 65–66, 67
Cashero, Jim, 78
Cassidy, Hiram, 22, 25
Cavalla, 19, 63, 88–89, 138, 142–44, 150, 156, 160
Christian, Cecelia, 126, 156
Christie, Ralph Waldo: appearance and character of, 47; Bend of the Road residence of, 47–48; bond between submariners and civilians, 128; exhaustion of skippers, judgment about, 103; Exmouth Gulf base, exploration of, 56–57; *Harder* loss effects on, 104, 128; local women working for, 50; mines, submarines lost to, 102; opinion of Manning Kimmel, 97; opinions about, 47, 48; photo of, 46; promotion of and move to Brisbane, 45; relationship with Lockwood, 45–47; relief of, 127–28; relief of Ramage, 53; staff of, 48, 68–69; star skippers under, 83, 84; successor to Lockwood, 45; tanker sinking, reaction to, 125; torpedo policy change, 65–66, 69; Torpedo Station, transfer to, 47; transfer of, 128; venereal disease, concern about, 60–61; war patrols of, 69, 87–88
Cisco, 56, 138
Claggett, Bladen D., 121
Clark, Albert H., 57
Clytie, 154
Cocking, Jack, 133
Cod, 146–48, 150
Coe, James Wiggins "Red" "Jim," 38, 56, 98, 138
Coley, Robert, 35
Colvin, Chuck, 64
combat pins, 82, 87

Cook, George Carlton, 24
Cook, Harold Oliver, 23
Coral Sea, Battle of the, 26, 28
Cornford, Roy, 134
Corregidor, 21, 22, 25, 67
Cottesloe, 8, 29, 78, 93
Cox, Gordon "Gordy," 17, 19, 33, 152–53
Crevalle, 33, 35, 36, 84, 89–92, 97, 127
Crowley, John Daniel, 99–101
Curtin, John, 3, 5, 8–9, 15, 26, 29, 94, 124, 161
Curtis, Derek William, 144
Cutter, Slade, 103

Dace, 120–22, 147
Darter, 120–23, 147
Darwin, 1, 6, 124, 135
Davenport, Leo, 147, 148
Davis, James, 89
Davis, Landon L., 133
Dealey, Samuel D. "Sam," 2, 84–88, 102–4, 128
Demers, Maurice L. "Doc," 132
depth charges, 11, 12, 69–71, 103, 135, 136–37, 143, 160
Diamond, William Vernon, 102–3
Dodds, Stan W., 85–86, 88
Dornin, Robert "Dusty," 70
drinking: accidents related to, 79; Australian beer, 77–78, 96, 110; fighting and, 77, 78–79; loss of inhibitions associated with, 79–80; rum rations, 108, 144; on submarines, 108
Dutch East Indies, 1, 5, 7, 10–13, 22–25, 152, 160
Dutch submarine force: cooperation with US forces, 146–48; decimation of, 160; logistical support for, 161; loss of submarines and men, 12, 13; move to Fremantle base, 1, 12–13; number of submarines in Far East, 12; number of war patrols from Fremantle base, 1–2; reconnaissance patrol operations, 44; success of, 12, 13
Dutch submariners: food and supplies for, 96; marriages to Australian

women, 18, 159; relationship with US submariners, 78

Edwards, Richard S., 47
Evans, Leonard "Chickie-Bub," 79
Exeter (Great Britain), 3
Exmouth Gulf, 56–57, 58, 60, 90

Farmer, Frank, 134
Fenner, Donald, 34–35
Field, Charles Ross, 41
Fife, James "Jimmy," 38, 47, 61, 127–28, 129–30, 138, 141, 146
Fisk, William, 133
Fitzgerald, John A. "Jack," 52, 53–56, 153
Fitzpatrick, Edward "Fitz," 31
Flasher, 50, 51, 83–84, 89–92, 124–25, 126
Flier, 2, 48, 93, 97, 99–102, 152, 153
food supply, 93–96
Fraser, Bruce, 106, 152
Fred C. Ainsworth, 156
Fremantle: air raid alerts in, 8; air raid shelters and trenches, building of, 8; air raid shelters in, 8; arrival of refugees in, 6; attack on, threat of, 6, 15, 76–77, 83; blackout conditions in, 8; bond between submariners and civilians, 4, 16–19, 161; charts for how to reach, 11–12; defenses to protect, adequacy of, 76–77; dispersion of ships and submarines from Harbor, 76; evacuation plans for citizens of, 6; fire on ship in harbor, 133–34, 135; hospitality offered to submariners, 16–19, 109–13, 155; lights ashore, 110; merchant vessels and warship in harbor, 12; movement of families from, 8; protection of by Royal Australian Navy, 20
Fremantle submarine base: advantages and disadvantages of, 1, 43; antisubmarine net system at, 20; arrival of British submarines, 105–6; arrival of US submarines, 9–12; Australian support for, 3, 93–96, 154–55, 161; civilian workforce at, 41–42, 93, 161; contributions to Pacific War, 1–4; cooperation between allies and success of, 3–4; importance of, 160–61; last US submarine to leave, 154; morale at, 4, 27–28, 29, 44, 155; move of submarines to, 1, 10–13, 160; move to Subic Bay from, 138, 139, 141; number of British submarines at, 105; number of US submarines at, 20, 37, 43–44, 59; number of war patrols from, 1–2, 44, 53, 58–59, 66–67, 83, 104; overhaul of submarines at, reinforcements for, 29; repair and machine shops at, 20–21; US submarine force office at, 20

gambling, 48, 80
Gamby, Dick, 82
Gillespie, Albert, 107–8, 141, 154
Glebbon, Phil, 126
Goens, Robert, 35
Golay, Frank, 80, 96
Goldman, Isaac "Gerry," 126, 158–59
Goossens, H. A. W., 116–17
Graham, Ace, 102–3
Grampus, 2, 35
Grashio, Samuel C. "Sam," 67, 68
Grayling, 2, 55–56, 97
Great Britain, relationship with Australia and entrance into war, 5
Great Lakes Naval Memorial and Museum, 102
Greenup, Francis, 141
Grenadier, 2, 18, 52, 53–56, 58–59, 61, 97, 152, 153, 157
Grider, George, 50, 62, 120, 124–25, 126
Griffin, 105, 138
Griffith, Walter Thomas "Walt," 2, 68–69, 149
Growler, 2, 131, 158
Guadalcanal, 43–44, 53
Guam, 5, 87, 104, 149, 156, 157
Guardfish, 18
Gudgeon, 2, 22–25, 51, 59, 70, 73
Gunnel, 18, 89

Haddock, 66
Hake, 87, 102, 103
Harder, 2, 84–88, 97, 101, 102–4, 128, 158
Hardhead, 141
Haseley, Don, 19, 63, 78, 80, 144
Haughey, Gwen, 34, 157–58
Hawkbill, 120, 124
Hawkins, Ona D., 79
Headington, Wes, 16, 62, 94
Hebditch, Nancy, 159
Helfers, Fred, 158
Hess, Franklin Grant, 90–92
Hewett, Dorothy, 7, 62
Hezlet, Arthur Richard "Baldy," 107, 144–46
Hirotama Maru (Japan), 49
Holland, 12, 13–14, 158
Hollywood Military Hospital, 76
Holt, Edward Rowell, Jr., 149–50
homicide cases, 78–79
Houston, 3, 48
Howard W. Gilmore, 36, 138
Hunt, Bob, 31, 64, 78

intelligence: Coral Sea battle, signals intelligence before, 26; landing and evacuation of intelligence operatives, 44, 73; radio intercepts and crypto-analysis activities, 66, 98, 99; reconnaissance patrols and information, 44, 76, 86–87

Jacobs, Tyrell Dwight, 9–11, 29
Jacobson, Alvin, 48, 93, 100, 101, 153
Japanese fleet: antisubmarine warfare, 56, 103, 149–50; attack on Fremantle, threat of, 76–77; warship movement to Singapore, 76
Java, 1, 6, 10, 44
Java Sea, Battle of, 2–3, 6, 154, 161
Java Sea, patrols in, 142–44
Jaywick, Operation, 117–18
Jensen, Marvin John, 70
Jinkins, William T. "Bill," 85–86, 88, 101, 102
Johnson, John Lewis, 35
Jongejan, Ary, 159
Jongerling, Peter, 79

kangaroo hunting, 31, 51, 126, 158
Kean, P. J. "Phil," 24–25
Kennaly, Frank C., 127
Kimmel, Husband, 97
Kimmel, Manning Marius, 97–99
Kimmel, Thomas Kincaid, 99
King, Arthur, 157
King, Cecil S., 19
King, Ernest, 3, 84, 99, 105, 106, 127–28
King, W. D. A. "Bill," 153
King, William, 2, 107, 118–19
Kinkaid, Thomas Cassin, 66, 69, 73, 75, 123, 127–28
K-IX (Netherlands), 12, 13, 28, 65
Kossler, Herman J., 88–89, 143–44, 150, 160
Kuder, Edward M., 67–68
Kuttabul (Australia), 28
K-VIII (Netherlands), 12–13
K-XII (Netherlands), 12, 13, 44, 79
K-XIV (Netherlands), 57
K-XV (Netherlands), 159

Larkin, Richard "Barclay," 75
Laughlin, Floyd, 98
Lauten, Henry Dewey, 151
Lawrie, William, 126
Leary, Herbert F., 32, 37
leave: African American experiences on, 35; Albany accommodations and activities at, 51; drinking while on, 77–80; encounters between officers and crew during, 52; experiences in Pearl Harbor, 16–17; female companionship during, 17–19, 60–64; fighting while on, 77, 78–79; gambling while on, 48, 80; hotels for crews, 29; local police response to behavior on, 79–80; Midway rest center for, 60; Pearl Harbor accommodations and activities, 16–17, 50; punishment for behavior on, 80; recreational activities for servicemen, 29–31, 50–52; reputation of Fremantle and Perth as best leave center, 4, 18–19, 44, 49–52, 109–13, 161; Subic Bay R & R camp, 138; tolerance of citizens

for misbehavior during, 80–81; two weeks of R & R after patrols, 29; wild behavior during, 52, 78, 92; wolf pack celebration in Perth, 92
Lee, Harold "Hal," 158
Leithhead, Vivian Charles, 23
Lempiere, Geoffrey, 55
Lend-Lease aid agreement, 93–94, 154–55
Leonski, Edward, 80
Leyte Gulf, Battle of, 119, 120–23, 135
Liddell, James W., 100
lifeguard duty, 142
Lintz, Johnny, 24
Lloyd, Edward R., 151
Lockwood, Charles Andrews, Jr.: appearance and character of, 27, 41, 47; civilian workforce, relationship with, 41–42; command of Fremantle base by, 27–28, 30; early life and education of, 27; enemy ships, sinking of, 138–39; Exmouth Gulf base, exploration of, 56; Midway rest center, support for, 60; mines, submarines lost to, 102; morale of submariners, concern about, 27–28, 29; nickname for, 27; opinions about, 27, 47; overhaul of submarines, reinforcements for, 29; Perth, opinion about, 27; Perth home of, 47; promotion of, 28; promotion of and move to Pearl Harbor, 45; relationship with Christie, 45–47; relief of Wilkes by, 27; response to Pearl Harbor attack, 27; staff of, 41–42, 48, 130, 149, 152; stewards on submarines, replacement of, 34; submarines, concern about number and condition of, 37; torpedo performance, concern about, 37, 38–39, 47; torpedo policy change, 65; waiting period for marriages, 32; work days of, 41
Lockwood, Phyllis, 28
Loep, Johannes, 12, 159
Logan, Sam, 102, 104
logistical support, 105, 106, 161

Lombok Strait, 57–58, 90, 114–15, 118, 135, 144, 149
Lowder, Hughston, 16, 18
Lucas, Richard, 35
Lynch, Beryl, 63–64
Lynch, Frank Curtis, Jr., 102
Lyon, Ivan, 117

MacArthur, Douglas: award for Dealey from, 88, 128; Biak offensive, intelligence about ship movement and, 87; Brisbane, movement of headquarters to, 80; cat named for, 52; cooperation between allies, 73, 75; evacuation from Corregidor, 21, 67; Leyte Gulf battle, 120; Melbourne arrival of, 21–22; relationship with Curtin, 3; Southwest Pacific forces, command of, 26
Mackenzie, Hugh, 111, 113, 114, 118
Mackerel, Operation, 44
Maidstone (Great Britain), 105, 106, 108, 109, 110, 134, 141–42, 146, 154, 159
Mar, Delbert, 140
Mariana Islands, 34, 83, 84, 87, 104
Markeson, Swede, 24
marriages: bride ships, 156–57, 158; British submariner couples, 126–27, 158–59; Dutch submariner couples, 18, 159; reunion and settlement of couples in US, 127, 156–58; separations endured by couples, 156; settlement in Australia after the war, 158; US submariner couples, 18, 31–34, 62, 63–64, 126, 156–58, 160; waiting period for, 32–33; War Brides Act, 158; widows from accidents at sea, 127
Mars, Alastair, 33, 110, 111, 126, 150–51
Martin, Wallace Keet, 98
Mayo, Elvin, 35
Mays, Hosey, 35, 36
McCain, John, 18
McCallum, James L. P., 135–36, 137
McCann, Allan R., 45
McClintock, David Hayward, 121–22

McCoy, Tim, 17, 157
McGrievy, Joseph, 24, 25
McGuire, Charles A. "Red," 35
McKittrick, Bill, 134
McLean, Heber Hampton "Tex," 41, 48, 49, 54, 98, 101
McNabb, Eric, 80
McPherson, George "Tag," 63, 78
Medal of Honor, 104, 128
memorials to Allied submarine force, 102, 159–60
Mendenhall, Corwin, 16, 50, 56
Menzies, Robert, 5
Midway, Battle of, 28–29
Midway Island, 60
Miers, Anthony "Tony," 71–75, 106, 109, 127, 146
Miller, Laurel Brenda "Babs," 63, 156, 157
Miller, Patricia, 127
Miller, Wesley, 100
mines and minelaying operations, 88, 98, 99–101, 102, 103, 117–18, 135, 145, 146
Missouri, 152
Montevideo Maru (Japan), 39–41
Morgan, Luis P., 67
Morton, Dudley "Mush," 103
Mosby, John, 32
Munson, Henry Glass, 6, 104
Murray, Stuart S. "Sunshine," 11, 31, 41–42, 152
Murray, Stuart "Sunshine," 48

Napolillo, Francis J., 68
Navy, U.S.: success of, 123; superiority of ships, 106–7
Navy Cross, 69, 127, 153
Navy submarine force, U.S.: Australian commandos on US submarines, 3, 85–86, 88, 101, 136–37, 161; command offices at Fremantle and Perth, 20; commanders of, 20, 27, 45, 128, 129; concentration of submarines and decision to split force, 13–14; cooperation with British forces, 3–4, 73, 75, 142–46; cooperation with Dutch forces, 146–48; homes loaned to in Perth, 47–48; last submarine to leave Fremantle, 154; move to Fremantle base, 10–12; number and condition of submarines for, 37; number of war patrols from Fremantle base, 1–2; officers and crew, relationships between, 52; overhaul of submarines at Pearl Harbor, 21; performance of, 38; success of, 12, 39–40, 44, 58–59, 69, 160; superiority of submarines, 106–7, 108
Navy submariners, U.S.: bond between submariners and Australian civilians, 16–19, 128, 160; food and pay for, 82, 94–96, 108; hospitality offered in Western Australia, 4, 16–19, 50–52, 155; love affairs with and marriages to Australian women, 17–19, 31–34, 61–64, 126, 127, 156–58, 160; memorials to recognize contributions of, 102, 159–60; morale of, 27–28, 29, 44, 140, 155; relationship with British submariners, 130, 142–46, 161; relationship with Dutch submariners, 78; social interactions British submariners, 108–9; survivors of lost submarine, 100–101; swimming skills of, 100
Netherlands East Indies. *See* Dutch East Indies
New London submarine school, 81
Nicholls, Stanley J., 95
Nichols, Philip, 103
nickel ore ships, 87–88
nightmares, 153
Nimitz, Chester W., 60, 65, 83, 97
Nimitz, Chester W., Jr., 39, 120

O-19 (Netherlands), 2, 105, 115, 135, 145, 146–48
Odom, Charley, 31, 58, 94
Otus, 34–35
Ovens (Australia), 43
Owens, Paul A., 68

Pacific War: contributions of Allied submarine force to, 152, 154–55, 159–61; Coral Sea battle as

turning point, 26; human cost of, 150, 152–53; island-hopping strategy, 83; map of Pacific Theater, x; retreat of and lack of success by submariners, 4; success of naval operations, 123; war of attrition, 43–44, 83–92
Packwood, Ed, 158
Pampanito, 35, 95, 130–34, 138, 160
Parks, Tom, 16
Parrot, 14, 25
patrol operations: bombing hazards while on, 160–61; British submarine patrols, 114–16; cheer ship for successful missions, 146; Christie war patrols, 69, 87–88; combat pin after successful war patrol, 82, 87; destroyers, attacks on, 84, 86, 87, 124; discomfort and dangers of, 161; Dutch submarine patrols, 44, 115, 116–17; enemy ships sunk during, 44, 53, 54, 58–59, 66–67, 69, 83, 84, 90–92, 104, 115–16, 123, 124–25, 138–40, 145, 148, 152; eternal patrol, 2; first and fifth patrols, likelihood of boat loss on, 103; Flaming Action patrol, 124–25; German submarines sunk during, 116–17, 144–45; Java Sea, patrols in, 142–44; longest patrol of the war, 146; loss of submarines and men, 2, 12, 13, 53–56, 58, 97–104, 149–50; next patrol as last, concern about, 78; number and condition of submarines for, 37; number of deaths from war patrols, 150; number of war patrols from Fremantle base, 1–2, 44, 53, 58–59, 66–67, 83, 104; oil tankers, sinking of, 124–25; radar for locating enemy targets, 66, 90, 97; reconnaissance patrols and information, 44, 76, 86–87; senior staff on war patrols, 41; sinking of prisoner ships, 39–41; wolf pack patrols, 88–92, 131. *See also* special missions
Pearl Harbor: attack on, 1, 5, 160; leave accommodations and activities at, 16–17, 50; Lockwood promotion and move to, 45; Lockwood response to attack on, 27; overhaul of submarines at, 21; submarine base at, 1; transfer of submarines to, 53
Pelias, 9, 51, 56–57, 76
Pennyman, Timothy, 35
Penzenik, William, 78–79, 101
Perske, Cliff, 136–37
Perth: air raid alerts in, 8; air raid shelters in, 8; attack on, threat of, 8; British submariner experiences in, 109–13; homes loaned to Navy in, 47–48; hospitality offered to submariners, 16–19, 50–52, 109–13, 155; Lockwood feelings about leaving, 45; Lockwood opinion about, 27; movement of families from, 8; US submarine force office at, 20; VJ day/week in, 150–51; wolf pack celebration in, 92
Perth (Australia), 3
Perth Perambulator, 156–57
Philippine Sea, Battle of the, 87
Philippines: attack on and fall of, 5, 22; attack on submarine base in, 11; attack on submarine base in and move of submarines to Dutch East Indies, 1, 10; attack on submarine base in and move of submarines to Fremantle, 160; Bataan surrender and escape of forces from, 22; Subic Bay base, 138, 141–42; torpedoes left during evacuation of, 37–39
Pickett, Harry, 133
Pigeon, 25
Pollack, 60
Pompon, 95
Porpoise (Great Britain), 2, 105, 117–18, 126
Post, William S., Jr., 59
Poston, Collie, 98
prisoners of war (POWs): Australian forces captured at Timor, 22–23; Bataan surrender and forces captured as prisoners, 22; effects of treatment on, 152–53; end of war announcement to, 152; *Grenadier* crew, 55, 157; *Maidstone*

transport of liberated, 154; prison camps, 55; release of and return to US after war, 152–53; rescue of Australian, 160; rescue of by *Pampanito*, 130–33, 134; *Robalo* crew, 98–99; Singapore surrender and soldiers taken as, 5–6; sinking of prisoner ships, 39–41; treatment of, 55, 68, 131, 137, 153; War Crimes Trials for treatment of, 153
Pruitt, John Alden, 79
Pryce, Roland Fremont, 11
Puffer, 61, 63, 70, 71, 79, 96, 101, 145–46
Python commandos, 85–86, 88

Queenfish, 132
Queensland, 80–81

Rabaul, New Britain, 26, 40–41
Radwick, Victor, 19
Rakuyo Maru (Japan), 130–33, 160
Ramage, Lawson Peterson "Red," 48–49, 53, 58
Rasher, 104
Raton, 35, 89, 126
Ray, 158
reconnaissance patrols and information, 44, 76, 86–87
Redfin, 100–101
Redmond, Eddie, 158
Ridgway, George, 51, 158
Robalo, 2, 97–99, 100, 101
Rock, 58
Roosevelt, Franklin D., 4, 15, 97, 123, 161
Rose, James R., 127
Royal Australian Air Force (RAAF), 10–11, 23–25
Royal Australian Navy (RAN): antisubmarine training of, 65; Fremantle harbor charts, delivery of, 11–12; *K-IX* as training vessel for, 13, 28, 65; protection of Fremantle harbor by, 20; submarine missions of commandos, 3, 85–86, 88, 101, 136–37, 161; submarines for, 65; success of, 65
Royal Navy, 5, 6, 25–26, 106–7, 160

Royal Navy submarine force: Australian commandos on submarines, 85–86; commander of, 106; condition of submarines compared to US Navy, 106–7; cooperation with US forces, 3–4, 73, 75, 142–46; hospitality offered to submariners, 109–13, 155; logistical support for, 105, 106; move to Fremantle base, 1, 105–6; move to Subic Bay, 141–42; number of submarines at Fremantle, 105; number of war patrols from Fremantle base, 1–2; retreat from the Far East, 26; return to UK after war, 154; submarine liaison officer, 71–75
Royal Navy submariners: comradeship and loyalty to the group, 107–8; discipline of, 107; light duties of, 108; love affairs with and marriages to Australian women, 126–27, 158–59; memorials to recognize contributions of, 159; popularity of with Australian families, 112–13, 154; relationship with US submariners, 130, 142–46, 161; rum rations, 108, 144; social interactions us submariners, 108–9
Ruhe, William, 33, 92
Ruiz, Kenneth, 60, 153
Rupp, Albert, 18, 55, 152
Rush, Charles W., Jr. "Charlie," 33, 34, 71

Sachs, John, 136–37
Sailfish, 16
Saipan, 87, 131, 132
Sandridge, Lloyd, 79
Sargo, 9–11, 29, 41
S-boats, 37, 45, 115
Schuermann, Lloyd, 64
Sculpin, 2, 16, 18, 43–44
Seadragon, 44
Seahorse, 17, 18
Sealion, 1, 132
Sealion II, 131
Searaven, 11, 22–25, 44
Seawolf, 2, 140
Seilor, George, 31

Selby, Frank Gordon, 70, 89
Shadwell, Lancelot M., 105, 106, 116–17, 141–42
Shakespeare (Great Britain), 108
Sheridan, Barbara, 156–57
Sherwood, Richard, 133
Shropshire (Australia), 120
Sieglaff, William R. "Barney," 59
Silver Star, 25
Singapore, 5–6, 76, 160
Sirdar (Great Britain), 105, 114–15, 127
SJ surface radar, 66, 90, 97
Skeates, Ben, 113, 159
Skipjack, 38, 56, 98
Snapper, 25, 35
Snider, Tom, 158
Snyder, Paul, 18
Solomon Islands, 43–44, 53
Spanton, John, 158
Spearfish, 11–12, 22
special missions: evacuation and rescue missions, 2, 21–25, 67–68; landing and pickup of commandos and intelligence operatives, 2, 73, 85–86, 88, 117–19, 136–37
Spender, J. A. "Tony," 115, 127
Spiteful (Great Britain), 105, 159
Springer, Lyall, 158
Spruijt, Siem, 135, 147
Stimler, Spencer, 95
Stimson, Henry, 34
Stoic (Great Britain), 105, 115
Stone, Hamilton L., 25
Stone, Lowell, 89
Storm (Great Britain), 105
Sturdy (Great Britain), 105, 127
Sturgeon, 39–40, 94
Styer, C. W. "Gyn," 37
Stygian (Great Britain), 108
Submarine Old Comrades Association, 159
submariners: comradeship and loyalty to the group, 2, 107–8, 161; courage of, 2; physical requirements for, 81; promotion opportunities for, 82; psychological testing of, 81; recruitment and selection of, 81, 82; risks taken by, 2; silver combat pin for, 82; skill and discipline of, 82; socializing with other submariners, 18; special branch of the military, status as, 81–82; specials training, 81–82; training of, 81–82; underwater escape exercise, requirement for, 81
submarines: aggressive tactics of skippers, 103; attitude toward rank and discipline aboard, 82; communications between, 88–89, 106; enemy attacks on, 53–56, 57–58; family atmosphere aboard, 82, 108; loss of during patrols, 2, 12, 13, 53–56, 58, 97–104; noisy machinery and detection of, 103; oxygen supply on, 25, 70
Summers, Paul Edward, 131, 132
Sundra Strait, Battle of, 3, 154, 161
survivor's guilt, 153
Swordfish, 2, 11, 44
Sydney, 28, 65
Sydney (Australia), 5
Syme, David, 114

Tait, Gordon, 110, 111
Tambor, 15, 64
Tantalus (Great Britain), 105, 111, 114, 118
Taurus (Great Britain), 116
Tautog, 34, 59
Taylor, Charles, 61
Taylor, Clive, 109
Teede, Bruce, 102–3, 158
Teede, Guy, 102–3
Telemachus (Great Britain), 105, 107, 114, 118–19
Terrapin (Great Britain), 142–44
Thompson, Roscoe P., 126, 156, 158
Thresher, 16, 57, 62, 71, 94
Thule (Great Britain), 110, 126
Tichenor, Murray Jones "Tich," 86, 101
Tidd, Ross, 101–2
Timor, 22–25, 40
torpedoes: Christie role in development of, 46–47; depth calibration and running deeper than set, 9–10, 38, 39; down-the-throat shot, 86; memorial to US

submariners, 159–60; performance and reliability of, 9–10, 11, 37, 38, 44, 47, 49, 69, 160; policy change on magnetic exploders, 65–66, 69; production of, 39; shortage of, 37–39, 44
Trenchant (Great Britain), 106, 110, 111, 113, 114–15, 142, 144–46, 148, 150
Trigger, 70
Trout, 2, 49, 53, 57, 58, 153
Turpin, 154

Ultra, 66, 98, 99
United States (US): assistance for defense of Australia, 8–9; force strength of in Australia, 26; Midway battle successes, 28–29; reunion and settlement of couples in, 156–58

Vasey, Lloyd R. "Joe," 43
venereal disease, 60–61
Vervalin, Chuck, 33–34, 52, 157–58
Victoria Quay marine slipway, 43

Walker, Francis David, Jr., 90–92
Westbrook, Edwin M., Jr., 147
Western Australia: air attacks on, 6–7, 14; air raid shelters and trenches, building of, 8; attack on, decline in threat of, 14–15, 25–26; attack on, threat of, 5–6, 76–77; bond between submariners and civilians in, 4, 16–19, 128, 154, 160, 161; civilian workforce, Lockwood relationship with, 41–42; defenses to protect, adequacy of, 6, 76–77; defenses to protect, responsibility for, 25–26; employment of women in, 50, 62; hospitality offered to submariners, 4, 16–19, 50–52, 109–13, 155; love affairs and marriages between local women and US submariners, 17–19, 31–34, 61–64, 126, 127, 156–58, 160; map of, x; memorials on Monument Hill, 159–60; overseas military service for men, 19, 63; population of, 6; road signs along coast, removal of, 8; Southwest Pacific Area, incorporation into, 25; submarine assaults on coast of, 7, 14
Western Australia Maritime Museum, 13, 43
Weston, Roy, 109, 159
Whitaker, Reuben T., 2, 47, 83–84, 89–92, 103, 124
White, Doreen, 62
White, Homer, 32, 158
Wilkes, James, 81
Wilkes, John, 11, 20, 21, 27, 47
Will, John Mylin "Dutch," 41
Willcock, John, 15
Willingham, Joseph Harris, 67, 68–69
Wingfield, Mervyn, 11, 116
wolf pack patrols, 88–92, 131
Wood, Peter, 106, 110, 146
World War II (WWII): Australia entrance into, 5; cable announcing end, 150, 199n20; celebrations at end of, 150–51; D-day invasion, 88; end of, 150–52; parades for returning vets, 153; surrender ceremony, 152; winning of, no question about, 83. *See also* Pacific War
Wright, William "Bull," 39, 94

Young, Edward, 71–72, 105, 106–7, 111, 112, 130
Young, Edwin J., 111–12, 113, 115, 150

Z Special Unit, 85
Zellmer, Ernest "Zeke," 19, 63, 77, 108, 150, 156, 157
Zwaardvisch (Netherlands), 105, 115, 116–17

About the Author

Michael Sturma is a professor of history and leader of humanities at Murdoch University in Perth, Australia. He is the author of six previous books, including *Death at a Distance: The Loss of the Legendary USS Harder* (Naval Institute Press, 2006). He served as editor of *The Great Circle*, the peer-reviewed journal of the Australian Association for Maritime History, from 2008 to 2013.

The Naval Institute Press is the book-publishing arm of the U.S. Naval Institute, a private, nonprofit, membership society for sea service professionals and others who share an interest in naval and maritime affairs. Established in 1873 at the U.S. Naval Academy in Annapolis, Maryland, where its offices remain today, the Naval Institute has members worldwide.

Members of the Naval Institute support the education programs of the society and receive the influential monthly magazine *Proceedings* or the colorful bimonthly magazine *Naval History* and discounts on fine nautical prints and on ship and aircraft photos. They also have access to the transcripts of the Institute's Oral History Program and get discounted admission to any of the Institute-sponsored seminars offered around the country.

The Naval Institute's book-publishing program, begun in 1898 with basic guides to naval practices, has broadened its scope to include books of more general interest. Now the Naval Institute Press publishes about seventy titles each year, ranging from how-to books on boating and navigation to battle histories, biographies, ship and aircraft guides, and novels. Institute members receive significant discounts on the Press's more than eight hundred books in print.

Full-time students are eligible for special half-price membership rates. Life memberships are also available.

For a free catalog describing Naval Institute Press books currently available, and for further information about joining the U.S. Naval Institute, please write to:

> Member Services
> **U.S. Naval Institute**
> 291 Wood Road
> Annapolis, MD 21402-5034
> Telephone: (800) 233-8764
> Fax: (410) 571-1703
> Web address: www.usni.org